Principled Action

Also by James D. Best

The Shopkeeper
The Shut Mouth Society
Leadville
Tempest at Dawn
Murder at Thumb Butte
The Digital Organization

Principled Action

*Lessons from the Origins
of the American Republic*

James D. Best

Principled Action: Lessons from the Origins of the American Republic

Cover design by Wayne Best

Cover photo by Mole and Thomas, 1918, The Human U.S. Shield, 30,000 officers and men, Camp Custer, Battle Creek, Michigan

Published by Wheatmark®
1760 E. River Rd, Suite 145,
Tucson, Arizona 85718 USA

ISBN: 978-1-60494-716-8
LCCN: 2011946015

To Diane and our children

"The infant periods of most nations are buried in silence, or veiled in fable, and perhaps the world has lost little it should regret. But the origins of the American Republic contain lessons of which posterity ought not to be deprived."

—*James Madison*

Contents

Part I
The Founding

Part II
The Founders

Part III
The Founding Principles

Acknowledgements

I am indebted to many people for helping me with *Principled Action*. Jordan Cash, Michael Newton, and Roger Bruning provided invaluable assistance. Martin Sielaff and the folks at *What Would the Founders Think?* gave appreciated advice, as well as providing me with a platform to develop ideas. Marcia Sielaff's research was particularly helpful with K–12 education. Thanks go to Wayne Best for an excellent cover design.

My wife, Diane, was an enthusiastic supporter who gave generously of her time and talents to help me—thank you.

I would also like to thank Glenn Beck for inviting me to conduct a class on his web-based Glenn Beck University. My class on Founding Principles eventually led to *Principled Action: Lessons from the Origins of the American Republic*. All errors of fact or interpretation are mine alone.

Introduction

The theme for this book came from a letter James Madison wrote to Dr. William Eustis in the summer of 1819: "The infant periods of most nations are buried in silence, or veiled in fable, and perhaps the world has lost little it should regret. But the origins of the American republic contain lessons of which posterity ought not to be deprived."[1] *Principled Action* revisits these lessons—the ideas and principles that served as the basis for the American founding.

Throughout history, new nations have come into being because of conquering armies, internal rebellion, or the edict of a great power. But not the United States of America. Although our nation was conceived in revolt, our governing institutions were born in calm reason. Our Constitution comes from a convention and ratification process where rational debate eventually led Americans to establish a new and unique government—a limited, representative republic.

Not only was the process of our founding unique, but the type of republic we formed was also profoundly foreign to most of the world. With a few brief exceptions, world history had been written about kings and emperors. The American experiment in self-government rudely shook up a world used to rule by nobility. Not only did we break away from the biggest and most powerful empire in history, we took the musings of the brightest thinkers of the Enlightenment and implemented them in the New World. Our founding was simultaneously an armed rebellion against tyranny and a revolution of ideas—ideas that changed the course of world history.

It doesn't take much study to conclude that early Americans held dear a few key principles and risked their lives, families, fortunes, and honor to build a republic based on those very same principles. Washington, Franklin, Jefferson, Madison, and most of their contemporaries believed they had witnessed and participated in events that were more than merely unusual. Our forefathers repeatedly said that the founding of the United States of America was truly historic—a unique event in human history. They believed this because they had lived in the world before our Revolution and they lived in the nation they had built after they won independence. They saw the *before* and *after* pictures.

The Founders encompassed all of the frailties of humankind, but in an era when honor meant everything, they were highly honorable and took principled action for the betterment of their fellow citizens and their progeny. The origins of the American Republic followed on the tail end of the Age of Enlightenment, and the founding of the United States served as the climax for that great intellectual movement. It could have happened no place else on earth. The American continents represented a fresh start for the whole world, and in the late eighteenth century, a confluence of historic magnitude occurred along the eastern seaboard of a vast wilderness.

In well under two hundred years, the people living in these North American British colonies had produced great cities, productive farms, and profitable industries. They built harbors, roads, and canals to make transportation along the coastal areas as easy as any place on earth. Philadelphia had become one of the largest English-speaking cities in the world. The colonists also built untold numbers of churches and taverns—which became the incubators of polite and impolite debates about the kind of republic they wanted for themselves and their children.

The American colonists were wealthy in comparison to most of the world. Meat, a rarity for the lower classes elsewhere, was cheap and plentiful. Land was available to anyone with industry enough to buy it or the gumption to venture westward to stake a claim. Trade with the colonies flourished along the Atlantic coasts of three continents and with the Caribbean islands, encouraging New England to create one of the greatest shipbuilding and maritime industries in the world.

Americans were well fed, well housed, and especially well educated—perhaps the best educated people in the world. Benjamin Franklin said, "We are more thoroughly an enlightened people, with respect to our political interests, than perhaps any other under heaven. Every man among us reads, and is so easy in his circumstances as to have leisure for conversations of improvement and for acquiring information."[2] And John Adams wrote, "A native of America who cannot read or write is … as rare as a comet or an earthquake."[3]

Opportunities for education were abundant in cities and towns, and colonists had established a culture of lifelong study. Most homes had at least a Bible and almanac in an era when books were expensive luxuries. Dartmouth, Harvard, Rhode Island College (later Brown University), Yale, King's College (later Columbia), the College of New Jersey (later Princeton), Queen's College (Later Rutgers), and William and Mary were all thriving institutions of higher education. Not just college graduates, but many of the self-educated had read Locke, Hume, Montesquieu, Blackstone, Voltaire, Rousseau, and the classics of ancient Greece and Rome.

The colonists did not only revolt against taxes; they revolted to stop the British from taking away the self-governance they already had been exercising since the earliest colonization. The crown appointed governors for the colonies, but over three thousand miles of ocean in the day of wind-powered ships gave ordinary Americans more freedom than a minor noble living in Bristol, England. (Connecticut and Rhode Island even elected their own governors.) Americans bristled over dictates from Parliament because colonial legislatures had been exercising substantial power for well over a century.

Even before they created a unique republic, Americans were a different breed than their European cousins. Pioneers who ventured far from home across a dangerous ocean were, by nature, adventurous and ambitious. Unhampered by close government scrutiny and blessed with abundant resources and relatively free markets, raw energy and ambition drove astonishing growth. Best of all, nobility did not have the sole claim to created wealth. Everyone, independent of station, could participate in any enterprise they chose and own the fruits of their labor or wits. Thus was born the American Dream.

Our forefathers bequeathed to us far more than a republic. They willed to us an enduring Constitution that incorporates more thought and brainpower than any document ever written by man. After fifty-five convention delegates worked on it ceaselessly for four months, three million people argued about it for two years, and only then was it ratified by conventions of the people so it could become the supreme law of the land. And immediately after it was put in force, Congress acceded to popular demand by proposing ten amendments that restricted the government from abridging the rights of the governed.

Was the American Dream open to all? Sadly, no. It's not possible to write a book about the founding and ignore slavery. Slavery is part of our heritage, and it deserves a candid assessment. However, judging the late eighteenth century from today's perspectives does not allow us to dismiss all of their work. Focusing on the faults of early Americans misses the entire point of the founding. The United States was founded on solid, idealistic principles, but at the time these principles were largely aspirational. The Founders bequeathed to us a republican form of government dedicated to individual liberty. Through Constitutional amendments, we have strived to expand liberty to one and all. While the effort was sometimes tumultuous, it was through the rule of law that liberty expanded.

Our inherited culture encourages us to extend the American Dream to everyone. We may occasionally forget the Founding Principles and misstep, but we invariably return to the path set out by our Founders. This makes Americans very different from the rest of the world.

Principled Action

PART I

The Founding

1

The Founding of the American Republic

"Objects of the most stupendous magnitude, and measure in which the lives and liberties of millions yet unborn are intimately interested, are now before us. We are in the very midst of a revolution the most complete, unexpected and remarkable of any in the history of nations."

—*John Adams*[4]

Building a new nation is a complex event, so what really encompassed the founding? Many people assume the United States of America was founded on July 4, 1776. This was the date the Declaration of Independence was signed by most of the delegates to the Continental Congress, but as the name implies, it was only a declaration. It took seven additional years of war to make that declaration a reality. But war alone does not found a nation. The Revolution was neither the start nor the conclusion of the founding. Prior to the Declaration, a consensus had to be developed within the colonies to seek independence; otherwise there would never have been enough volunteers to fight the powerful British Empire. After the Treaty of Paris in September of 1783, the fledgling United States still needed a government that could function well enough to retain the country's newly won independence. An American Republic under a constitution authorized by the people took many more years to design and put in place.

This book defines the founding as extending from the Stamp Act (1765) through to the end of George Washington's second term as president (1797). These thirty-two years include the growth of a revolutionary spirit, the war for independence, a few non-war years governed under the Articles of Confederation, the adoption of the Constitution, and the two precedent-setting terms of Washington's presidency. It took all of these events and developments to found the United States of America as a full nation with a governmental system that could be passed down from generation to generation.

A Growing Rebellion

In the five centuries following the Magna Carta (1215), Englishmen had gradually gained individual rights, so that by the late eighteenth century, the English were beginning to exercise a degree of self-government. The King and nobility still wielded substantial power, but Parliament had gained increasing authority, especially in the elected House of Commons. Toward the end of this period, the opinions of those outside the aristocracy were increasingly influenced by the Enlightenment, an intellectual movement of the seventeen and eighteenth centuries. Enlightenment thinkers began to challenge existing religious, government, and social norms, and pushed for additional individual liberty and the free exercise of natural rights. They argued that mankind not only had a capacity for self-government, but that it was a natural right. Through an evolutionary process, Englishmen grew to enjoy an ever-increasing say over who made the laws that governed their lives. That is, those Englishmen who lived in England. If an Englishman happened to live in one of the British colonies, he was still a mere subject of the crown with no representation in Parliament.

This second-class citizenship chafed the American colonists. The irony is that even without representation in Parliament, the colonists still enjoyed more personal liberty than their English counterparts. In order to have the colonies function effectively three thousand miles away from the mother country, the colonists were allowed to make many of their own rules through locally elected legislatures. The colonists had developed a strong history of self-government, and had gotten used to being somewhat independent from the rulers of the British Empire. They viewed themselves as English, and took an Englishman's rights more seriously than those surrounded by nobility that constantly strived to enforce the status quo.

Despite enjoying greater liberty than their English cousins, the colonists grew increasingly annoyed because of the palpable disrespect they received from London. Two examples will help illustrate this point. George Washington served honorably as a colonial officer in the French and Indian War, but no matter how incessantly he pleaded, he could not secure a regular commission in the British Army.[5] No matter how well they fought, a colonist could never be considered the equal of an English officer. Washington suffered innumerable other slights from his British overlords until they eventually drove him to become a committed rebel. Benjamin Franklin also suffered poor treatment from the English. As relations grew tense between England and the colonies, Franklin, who had lived in London for eighteen years, tried to smooth things over as an unofficial envoy. He was so angered by his ill-treatment at a Privy Council session that it is rumored he told the British solicitor general, "I will make your master a little king for this."[6] Franklin made good on his word. Upon returning from England, he was appointed to the committee that wrote the Declaration of Independence.

A Tax That Riled the Colonists

The view was different from London, of course. The rulers of the British Empire saw the colonists as getting a free ride. The great British Navy kept the seas safe for New England ships, and the mercantilist Parliament regulated trade so that the American maritime industry prospered. To keep the colonies safe from foreign invasion, England had built forts and posted troops throughout their North America holdings. The French and Indian War caused a major drain on the British treasury. Parliament looked at all of these costs and saw colonials acting like ungrateful, spoiled children who had grown large enough to pay their own way. So in 1765, Parliament passed the

Duties in American Colonies Act, more commonly referred to as the Stamp Act.

This new act was relatively simple, but would pervade the colonies. Printed documents and materials were required to use paper manufactured in London with an embossed revenue stamp. The tax also had to be paid in scarce British currency, not colonial money, which had severe economic consequences. Because of protests and harassment of stamp tax officials, the tax was rescinded the next year. But Parliament simultaneously passed the Declaratory Act, stating that Parliament had unconstrained authority to pass legislation that would have the full force of law in the American colonies. This throwing down of the gauntlet by Parliament put the two countries on the path to war.[7]

A Failure to Communicate

The loyalist lieutenant governor of Massachusetts, Thomas Hutchinson, tried to explain colonists' resistance to the Stamp Act: "[The] prevailing reason at this time is, that the Act of Parliament is against the Magna Carta, and the natural rights of Englishmen, and therefore, according to Lord Coke, null and void."[8] Explanations didn't matter. In the ensuing years after the abortive Stamp Act, Parliament tried to impose a series of new taxes on the colonies. The results on the American side of the Atlantic were protests, boycotts, and scattered violence, gradually escalating until 1775, when the "shot heard 'round the world" ignited a war.

The decade between 1765 and 1775 was a test of wills in which neither side would compromise. Members of Parliament felt they had a right to impose taxes on the colonies, and that the colonies were obligated to contribute to the costs of running the empire. Parliament also wanted to assert its authority to manage trade between different outposts of the empire. Parliament hotly asserted that they had an absolute authority to control taxes and commerce between territorial possessions. The Americans, on the other hand, wanted the respect and rights of an English citizen, which included representation in any body that made laws governing their lives. To them, only colonial legislatures had the right to impose taxes on them.

New Englanders were especially incensed at restrictions Parliament had put on trade.

Neither side seemed to understand or acknowledge what the other wanted. London wanted money and to demonstrate authority over its territorial possessions. Protecting a huge empire was expensive, and Parliament believed it was only fair that every part of the empire should contribute to maintaining safe sea lanes, providing security against indigenous populations, and holding other world powers at bay. The British never really understood that it wasn't taxes per se that roiled the colonists; it was an idea.

That idea was self-government. John Adams wrote, "The Revolution was effected before the war commenced. The Revolution was in the minds and hearts of the people; a change in their religious sentiments of their duties and obligations … This radical change in the principles, opinions, sentiments, and affections of the people, was the real American Revolution."

American colonists believed self-government was a natural right. With no colonial representation in the House of Commons, Parliament had no authority over Americans. The Revolutionary slogan "No taxation without representation" embodied this principle. An illustration of the importance of this principle is that in 1765, Patrick Henry got the Virginia House of Burgesses to pass the Virginia Stamp Act Resolutions, which asserted that the British constitution guaranteed Englishmen the right to be taxed only by their own representatives, and for that reason colonial assemblies had the sole and nonassignable authority to impose taxes on colonists.[9]

Fear of an Idea

Although the two parties were talking at cross-purposes, it was more complicated than that. In Britain, voting rights were far more limited than in the colonies. Only about 3 percent of men could vote in Britain, and those who could vote were selected by local nobility. A larger segment of men could vote in the colonies and the requirements were set by law, not officials. Voting rights traced back to the earliest history of the colonies. Within days of landing in Jamestown, for instance, the first colonists elected an executive officer. Only six men were allowed to vote in this embryonic colony, but from that moment forward, colonists expanded the right to vote to broader segments of the population. Despite obvious shortcomings, by 1775, the American colonies were the most democratic places on earth. The British did not want this egalitarian principle spreading to other parts of the empire, especially not to England.[10]

Property Requirement to Vote

It's a myth that prior to the mid-1800s only property owners could vote throughout the United States. It varied by state. At the time of the Constitutional Convention in 1787, several states had already dropped the property requirement. That is why the convention didn't establish a standard for national elections. States that had expanded the voting franchise to non-property owners didn't want to deny their citizens the right to vote for members of the House of Representatives, while the states that retained a property requirement didn't want the new government to rescind the qualification. The convention resolved this conflict by letting the states set voting rights for national elections.[11]

To Set a Country Free

Measured from the skirmishes along the Concord/Lexington/Boston road to the Treaty of Paris, the American Revolution lasted eight years. It was a war we weren't supposed to win. The British army was formidable and its navy the most powerful military force that ever set to sea. A ragtag bunch of farmers and tradesmen should have been easily suppressed. But the American rebels had several advantages. Many of them were good marksmen—they had to be, or they didn't eat. They also didn't fight using European rules of engagement. They shot officers first, and saw no stigma in shooting from behind cover. But beyond their fighting prowess, the Americans had other key assets—the leadership of George Washington and Benjamin Franklin and the power of an idea.

George Washington must have been temporarily addled to accept the position of commander in chief of the Continental Army. When he set off from Philadelphia to Boston, the army officially consisted of one person—himself. He had no troops, little weaponry or gunpowder, and not even the cloth needed to make uniforms. In previous years, he had obsessively built one of the grandest estates in the country, yet he chose to put his life, fortune, and family at risk for independence. He managed to win the war through raw tenacity and unbroken leadership. He wouldn't give up, and despite unbelievable hardships, his stalwart leadership kept his army intact enough to continue the fight. Luckily, he got some invaluable help from Benjamin Franklin.

While George Washington was accomplishing the seemingly impossible in the field, Benjamin Franklin was doing the same in the world of diplomacy. The two things necessary to wage war are men and money. Franklin surprisingly got both from the arrogant and recalcitrant French. With this diplomatic achievement, Franklin had pulled off a triumph of immeasurable proportions. Instead of an easily handled backwoods insurrection, the American Revolution became a full-scale war between the world's two greatest powers. Washington could not have won without the French, and Franklin could never have convinced the French to join the war if Washington hadn't shown endurance and accomplishment in the field.

There were many other Founders that made significant contributions to winning the Revolution, but an idea proved more important than any of these people. The Declaration of Independence expressed this startling concept with the phrase *consent of the governed*. If America could not achieve the Englishman's right to self-governance under the British, then it would seek independence. Colonists firmly believed that the definition of tyranny was edicts from above without representation. In their minds, the way Parliament had been treating them restricted their liberty and denied them natural rights. Thomas Paine wrote, "We fight not to enslave, but to set a country free, and to make room upon the earth for honest men to live in."[12]

The Great Business Now before Us

The truly exceptional work in the founding began after the war for independence was won. During the Constitutional Convention, George Mason wrote, "The revolt from Great Britain and the formations of our new governments at that time, were nothing compared to the great business now before us; there was then a certain degree of enthusiasm, which inspired and supported the mind; but to view, through the calm, sedate medium of reason the influence which the establishment now proposed may have upon the happiness or misery of millions yet unborn, is the object of such magnitude, as absorbs, and in a manner suspends the operation of the human understanding."[13]

The writing and ratification of the Constitution made the United States of America unique. The origins of our republic were not by the sword, but through the *calm, sedate medium of reason*. There was a long and bloody revolution, but four years of peace had calmed the infant nation before the Founders collectively sat down to debate the design of a republic for millions yet unborn.

Principled Action

The Founders were brave and principled. They first stood against tyranny, and then went against the grain of world history to risk their future on an idea that had been tried and failed many times before. Previous experiments in self-governance had flamed bright only to be doused by powerful factions driven by self-interest.[14] Absolutist rulers invariably emerged to replace unbridled democracies. In time, a consensus developed that the divine right of kings was a far more attractive option than rule by the most ruthless.

The scholars of the Enlightenment brought self-governance back into fashion by audaciously proposing that individuals, not kings, were *endowed by their Creator with certain unalienable rights*. This simple principle is the earth-shaking idea that guided the Founders' actions before, during, and after the Revolution. But the American Founders didn't want to repeat the mistakes of previous republics, so they studied the governments of the past and designed a balanced system with numerous checks on the exercise of power.

Many of the Founders committed their entire life to the creation of the American Republic. They were bright, educated, and principled men and women who had their countrymen's interests at heart. They certainly weren't perfect, but their motives were near perfect, even when their actions fell short of their aspirations. Why do some disparage the Founders? To a great extent, the Founders purposely put shackles on government. They feared an overreaching government and wanted it constrained. As we'll see, the Founders had solid reasoning and a few key principles to back them up. Today, some want the government to do more, much more. The justification for an increase in government authority is usually cloaked in the cause of improving the general state of mankind. Those who look to government for answers to world disorder constantly see those pesky Founders getting in their way.

The Founders would be proud.

2

Which Principles Guided the Founders?

"What is a Constitution? It is the form of government, delineated by the mighty hand of the people, in which certain first principles of fundamental law are established."

—William Paterson, Delegate to the Constitutional Convention and author of the New Jersey Plan[15]

Historians make references to the Founding Principles—also called First Principles—but what are they? They are the bedrock values that guided the Founders and formed the basis of the American Experiment. They are derivative of natural rights. Enlightenment doctrine held that natural rights are universal, and although they might be suppressed, they cannot be taken away. Today, we usually call this collection of natural rights *freedom*, but during the founding period, they more accurately called the exercise of natural rights *liberty*. Nature—or nature's God—endows every human with certain inalienable rights, and these natural rights are superior to those granted by government with man-made laws. Natural rights are superior to man-made rights because rights granted by government can be taken away—they are not inalienable.

When the colonies felt it necessary to declare their independence from Great Britain, they based their action on natural rights. The first paragraph of the Declaration of Independence reads:

"When in the Course of human events it becomes necessary for one people to dissolve the political bands which have connected them with another and to assume among the powers of the earth, the separate and equal station to which the Laws of Nature and of Nature's God entitle them, a decent respect to the opinions of mankind requires that they should declare the causes which impel them to the separation."

The *Laws of Nature and of Nature's God* was a direct reference to natural law. This was the grand justification that allowed the colonies to separate from Great Britain. Next came what may be the best-known sentence in the English language:

"We hold these truths to be self-evident, that all men are created equal, that they are endowed by their Creator with certain unalienable Rights, that among these are Life, Liberty and the pursuit of Happiness."

All humans are endowed with equal, unalienable rights, and these rights come from their Creator. There has never been an agreed-upon list of specific natural rights, but life, liberty, and the pursuit of happiness is a tidy summation that has served mankind well. Although the exact boundary between natural rights and man-made rights may be unclear, it is possible to identify the Founding Principles by a simple technique. In the spring of 1787, fifty-five men came to Philadelphia to attend a Federal Convention, which eventually presented a constitution to the people of America for ratification. On the surface, these men appeared to agree on very few issues; after all, they argued for four months about every detail of the Constitution. But on arrival, it is safe to say that there were five principles firmly held by all fifty-five delegates—principles about which there was no disagreement. During the course of the deliberations, a sixth principle was adopted by nearly every member. These six principles can be rightly called the Founding Principles because they guided the design of the Constitution of the United States of America and its first ten amendments.

This chapter will introduce the six Founding Principles. Part III, The Founding Principles, will go into greater detail with a chapter dedicated to each of the principles.

The Six Founding Principles

The six Founding Principles are:
1. Rights come from God, not government.
2. All political power emanates from the people.
3. A limited, representative republic protects liberty.
4. Consent of the governed requires a written constitution.
5. Liberty depends on the right to private property.
6. Power must be balanced and checked.

These principles may seem commonplace to informed Americans today, but in 1787, they were revolutionary ideas. In fact, they were so radical that the British rulers saw them as treasonous, and feared that these principles might foment rebellion throughout the empire. Despite losing the war, Britain did not believe the American states could survive under the Articles of Confederation. Like a rebellious youth who had run away from home, they expected the colonies to return to the fold when confronted with the harsh world outside of their protection. It must have been sobering for Britain to watch the Constitution and Bill of Rights being adopted. It meant that the United States was more mature than they had supposed, and worse, that ideas could be contagious. Luckily for the empire, the contagion first extended not to their own people, but to the French, whose revolution turned out so badly that it gave pause to the rest of the world.

Principle 1: Rights Come from God, Not Government

The first Founding Principle is embedded in the second paragraph of our Declaration of Independence: "We hold these truths to be self-evident, that all men are created equal, that they are endowed by their Creator with certain unalienable rights, that among these are life, liberty and the pursuit of happiness." Throughout most of history, rulers and their governments bestowed rights. The Founders, however, didn't believe that governments conferred rights, nor did they believe that governments protected rights. Governments and rulers were the ones that threatened and abridged rights. The Founders had learned this lesson from their study of history and as subjects of the British Empire.

This principle of natural rights came directly from the Enlightenment. It was a revolutionary concept because the divine right of kings held that God designated certain bloodlines to rule; then with the grace of God behind them, kings would bestow rights and privileges onto their subjects. To believe that rights came directly from God to each human, and not through the ruling elite, meant there was no intermediary. This was a direct challenge to the existing order.

Principle 2: All Political Power Emanates from the People

The Founders believed that they held a natural right to select their leaders and government. The phrase *consent of the governed* in the Declaration of Independence encapsulates this concept. The power of the people is also declared in the first three words of the Constitution—*We the people.* The Founders were strongly influenced by John Locke, who advocated government as a social contract, which meant that the people decide who is to govern them and how they will be governed. Of the first two principles, this one was the more radical because it directly challenged the divine right of kings. It was the eloquent articulation of this principle that made the Declaration of Independence the most revolutionary document ever written.

Principle 3: A Limited, Representative Republic Protects Liberty

This principle is derivative of natural rights and the principle that all political power emanates from the people. The Founders saw a limited, representative republic as the only effective way to keep the people in charge of government and protect them from the inherent weaknesses of mankind. Power corrupts, and without ironclad limits, those with power will invariably force their will on the people. The Founders knew that unrestricted general power would lead to tyranny, so they believed in limited enumerated powers, and purposely designed structural limits on government. The second principle also dictated a republican form of government with elected representatives.

Most of the Founders distrusted direct democracy because they equated democracy with mob rule. James Madison constantly preached against a pure democratic system because it allowed special interests (factions) to gain control of the government. He showed that throughout history, pure democracies had failed because collusive factions gained control of the government and then tyrannized minorities, and it didn't matter whether those minorities were based on race, wealth, religion, or geography.[16]

Principle 4: Consent of the Governed Requires a Written Constitution

This principle may seem obvious today, but at the time England had no written constitution and it was the most powerful empire on earth. The Roman Republic also had operated with an unwritten constitution. The English believed a constitution needed to evolve and that a written constitution would be restricting. Of course, they were coming from a history of oppressive rule with a gradual transition toward more parliamentary powers, and they didn't want to inhibit the evolution toward additional liberties. We, on the other hand, were starting with a blank slate and insisted that our basic principles be codified. This American tradition of a written constitution actually went all the way back to the Mayflower Compact. While still aboard ship, the Pilgrims wrote and signed a short statement that combined the passengers "together into a civil body politic." At the time of the Constitutional Convention, the national government operated under a written Articles of Confederation and all thirteen states had written constitutions.

Thomas Paine, a strong proponent of a written constitution said, "An unwritten constitution is not a constitution at all."[17] The Founders believed that a constitution formally sets the rules for governance between the people and their elected representatives, and it should be in writing so people could make a formal delegation of powers. Additionally, a constitution must be approved by many people, so it needed to be in writing so everybody could examine what they were approving.

Principle 5: Liberty Depends on the Right to Private Property

The Founders saw the protected ownership of private property as one of the keys to liberty. The Founders believed this principle because of their personal experience and what to them was recent history. They equated central ownership of property with the divine right of kings, nobility, and serfdom. Until the time of the Renaissance, rulers or nobility owned everything. A middle class didn't emerge until the common man was allowed to own property. Property rights were intertwined with liberty because a person was not free if he had no confidence that he could keep what he produced. Without that assurance, he was a serf or slave to someone else. A just government would never permit a person's property to be arbitrarily taken away.

Private property rights had been highly protected in the colonies and the colonies had not only prospered, they had created an American Dream where anyone could achieve and hold on to success because they owned the fruits of their labor or wits. Private property rights had also built a relatively classless society, or at least a society where movement between the classes was generally unrestricted.

Principle 6: Power Must Be Balanced and Checked

Initially, most of the delegates had a strong bias toward the legislative branch. This was due to their fear of a king. After all, they had just escaped from the tyranny of George III. But James Madison convinced the Convention delegates that to guard against tyranny, power needed to be dispersed evenly among the legislative, executive, and judicial branches, with each branch of the government given formidable checks on the authority of the other branches. This check and balance wasn't just between the three branches of the national government; the Founders also wanted the states to act as a solid check on the national government.[18]

Through most of history, limits on the power of rulers and their governments would have been considered counterproductive, but the Founders didn't trust concentrated power. A system of checks and balances inhibits action until a consensus develops, and it puts restraints on the abuse of power. Madison argued his point successfully, and by the conclusion of the constitutional debates, the delegates accepted as a basic principle that power must be balanced and checked.

Reliance on the Founding Principles

These six Founding Principles provided the foundation for our constitutional government. The delegates to the Federal Convention didn't often agree. In fact, it's possible they only agreed on these Founding Principles. They argued endlessly over every aspect of their design, but these principles remained their sturdy guideposts throughout their debates. In Part III, The Founding Principles, we'll show how these principles were incorporated into the founding documents. From the Declaration of Independence to the Bill of Rights, the Founders remained faithful to these principles. There were detours along the way, but in the end they always took principled action.

Did the Founders believe these principles were important? George Mason, James Madison, Thomas Jefferson, and Patrick Henry certainly thought so when they collectively wrote the Virginia Constitution. "No free government, nor the blessings of liberty, can be preserved to any people, but by ... frequent recurrence to fundamental principles."[19]

PART II

The Founders

3

Who Were the Founders?

"Threading an idea into the slipstream of politics, then into government, then into history ... is a craft which I have since come to consider the most important in the world."

—*Theodore White,* In Search of History[20]

People frequently refer to the Founders as if they were a homogenous group. They did share a belief in key principles, but they were very different in other respects. For example, George Washington was a wealthy plantation owner, but his top officers in the Revolution included Major General Nathanael Greene, who entered the war as a militia private and was the son of a small farmer; Major General Henry Knox, a Boston bookstore owner who later became President Washington's secretary of war; and Lieutenant Colonel Alexander Hamilton, born illegitimate in the West Indies to a struggling mother who died when Hamilton was thirteen. Hamilton went on to become the first secretary of the treasury.

When you examine the Founding era, you find that the American Dream was already firmly implanted in the culture. As with Washington and his staff, this mix of so-called aristocracy and common man can be seen throughout society. The Constitutional Convention included physicians, shopkeepers, academics, farmers, merchants, bankers, lawyers, politicians, and even an educator who lived on the edge of the then-frontier.

The Founders differed also in their religions, preference for agrarian versus city lifestyles, whether they owned slaves or supported slavery's abolition, and most of all by their state of residence. At the time, Americans saw themselves as first being New Yorkers, Virginians, or Georgians. State allegiance was akin to national loyalty. Major Pierce Butler, a revolutionary officer and Constitutional Convention delegate from South Carolina said, "... the manners, mode of thinking, and interests of the North and South are as different as the interests of Russia and Turkey."[21]

How Many Founders Were There?

How many people were involved in founding the United States of America? It was hundreds of thousands of people. Just to start, here are the numbers from some of the more famous episodes in the thirty-two-year founding period.

- 437 were members of the Continental Congress or of Congress under the Articles of Confederation
- 56 committed treason by signing the Declaration of Independence
- 48 signed the Articles of Confederation
- 55 attended the Constitutional Convention as delegates
- 30 were members of the first Senate
- 67 were elected to the first House of Representatives
- 9 joined Washington's cabinet
- 6 secured appointments to the Supreme Court

If you eliminate those who served in multiple roles, there were still nearly five hundred people who could rightfully claim a Founder's role. In addition, more than one hundred twenty thousand served in the Continental Army, of whom about twenty-five thousand died due to action, disease, or prison conditions. Prior to and during the Revolution, many thousands more put themselves and their families in great jeopardy by serving in colonial or state governments. The Constitutional Ratification Conventions involved more than a thousand delegates across the states. Thomas Paine, George Whitefield, Noah

Webster, James Otis, Jr., and hundreds of others contributed to the Founding through their writings or sermons.

During the Founding, all official positions of authority were occupied by men, but that doesn't exclude women from a rightful claim to be called Founders. For example, fifty-one women from the Society of Patriotic Ladies at Edenton, North Carolina, signed a revolutionary statement. Esther Berdt Reed organized women in Philadelphia to raise $7,500 for the war effort, an enormous amount of money at the time. Women defended their homes against the British and Native American troops. Catherine Van Rensselaer Schuyler burned wheat fields around Albany, New York, to prevent British forces from harvesting them, and Mary Katherine Goddard printed the first official copy of the Declaration of Independence and personally paid post riders to carry it throughout the colonies. A few women even participated in battles and served as spies.[22]

Many blacks also were among the Founders. Washington's army was at times 10 percent black and not until the Korean War did America field an army as integrated as the Continental Army. Many free blacks in the North could vote, and some bought war bonds just like other Americans that supported independence. This obviously doesn't justify slavery, which was legal in twelve of the thirteen states.[23]

During the Founding, the United States population grew roughly from two to four million. While the war raged, there were probably more than a million people who contributed to the cause of independence. Once the Constitution was written and presented to the nation, practically the entire population participated in debates that raged for almost two years in taverns, halls, and churches.

Dead, Rich, White, Male Slave Owners

Some of today's armchair pundits want to dismiss the Founders and even the relevancy of the Constitution. The bill of particulars against the Founders is that they lived in a vastly different and ancient world; they really just wanted to protect their wealth; Founders only included white men, and many of them owned slaves. Some of the criticisms have validity, but none are universally true. If the Founders had not set such lofty goals for their country, perhaps the criticisms would have greater weight. The Founders should not be judged by the more egalitarian society of today, but by eighteenth-century culture and whether their principles lead us toward an ever-more-just society.

The Founders of the United States lived more than two hundred years ago. Many want to dismiss their ideas for this reason alone. Critics point out that the world was completely different in the latter-half of the eighteenth century. Granted, the technology of the world was different two hundred years ago, but the nature of government in that long-ago era was still defined by the frailties of mankind. The Constitution is not a list of laws. It is a system of government meant to restrain the worst impulses of man. It's the responsibility of Congress to pass legislation to accommodate a changing world. As James Madison warned us, "What is government itself but the greatest of all reflections on human nature? If men were angels, no government would be necessary. If angels were to govern men, neither external nor internal controls on government would be necessary." Despite unbelievable progress in technology and changing social norms, the risks associated with the rule of man over man have not changed in two hundred years.

Some denigrate the Founders by saying most of them were wealthy, yet wealth has never been a disqualifier in America. The American Dream is that anyone can rise to any level in our society, independent of their station, gender, or race. The highest achievers in almost every endeavor—whether sports, business, science, or any of the arts—are richly compensated. To disqualify the rich merely because of their success snatches the American Dream away from everyone. And not all of the Founders were rich; many struggled to feed and shelter their families. They were Americans from every walk of life, and they worked together to build this great country.

Critics also point out that many of the Founders—including eight of our first fifteen presidents—were slave owners. Slavery was an unconscionable violation of the Founding Principles, and it has caused soul-wrenching problems that linger to this day. (We'll address slavery as a founding issue later in this book.) It would be unfair, however, to dismiss the contributions of these men for acting within the norms of their time. Aristotle defended slavery, but we don't discard the remainder of his life's work for that reason.[24]

Others denigrate the Founders because women were excluded from positions of power. There has recently been extensive research into the contribution of women during the founding period. Although female involvement was more substantial than previously reported, there is no denying that men were at the forefront of the founding. Male dominance, however, was not unique to the American continent; it was a feature of almost all of the cultures of the world at that time.

Whether these criticisms have some validity or not, they are woefully misleading when applied to the great body of people who committed their lives and everything they owned to the idea of self-government.

Rabble-rousers, Warriors, Politicians, and Thinkers

One way to think about our Founders is to group them loosely into four broad categories: the agitators who incited revolution, those who picked up a gun and went to war, a political class who shaped government action, and the philosophers who imbued the founding period with first principles.

Samuel Adams, Patrick Henry, Thomas Jefferson, Thomas Paine, and John Hancock were articulate firebrands who fomented a revolutionary spirit throughout the colonies. Using their superb gifts for speaking and writing, they popularized the revolutionary cause until most of the people became emotionally tied to it.

Once the shooting started, a warrior class emerged. George Washington, William Anderson, Alexander Hamilton, Benedict Arnold, Nathan Hale, Ethan Allen, Nathanael Greene, Robert Howe, Henry Knox, Francis Marion, John Paul Jones, Daniel Boone, and over a hundred thousand others fought the British with ingenuity and valor.

A third group—those Americans who accepted a political role during the war—also committed treason. Their punishment, if America had lost, could have been as severe as death, but almost certainly would have included prison time and loss of property. Congressmen like John Adams and Thomas Jefferson, along with governors like Patrick Henry and George Clinton, were almost at as much at risk as soldiers in the field. This was true as well for the members of the state legislatures.

After the war, politicians and citizen delegates assumed responsibility for creating a lasting government system that would protect the Founding Principles. This included brilliant thinkers and political theorists like John Adams, James Madison, George Mason, Thomas Jefferson, Alexander Hamilton, and John Jay.

Some of these names fit into more than one category. For example, Benjamin Franklin could easily fit into three and he was also an indispensable war asset. Many others had multiple roles, like Benjamin Rush, who signed the Declaration of Independence, served as surgeon general of the Continental Army, and fought for ratification of the Constitution.

The point is the Founders were not a homogeneous group. Some were key figures throughout the thirty-two years, while others played an important role at one point in the founding, but were ill suited for the next step. This was especially true of the revolutionary agitators like Sam Adams, who could get a crowd excited about ending British rule and oppression, but was less effective when it came to building a nation. In fact, of the better-known rabble-rousers, only Thomas Jefferson made a full transition to political leadership.

How Do We Know What the Founders Thought?

Two hundred years ago, there were no televised speeches or proceedings, no one captured video of crucial events, and transportation was so bad that newspaper reporters needed to live near an event to report it. Frequently, political meetings were held in secret. In fact, the Constitutional Convention was closed to the public, held with windows nailed shut and guards posted to the doors. Secrecy was paramount—from among the fifty-five delegates in attendance, historians have never found a single instance of anyone among them leaking news of the proceedings to the outside world. For fifty years after this historic event, the only records of what happened inside the State House (which we now call Independence Hall) were terse official minutes and a few partisan reconstructions.

Pundits talk about the original intent of the Founders, but does anyone really have a clue what they thought? How would someone living today know the intent of the Founders? Actually, it's not difficult at all. They left an extensive record. We have a treasure trove of written material from the founding period. State militias and the Continental Army kept extensive records of the Revolutionary War. The Founders were prolific letter writers, and they often wrote about the Revolution, politics, and their opinions about events of the day. Washington kept an exhaustive diary of his expenses during the Revolution, which tells us where he was and what he was doing almost every day. The First Congress and the states recorded the entire process of adopting the Bill of Rights. Washington's two presidential terms are officially documented as well as recorded by a press that was free, combative, and widespread.

Every town had multiple newspapers that not only published local stories, but also reprinted national and world news. Opinion pieces were abundant in these newspapers and in independently published pamphlets. The secret proceedings of the Constitutional Convention were eventually made public. James Madison left instructions that after his death, Dolley Madison should publish his exceptionally comprehensive convention notes—in excess of 230 thousand words, each written by hand with a quill pen. In addition, modern students have access not only to the Federalist Papers, but a collection of opinion pieces we now call the Anti-Federalist Papers. The Constitution was ratified by conventions of the people in each of the thirteen states, and we have good-to-excellent documentation of all of these ratification debates.

In the three decades of the Revolution and the political founding of our country, the process of building a new nation captured the intellect and energy of an entire population. Like columnists and bloggers of today, newspaper writers and pamphleteers spread their opinions to the general populace. People gathered in churches, taverns, halls, and homes to argue the issues. Everyone debated the kind of government they wanted for themselves and for future generations. Debate raged across the nation for years as *We the People* rationally came to a decision on the best form of government to protect individual liberty.

We know what they thought—and we know their thinking was learned, intense, and at times acrimonious. Open debate gave everyone a voice, and opinions not only varied between different people, they often evolved over time within an individual person. Because that's what real debate does—it changes minds. One result of all this recorded history is that now when someone wants to justify a modern position, he or she can usually find a quote by one of the Founders that gives the impression the Founders once thought exactly as they do. This is disingenuous and unfair to the developing thought of the Founders. They studied endlessly, argued incessantly, and then made a choice, and that choice was based on what they genuinely believed was best for their country. Time and again, the Founders took principled action because they wanted to secure and protect liberty for generations.

Are the Founders Worthy of Our Admiration?

We owe the Founders more than admiration: we owe them our attention. Never before was there a group of people so dedicated to the task of creating a government that would insure "liberty and justice for all." They were educated about government systems, debated endlessly on the subject, and came to a national consensus on the best way to protect liberty and enrich lives. It's crucial we learn what the Founders thought so we can understand how they came to the conclusions they did—because the conclusions are the most important. Never in human history has so much study, thought, and debate gone into designing a government so it wouldn't grow to become oppressive. Our constitutional form of government was based on solid, well-thought-out Founding Principles. Tragically, these Founding Principles have been eroded to the point where they no longer provide guideposts to the citizenry or the government.

The Founders bequeathed to us a rational system of self-government, but they also gave us a loftiness of purpose that has continued to expand liberty. Their idealism and sense of fairness has made this country great. It's easy to denigrate societal inequities, but the Constitution includes a way to change and evolve. The people have used the amendment process to add a Bill of Rights, end slavery, give women the right to vote, and institute several other expansions of liberty to all citizens.

Some politicians today seem to violate or ignore the Constitution when it gets in the way of what they want to do. Worse, some would surreptitiously undermine key principles of our government to impose their will on our citizens. We must stop—and then reverse—this erosion of constitutional principles, but first we need to study the founding process so we can understand the lessons from the origins of the American Republic.

4

George, Ben, and a Few of Their Friends

"A good moral character is the first essential in a man, and that the habits contracted at your age are generally indelible, and your conduct here may stamp your character through life. It is therefore highly important that you should endeavor not only to be learned but virtuous."

—George Washington[25]

There were hundreds of thousands of people involved in the founding, but some were more essential than others. These were very unusual men. The thirty-two years of the founding were one of those rare historical moments where uncommon brilliance was the order of the day. Intelligent leaders not only seemed omnipresent, but those principled leaders were driven by a fervent desire to create something great and lasting—and many rose to the challenge. George Washington, Benjamin Franklin, Thomas Jefferson, James Madison, Gouverneur Morris, Alexander Hamilton, John Adams, and a host of others didn't just stage another revolution; they changed the course of history. Let's take a closer look at these great men.

George Washington, the Perfect Man for the Time and Place

By temperament, Washington was the perfect man to father a new republic. He could have easily claimed the mantle of Emperor; in fact, it would have been easier for him to do so than it was for Napoleon Bonaparte after the French revolution. But he did not seek such power for himself. Washington was truly the American Cincinnatus[26] and a moral, principled man.

Considering the resources he was given, he grew to become a brilliant field commander. He kept both his emotions and fiercely competitive nature in check until he had the opportunity to strike a blow that had a chance for success. His steady leadership with Congress and his troops succeeded in defeating the most powerful military force on earth—a feat no one in Europe had believed possible.

Washington was different from our stereotypical image of him. The popular perception of Washington is of a man of honor who won a war through strength of character and perseverance, and as a first president who gracefully stepped down from power after two precedent-setting terms. Most view him as cold and aloof. It's true that he was tall and stately, personally reserved, and preoccupied with his reputation, but he also loved to dance, play cards, and attend the theater. He was a superb horseman, ran his plantation with a sharp eye for profit, and attended church regularly. Washington was a vibrant, athletic man who wanted most of all to be loved by his countrymen.

We see his image in marble, stone, oil paint, and on the dollar bill. His name adorns counties, a state, cities, monuments, schools, and even a bridge leading into New York, a city he lost to the British. Amazon lists nearly two thousand biographies of George Washington, and we call him the father of our country. Despite these honors, some dismiss him as an aristocrat who owned slaves, and relied on others for creative thinking and grand ideas. Few historians give him credit for being a master politician, but whatever he became involved in, he actively managed, and he was an expert in public relations and image-making. He was open and vocal about his political beliefs, but closed and silent about his political manipulations.

Historians generally concede his military contributions and restrained leadership, but tend to dismiss him as a figurehead at the Constitutional Convention. What were Washington's contributions to the Constitution? First, he made the sacrifice of coming out of retirement and leaving his beloved Mount Vernon to attend. His mere presence ensured a quorum of states. He was unanimously elected as president of the convention, and presided over the sessions with a steady hand. The turning point of the convention was the Great Compromise, which was vastly more complicated than merely allowing each state two senators. Roger Sherman is credited with using this compromise to break the stalemate, but his idea had been sitting around for weeks. The small states just didn't have enough power to get it accepted by the convention. When the cast of characters and the breadth of actions are examined, the only possible conclusion is that George Washington played a major leadership role—and typically, he left no fingerprints.

Historians point out that Washington spoke only once during the convention, but they seldom mention what he said. He asked the delegates to approve a last-minute motion to give states a representative for every thirty thousand people instead of for every forty thousand.[27] This change provided the large states with some counterweight to the equal state representation in the Senate by granting the large states additional representation in the lower house. The timing was perfect. Everything was done, and everybody wanted to go home, so they quickly passed this stealth erosion to the Great Compromise. Washington deftly gave what was necessary to move the convention forward, but later mitigated what he perceived as an excess of state power in congress.

During ratification, Washington publicly endorsed the Constitution, putting his considerable reputation behind its public approval. He most likely encouraged many of the ratification initiatives, especially those of Alexander Hamilton and James Madison. Then there is the case of Edmond Randolph. Randolph was governor of Virginia and had refused to sign the Constitution, and even threatened to work with Patrick Henry against ratification. After Washington asked him to join his administration as attorney general, Randolph switched sides and joined forces with Madison.[28] Washington instinctively knew what actions to take to move events in the direction he wanted.

Because Washington always kept extremely bright people close at hand, some historians attribute his political positions and pronouncements to his subordinates. Dr. Glenn A. Phelps, professor of political science at Northern Arizona University, has written in *George Washington & American Constitutionalism* that Washington's "writings reveal a clear, thoughtful, and remarkably coherent vision of what he hoped an American republic would become. These notions began to emerge early in the 1770s, took on a sharper, clearer perspective during the Revolution, and changed little thereafter."[29] Washington knew his mind, and was not overly influenced by subordinates.

George Washington fought for independence, helped frame our Constitution, and then for eight years gave us a sterling example of limited Constitutional governance. He wagered his life and fortune in the service of his country, and he would be disappointed by our lack of knowledge about our founding history.

Benjamin Franklin, Renaissance Man

During the second half of the eighteenth century, the United States was blessed with numerous Renaissance men, but none could compare to Benjamin Franklin. Franklin's humorous aphorisms are so embedded in our popular culture, and he has been caricatured so often, that we sometimes think he must have been the class clown of the Revolution. Nothing could be further from the truth. Franklin was arguably the second most important person in securing our independence. Despite Washington's great efforts, our domestic military and treasury could never have defeated the British Empire. We needed help. As commissioner of the United States in Paris, Franklin did more than flirt with the ladies; he charmed a nation and gained access to the French court. Everything Franklin did had a purpose. Once granted access to the back rooms of Versailles, he achieved the impossible by getting the United States desperately needed money, warships, and international legitimacy.

Franklin started life as a poor apprentice printer but ended up exceptionally wealthy. Michael Klepper and Robert Gunther rank him in the top one hundred in *The Wealthy 100: From Benjamin Franklin to Bill Gates—A Ranking of the Richest Americans, Past and Present.*[30] How did he do it? With two grand entrepreneurial moves. In the first, he nearly perfected the current concept of franchising, setting up print shops in cities outside Philadelphia that were as standardized as an H & R Block office. But the bulk of his fortune came from his realization that content was more valuable than labor. Franklin went beyond the printer's craft to become a publisher. For nearly the entire twenty-five years of its publication, *Poor Richard's Almanac* was the #1 bestseller after the Bible, and the *Pennsylvania Gazette* was the most successful newspaper in the colonies.[31]

Franklin was also an inventor and world-renowned scientist. He invented bifocals, the Franklin stove, the lightning rod, a urinary catheter, swim flippers, a glass armonica, an odometer, and many other devices. He was especially renowned in Europe for his scientific achievements. His famous kite-flying episode was not a lark, but an experiment to confirm a portion of his well-developed theory of electricity. He was the first to map the Gulf Stream, which gave him something to occupy his mind during his eight voyages across the Atlantic. In 1727, Franklin founded a philosophical organization called the Junto. This civically minded group led to the nation's first volunteer fire department, public hospital, public library, and numerous other civic improvements, which all had a strong Franklin imprint. He later transitioned the Junto into the Philosophical Society, the country's first learned society.[32]

In the earlier stages of the Founding period, Benjamin Franklin had been a loyalist. As an informal envoy to England, he realized that Parliament was intractable and changed his mind.[33] Despite his jovial image, Franklin could hold a grudge, and he made those who slighted him or his country pay for their transgressions. During the war, Franklin did what the Continental Congress could not do—he delivered money, arms, and military forces to Washington. While the home politicians bickered endlessly, Franklin got what George Washington needed from France.

The Constitutional phase represented the true nation-building.

This convention was at times so acrimonious that the delegates several times nearly abandoned the endeavor. Each time the convention edged toward collapse, Benjamin Franklin was there to lighten the tone through humor, calls for help from the Almighty, or merely filibustering until tempers abated. Franklin did not add much substance to the constitutional design, but his interpersonal skills held the delegates together until the design was complete. He also hosted innumerable caucus meetings under his famed mulberry tree.[34] He played a unique role that no one else could fill.

Benjamin Franklin built things to last. The American Philosophical Society still resides next to Independence Hall. *Poor Richard's Almanac* and his autobiography have never been out of print. The Philadelphia Contributionship for the Insuring of Houses from Loss by Fire that he helped found still sells fire insurance. The University of Pennsylvania and the Pennsylvania Hospital still exist. And we still have our Constitution. If Franklin returned today, he would likely warn us not to let our priceless heritage slip away. He might put aside his own sacrifices and contributions, but his jovial image would not disguise his anger at those who flippantly discarded the work of his friends.

Thomas Jefferson, Rebel with a Cause

Thomas Jefferson was a planter, architect, revolutionary, author, agricultural scientist, inventor, and politician, among a few other things he did in his spare time. His tombstone is inscribed, "Here was buried Thomas Jefferson, author of the Declaration of American Independence, of the Statute of Virginia for Religious Freedom, and father of the University of Virginia."[35] The inscription says nothing about his presidency where he reduced spending, cut taxes, kept us out of war, and doubled the land mass of the country. He wrote the epitaph himself and included the accomplishments that he took the most pride in. The Declaration of Independence is simultaneously a bill of particulars against King George III, and possibly the most hopeful and eloquent statement of the Founding Principles.

On June 11, 1776, the second Continental Congress appointed a committee to write a declaration of independence. Besides Jefferson,

John Adams, Benjamin Franklin, Robert R. Livingston, and Roger Sherman were selected. One of these five was a renowned author. Benjamin Franklin's *Poor Richard's Almanac* and his newspaper articles in the *Pennsylvania Gazette* had made him the best-known writer in North America. But Franklin declined to draft the declaration, supposedly due to poor health, so the committee asked the thirty-three-year-old Thomas Jefferson to draft the document.

In less than three weeks, Jefferson completed this historic document and presented it to the rest of the committee. The committee mostly accepted the document as written, except that Franklin made some subtle but important revisions. For example, Jefferson had written, "We hold these truths to be sacred and undeniable," which Franklin revised to "self-evident." Some have suggested that Franklin was pushing the text toward the analytic empiricism of David Hume, but it's more likely that the master editor was wordsmithing for a more graceful rhythm to the words.[36]

On June 28, the Committee of Five reported out the declaration to Congress. Congress proceeded to make thirty-nine revisions, but thankfully left the preamble alone. Altering the list of grievances did not dilute the earth-shaking ideas in the first two paragraphs. Although Jefferson never publically uttered a word of complaint, he secretly fumed at the constant meddling.[37] Jefferson reported that afterward, Franklin told him that he avoided drafting papers that would be reviewed by a public body. You can almost hear the seventy-year-old patriarch chuckling as he gave this advice to the young Virginian. According to Jefferson, Franklin told him the following story.

An apprentice hatter was about to open shop for himself. His first concern was to have a handsome signboard, with a proper inscription. He composed it in these words, "John Thompson, Hatter, makes and sells hats for ready money," with a figure of a hat subjoined. He then submitted it to friends for their amendments. The first he showed it to thought the word "Hatter" repetitive, because it was followed by the words "makes hats." It was struck out. The next observed that the word "makes" might as well be omitted, because his customers would not care who made the hats. He struck it out. A third said he thought the words "for ready money" were useless, as it was not the custom of the place to sell on credit. The inscription now stood, "John Thompson sells hats." "Sells hats!" says the next friend. "Why, nobody expects you to give them away. What then is the use of that word?" It was stricken out, and "hats" followed it, as there was one painted on the board. So the inscription was reduced to "John Thompson" with the figure of a hat subjoined.[38]

The principles espoused in the declaration were not new. In 1822, John Adams answered a query about the Declaration of Independence. "We reported it to the committee of five. It was read, and I do not remember that Franklin or Sherman criticized anything. We were all in haste. Congress was impatient, and the instrument was reported, as I believe, in Jefferson's handwriting, as he first drew it. As you justly observe, there is not an idea in it but what had been hackneyed in Congress for two years before. The substance of it is contained in the declaration of rights and the violation of those rights in the Journals of Congress in 1774. Indeed, the essence of it is contained in a pamphlet, voted and printed by the town of Boston, before the first Congress met, composed by James Otis, as I suppose, in one of his lucid intervals, and pruned and polished by Samuel Adams."[39]

Jefferson himself told Henry Lee, "This was the object of the Declaration of Independence. Not to find out new principles, or new arguments, never before thought of, not merely to say things which had never been said before; but to place before mankind the common sense of the subject, in terms so plain and firm as to command their assent, and to justify ourselves in the independent stand we are compelled to take."[40]

Nearly every American recognizes the first sentence of the second paragraph of the Declaration: "We hold these truths to be self-evident, that all men are created equal, that they are endowed by their Creator with certain unalienable rights, that among these are life, liberty and the pursuit of happiness." Jefferson rightly deserves enormous recognition and praise for writing an eloquent and powerful expression of this revolutionary concept, but it was an idea more universal than one man—or even one generation. Harry Truman called the Declaration of Independence "the supreme expression of our profound belief."[41] Let's remember to take it out from under its glass case when we need it.

James Madison, Father of the Constitution

In his later years, James Madison protested being called the Father of the Constitution, saying that the document was not "the off-spring of a single brain."[42] Our Constitution was actually the offspring of fifty-five brains, although none of them as potent as Madison's. A few historians have denigrated Madison's informal title, saying he had merely outlived the other Founding Fathers and his convention notes gave him more credit than he would have received otherwise. These critics also point out that the final Constitution differed appreciably from the Virginia Plan that Madison initially supported as the correct governmental system.

This is an incorrect appraisal of Madison's contributions. James Madison was arguably the most important Founder before, during, and after the Federal Convention of 1787.

Before the Constitutional Convention

In 1786, the country was at peace, but teetering toward collapse. Congress called for a convention in Annapolis to offer amendments to the Articles of Confederation, but the meeting failed due to a lack of a quorum. James Madison and Alexander Hamilton made a pact to promote another convention for the following year in Philadelphia.

Madison immediately committed himself to making the Philadelphia convention successful. He renewed his study of historical republics, and the writings of government philosophers. He started corresponding with academics, clergy, and his fellow Founders. He was a major architect of the Virginia Plan and worked ceaselessly to build a coalition of big states that could push the plan through the convention. Perhaps most importantly, he worked tirelessly with Alexander Hamilton, Thomas Jefferson, and George Mason to convince General Washington to attend. With Washington's reluctant commitment to be there, Madison knew his renown would draw enough delegates for a quorum of the states.[43]

During the Constitutional Convention

Edmund Randolph, the governor of Virginia, presented the Virginia Plan, but everyone knew that it was Madison's plan. Madison attended every session, and took the floor to speak 161 times, third after Gouverneur Morris and James Wilson.[44] He sat in the front of the room so he could take extensive notes of all the deliberations. Madison also frequently influenced debate with speeches on first principles, historic republics, and theories of government. Toward the end of the convention, Madison sat on the key committees charged with consolidating the prior four months' deliberations and votes.[45]

During the convention, Madison changed many delegates' minds, but he also changed his own mind on many of the details of how the government ought to be designed. He felt confident in the results, but he knew their work was going to be an academic exercise unless they could get it adopted by their fellow Americans.

After the Constitutional Convention—Ratification

Madison played a key part in guiding the Constitution through the Continental Congress, a prerequisite to getting it out to ratification conventions. Once this was accomplished, they needed nine states to ratify, but New York and Virginia were crucial. These two large, prosperous states would split the country geographically if they decided to go their own way. So Madison pretended to be a New Yorker to help Hamilton and Jay write the *Federalist Papers*, which were the opinion pieces of the day. These papers, intended to persuade New York to ratify, were soon republished throughout all the states. Next, he raced home to Virginia to lead the Federalist charge in the Virginia ratification convention. Taking on Patrick Henry, an Anti-Federalist leader and reputedly the best speaker in the country, Madison led his caucus to victory.

But he wasn't done. Ratification in several states depended on a promise to add a Bill of Rights to the Constitution. Madison was the one who led the First Congress to make good on this promise— resulting in his second moniker, Father of the Bill of Rights. The Bill of Rights followed almost immediately after ratification and was a condition of ratification by many states. For this reason, the first ten amendments could almost be considered part of the original document. Americans should be thankful to James Madison for the greatest constitution in history. We owe him an enormous debt of gratitude.

Gouverneur Morris, Penman of the Constitution

Most Americans know that Thomas Jefferson wrote the Declaration of Independence, but fewer know that Gouverneur Morris wrote the Constitution. In both cases, men gathered at the Pennsylvania State House and voted for each element of the respective documents, but it was up to Jefferson and Morris to edit the language of the resolutions, organize the presentation, and prepare a preamble. Both men wrote with such consummate skill that their words have reverberated across time and distance.

At the end of the Constitutional Convention, Morris was assigned to the Committee of Style. This committee's task was to take the work of the Committee of Detail and compose a clear and coherent constitution. For example, the preamble from the Committee of Detail read:

"We the people of the States of New Hampshire, Massachusetts, Rhode-Island and Providence Plantations, Connecticut, New-York, New-Jersey, Pennsylvania, Delaware, Maryland, Virginia, North-Carolina, South-Carolina, and Georgia, do ordain, declare, and establish the following Constitution for the Government of Ourselves and our Posterity."

Morris volunteered to take this draft home and prepare a more polished version. He did a masterful job. Beyond organizing the document and clarifying the language, Morris wrote a short, but eloquent preamble.

"We the People of the United States, in Order to form a more perfect Union, establish Justice, insure domestic Tranquility, provide for the common defence, promote the general Welfare, and secure the Blessings of Liberty to ourselves and our Posterity, do ordain and establish this Constitution for the United States of America."

James Madison, another member of the committee, gave Morris

credit for "the finish given to the style and arrangement of the Constitution."[46] William Pierce, a fellow delegate, wrote, "Mr. Morris is one of those genius's [sic] in whom every species of talents combine to render him conspicuous and flourishing in public debate: he winds through all the mazes of rhetoric and throws around him such a glare that he charms, captivates, and leads away the senses of all who hear him."[47] Perhaps his speaking prowess was one reason why he spoke more than any other delegate at the convention (173 times).[48] The other reason was that he was a man of firm opinions. He was a strong proponent of separation of powers, with effective checks and balances. Morris was an abolitionist, saying he would gladly pay taxes to free all Africans, and called slavery the "curse of heaven." Before the Bill of Rights, he fought for a Constitutional guarantee that anyone could practice their chosen religion without interference.[49] Gouverneur Morris was an unequivocal believer in the Founding Principles.

Alexander Hamilton: A Plan for Solvency and Survival

As Americans celebrated New Year's Day in 1790, the new nation's economy was on the brink of collapse. The cumulative debt of the states and nation was enormous, soldiers who had served in the Revolution hadn't been paid, farm foreclosures were so rampant that mobs burned down courthouses, there was no national coin or currency, inflation raged out of control in many states, and international trade was near impossible because the nation had no credit. It seemed all but certain that the American experiment would fail.

The newborn country might have failed if it were not for the three enormous assets the United States had not possessed just ten months earlier. A new government had been formed under the recently ratified United States Constitution, George Washington had been sworn in as the first president, and Washington had a cabinet member with a plan. That man was Secretary of the Treasury Alexander Hamilton.

On January 14, 1790, the secretary presented his economic plan to Congress. Hamilton's goal was to renew confidence in the government, and "to promote the increasing respectability of the American name; to answer the calls of justice; to restore landed property to its due value; to furnish new resources both to agriculture and commerce; to cement more closely the union of the states; to add to their security against foreign attack; to establish public order on the basis of an upright and liberal policy."[50]

The major elements of Hamilton's plan included: 1) national assumption of all war debts—the U.S. had state, national, and foreign debts of about $80 million, 2) issuance of tiered debt instruments to finance the retirement of existing loans, 3) retirement of all prior debt at face value, 4) a national bank 80 percent privately owned, 5) a sinking fund to retire new debt, 6) a sound national currency backed by gold and silver specie, and 7) tariffs to raise revenue and protect fledgling commerce.

Economic collapse has not been uncommon in world history. Even when everyone can foresee a looming calamity, it requires courage to take the steps needed to re-instill confidence. Hamilton's plan was hugely controversial. Critics screamed that it wouldn't work, or that it was unfair. They said it wouldn't work because growth could never be fast enough to retire the debt, and it was unfair because his plan rewarded speculators who had bought bonds from soldiers for pennies on the dollar. Hamilton argued in return that a country's reputation for fiscal responsibility was more important than perceived fairness. (He actually believed speculators had performed a service by providing cash for what many believed was worthless paper.)[51]

The critics were wrong. Hamilton's plan worked exceptionally well. With renewed confidence, the economy boomed; foreigners engaged in expanded trade with the new nation; a trustworthy currency dampened civil unrest; jobs became plentiful; and debt as a percent of gross domestic product dropped to negligible levels. James Monroe later said, "The circulation of confidence is better than the circulation of money."[52]

When Washington retired seven years later, he handed over to John Adams a healthy, robust economy.

John Adams, the Philosopher Rebel

John Adams was the greatest expert on government in the colonies...at least until James Madison stepped to the forefront. Harvard educated, Adams was a champion of the Founding Principles, a firm proponent of Enlightenment teachings, and a constitutional scholar. Granted, he could be argumentative and self-righteous, but he was a pious man of honor and character.

Adams was an early and fervent advocate for independence. He opposed the Stamp Act in speeches, articles, and his widely circulated dissertation, *Essay on the Canon and Feudal Law*. He served in the first and second Continental Congresses, where he took part in more than ninety committees, many of which he chaired. Adams nominated George Washington to be commander-in-chief, and headed the Board of War and Ordnance, which was responsible for supplying Washington's army. He succeeded in getting an early resolution for independence passed that eventually led to the Declaration, and then served on the committee that wrote the Declaration of Independence. Twice during the war he served as an envoy in Europe. In later years, Thomas Jefferson said that Adams was "the pillar of [the Declaration's] support on the floor of Congress, its ablest advocate and defender against the multifarious assaults it encountered."[53]

Despite his revolutionary credentials, Adams's greatest contributions were as a thinker and writer. In 1772, he wrote *Dispute with America, From Its Origin, in 1754, to the Present Time*, arguing persuasively against British imperial policy. His 1776 *Thoughts on Government* influenced numerous state constitutions. The treatise defended bicameralism, and argued for separation of power between three branches with checks and balances. In 1780, Adams largely wrote the Massachusetts state constitution, which included a strong executive with limited veto authority and a bicameral legislature. While in London (1787), Adams published *A Defence of the Constitutions of Government of the United States,* which was so popular with delegates to the Constitutional Convention that Adams could almost be considered the fifty-sixth delegate. Adams strongly pushed the idea of "checks and balances" and his thinking had a strong influence on James Madison.

John Adams was possibly the hardest working person during the founding. He was everywhere, doing everything during each and every one of the thirty-two years and beyond. In all his activities, he always tried to keep the best interests of his country in mind. An ardent Republican, he was an honorable man who truly believed his countrymen were up to the task of self-government.

The First Essential—Good Moral Character

John Adams's second cousin, Samuel Adams, said, "Nothing is more essential to the establishment of manners in a state than that all persons employed in places of power and trust must be men of unexceptionable characters."[54] The language may be old-fashioned, but the meaning is clear. People in places of power need to be honorable. Character does matter. The United States of America was indeed lucky to have a large cadre of *unexceptionable characters* to take principled action during the early days of our country. Then again, perhaps *lucky* is not the proper word.

5

Who Wrote the Constitution?

"The greatest single effort of national deliberation that
the world has ever seen."

—John Adams[55]

The Articles of Confederation had proved barely adequate during
the imperative of war and a failure after independence was
achieved. A few years after the Paris Peace Treaty, our military had
been reduced to almost nothing and the economy was in such bad
shape that there appeared to be no way to rebuild it. England believed
that the United States would soon come crawling back to the British
Empire after the French and Spanish showed their former colonists
what a nasty world it was outside of English protection.

It appeared as if the United States was doomed. The union was
a weak confederation of bickering, semi-independent states that
in some cases were actually shooting at each other. There was no
common money for the nation. Each state was trying to figure out
ways to extract funds from neighboring states through tariffs, trade
barriers, and exorbitant harbor fees. The new country was broke—or,
more accurately, bankrupt—because it was deeply in debt to foreign
powers and its own citizens. In fact, the country couldn't even make
good on the back pay owed to Revolutionary soldiers. To add insult
to injury, the states did little to halt the numerous farm foreclosures

that were occurring because of unpaid taxes. Malcontents like Daniel Shays had no difficulty fomenting violence against the states.[56] In taverns across the thirteen states, Americans complained that their British overlords had never treated them this unfairly.

It looked hopeless. Then in May of 1787, delegates came to Philadelphia with a congressional charter to revise the Articles of Confederation. But they didn't revise the Articles. Instead they wrote a constitution for a totally new government. These men carried out a bloodless coup. Most governments evolve over decades or centuries, or find order under a strong ruler who bends the populace to his will through force of arms. Never before had people gathered in a room to design a government from scratch. Certainly that couldn't work. But it did. The Constitution of the United States of America brought order out of near anarchy without a shot. It did this without violating the Founding Principles, without installing a king, and without any help from a foreign power. And it did all of this with permission from the people. It was a miracle. Unlike the Articles of Confederation, this new republican government worked so well that England waited in vain for its wayward children to return to the fold.

Revolutionaries, Patriots, and Demigods

Fifty-five men attended the Federal Convention of 1787, what we now call the Constitutional Convention. When Thomas Jefferson read the list of attendees in France, he called them an "assembly of demigods."[57] Not exactly, but they were staunch revolutionaries and patriots. They were also highly successful, well educated, and unswerving in their support of a republican form of government and the Founding Principles. They came to Philadelphia committed to rescuing American from its slide into anarchy. (The delegates to the Constitutional Convention are often called Framers.)

While the names of many of the delegates have been forgotten, a few remain household names. George Washington was unanimously elected to preside over the convention. James Madison, Benjamin Franklin, Alexander Hamilton, Gouverneur Morris, James Wilson, George Mason, and Roger Sherman were all key delegates. Most of these men knew each other from years of politicking or war. Twenty-nine served in a military capacity during the Revolution and another twenty-three risked their fortunes and lives by taking an active political role during the war. Eight of them had already committed treason by signing the Declaration of Independence, and four had been assigned to the committee that wrote the Articles of Confederation. This was more of an assembly of tired revolutionaries than of demigods, except that the firebrands were noticeably absent. Sam Adams, Patrick Henry, John Hancock, and Thomas Paine were not in Philadelphia that summer. It was a time for nation builders.

Highly Educated and Generally Wealthy

In colonial America, college degrees were rare, yet twenty-nine delegates held college degrees and many others were self-educated in the classics and modern political thought. Almost all of the delegates were knowledgeable about Aristotle, Cicero, Locke, Hume, Smith, Blackstone, and Montesquieu. Ten had degrees from the College of New Jersey (later to become Princeton), six from European universities, four from Harvard, four from Yale, four from William and Mary, two from the College of Philadelphia, and one from Kings College (later to become Columbia University).

Eleven were businessmen, eight owned large plantations, three were physicians, one was a professor, and six could be called professional politicians. Thirty of the delegates were lawyers in an age that revered the rule of law and reason. They came from all walks of life and social stratums, but the majority of them were wealthy. In fact, forty-five of the delegates could be considered rich, or at least well-off. Thirty-one had the good fortune of being born to wealthy or prominent families. Twelve were self-made and two married into money. It was expensive to travel and be away from a person's livelihood, so the delegates tended to be individuals who could afford to spend months in the most expensive city in America. Ten of the delegates struggled to make ends meet and had to rely on a stipend from their state legislatures.

English Spoken Here, but...

All of the delegates spoke English, but the accents could be confusing. Eight were born in other counties, as were many of their parents. In a day when traveling more than a few miles was rare, regions tended to incubate strong local accents. Delegates from the Deep South thought that the New England twang was shrill and that people from the North talked too fast. Accents even varied within regions, with Virginians as perplexed by a rural Georgian accent as someone from Connecticut.

Washington and Franklin were the only delegates who had held positions representing all of the states. In general, the other fifty-three delegates had a weak allegiance to the national government and thought of themselves as more attached to their respective states. At least this is the way they felt at the beginning of the convention. By September 17, 1787, when they held the signing ceremony for the Constitution, most of them had come to think and act on a national scale. They had made the leap to becoming Americans.

A Republic for the Ages

The delegates were staunch republicans, but they also were practical men. All of them had already invested a good portion of their lives to independence and the republican cause. Now they were desperate to make it work. Some wanted to adjust the Articles, while others arrived convinced they needed something completely new. Their original disagreements were huge, but they shared a belief in the Founding Principles, which provided a common foundation to resolve their differences. They often argued about who was being the most faithful to their core beliefs, but unlike other revolutionaries, they didn't abandon their principles in a quest for power, or disintegrate into self-consuming warfare because they didn't know when to quit fighting and start building.

These were not demigods, but real men with human frailties and weaknesses. They also were honorable men in an era when honor defined a man. They sequestered themselves for four months in a hot, closed room and argued endlessly over every detail of the government plan. They often talked about future generations. They insisted on liberty for themselves, but also wanted a system that protected liberty for posterity. More than anything, they wanted a republic that would never threaten its own people. That meant they had to craft it with precision. Man was naturally a power-seeking animal, and this impulse had to be thwarted by a system of checks and balances. They succeeded. Over two hundred years later, constitutional restraints have been eroded, but not completely overturned.

Did the delegates believe that the Constitution could protect the liberty of Americans for all time? Washington wrote, "No wall of words, ... no mound of parchment can be so formed as to stand against the sweeping torrent of boundless ambition on the one side, aided by the sapping current of corrupted morals on the other."[58] The longevity of the Constitution has never been solely or even primarily based on the mechanisms embedded in the document. The greatest credit goes to Americans who restrain the worst impulses of power seekers. The Founding Principles are so deeply embedded in our psyches that Americans automatically rise to the occasion whenever they see them challenged.

What Ever Became Of...

Each of the Constitutional Convention delegates had extensive political experience and many went on to take substantial roles in the government they created. Two became president, twenty-five served in Congress, five gained appointments to the Supreme Court, four became foreign ministers, and four held cabinet positions.

Not every delegate went on to further success, however. Six wealthy delegates died impoverished and fleeing creditors. One was indicted, but not tried, for treason. One barely escaped impeachment by the Supreme Court, and another was expelled from the Senate. Two died in duels, another mysteriously disappeared in the middle of New York City, and another was rumored murdered by a grand-nephew impatient for his inheritance.

A Legacy for All of Us

That long-ago summer was truly amazing. Many question whether the Founders understood the full ramifications of what they were doing. Those people have obviously not read Madison's extensive notes from the convention. They knew. They set their sights incredibly high. They understood they were doing something big—really big.

Now it is up to us to remain worthy of their legacy. How? The first step is to read this precedent-shattering document—the United States Constitution. Next, study the debates, the Federalist Papers, the Anti-Federalist Papers, and the records of the ratification conventions. Together, these are an astonishing account of how an entire nation applied its collective intellect to design and enact a system of checks and balances that prevented the dangerous concentration of power. Our Founding Fathers understood that liberty would not survive centralized political power. When humans get possession of power, they seldom relinquish it without a major struggle. It has been the same way throughout history, and human nature has not changed in the last two hundred years. The United States Constitution is based on a few solid principles that have been rigorously tested and found crucial for the preservation of liberty. That's why our Constitution is as valid today as it was in 1787.

PART III

The Founding Principles

6

Rights Come from God, Not Government

"Can the liberties of a nation be thought secure when we have removed their only firm basis, a conviction in the minds of the people that these liberties are the gift of God?"

—*Thomas Jefferson*[59]

The Founders didn't believe rights were handed down by governments, kings, or rulers. Instead, they believed every individual was endowed by their Creator with certain unalienable rights. In their experience, governments didn't protect rights; governments threatened rights. World history had been an unbroken string of ruler upon ruler suppressing rights and liberty.

Rights endowed by God was not a new concept. It went back at least to Marcus Tullius Cicero and the Roman Republic. Cicero searched for what he called natural law.[60] John Locke and the Enlightenment magnified awareness that rights came from God. Locke wrote that the natural rights enjoyed by prehistoric humans were the ones that came from God. He believed that the state of nature is governed by the law of nature, which seventeenth-century man could discover through reason. Locke concluded that humans were "by nature free, equal and independent."[61]

Locke's teachings didn't mean that natural rights couldn't be suppressed. It was the exception when they were not. Thomas Jefferson said, "The God who gave us life gave us liberty at the same time; the hand of force may destroy, but cannot disjoin them."[62] This means that force can be used to suppress rights, but they remain intrinsically joined to our human spirit. That is why the history of the world is not only the history of despots; it's also the history of man's constant struggle to reassert his natural rights. John Adams agreed, "You have rights antecedent to all earthly governments; rights that cannot be repealed or restrained by human laws; rights derived from the Great Legislator of the Universe."[63]

This was not an academic problem for the Founders. They had personally experienced the British government trampling their rights. They knew rights were fragile. They could be suppressed by force, gradually eroded, or simply lost through neglect. Since some amount of governance was necessary, restraining this perpetual threat became an overwhelming concern when the time came to design a new government. The Founders' study of history taught them that power was the essential prerequisite for oppression: the more power was centralized and concentrated, the more at risk were rights and liberty.

No Bill of Rights?

The original Constitution included no Bill of Rights because delegates didn't believe one was necessary. They had chosen to protect rights through another method. When George Mason made a motion for a committee to draft a list of rights, it was unanimously defeated. In their minds, rights were not protected by words on a piece of paper, but by limiting governmental power.

Montesquieu and Hume advocated separation of power into three equal branches, with each branch having potent checks on the two other branches.[64] Although this was a well-established theory at the time, no government in the world had been designed along these principles. (In most of the existing state constitutions, overwhelming advantage was given to the legislative branch.)[65] Delegates to the convention believed that if they could construct a system consistent with the separation of powers doctrine, limit the national government to enumerated powers, and effectively set up the states as checks on the national government, then the national government would be restrained from trampling rights or intruding into peoples' lives.

Before the Constitution could become the supreme law of the land, it had to be debated and ratified by conventions of the people. The ratification debates—and accompanying newspaper and pamphlet opinion articles—were always contentious. Success was never assured. One of the Anti-Federalist arguments that gained support was that the Constitution was flawed because a Bill of Rights was missing. Although not a legal condition of ratification, several conventions approved the Constitution based on a promise that a Bill of Rights would be immediately added. As a result, the First Congress proposed a set of amendments, and the states ratified ten, which we now call the Bill of Rights.

A bill is a list, but is our Bill of Rights a list of government-guaranteed rights? No. These ten amendments remained consistent with the Founding Principles. The first eight amendments are filled with phrases like, "Congress shall make no law, shall not be infringed, shall not be violated, nor be deprived, shall not be required." These are not a list of rights generously bestowed by a benevolent government. They are, instead, directives from the American citizenry to those in government not to infringe upon their God-given rights. Some commentators have noted the Bill of Rights would be more accurately called a "Bill of Restrictions." If the first eight weren't clear enough, our Founders added two more amendments:

Ninth: "The enumeration in the Constitution, of certain rights, shall not be construed to deny or disparage others retained by the people."

Tenth: "The powers not delegated to the United States by the Constitution, nor prohibited by it to the States, are reserved to the States respectively, or to the people."

The Founders did not look to government to define or protect rights. They fulfilled their promise to propose a Bill of Rights by giving the government a list of rights that were never to be abridged by the government itself. As a safety measure, they added the caveat that this was not a complete list. Thomas Jefferson, as usual, artfully encapsulated the Founders' thinking on rights: "Rightful liberty is unobstructed action according to our will within limits drawn around us by the equal rights of others. I do not add 'within the limits of the law,' because law is often but the tyrant's will, and always so when it violates the rights of the individual."[66]

Rights at Risk

Today, rights are becoming increasingly at risk because power has become highly concentrated at the national level. Rights can only be abridged by a government that possesses unchecked power. Our American heritage is to fear concentrated power, so those who seek control have worked hard to convince many of us that it is the government that grants and guarantees rights. They are in essence saying that there is nothing to fear here—we are the ones that make you free, and we can even enlarge your freedoms. Just give us enough power.

Except that this has never been true in the history of the world. Oppression always comes from government. It always has, and always will. What about those mean, selfish corporations? In one-company towns, corporations wield enormous power, but the oppression comes from their exercising governmental power, not business power. It's the same with religion. Religions become oppressive when they extend themselves into a governmental role. This was true in the Middle Ages, and it's true today for those under Sharia law.

Since oppression always comes from government, or organizations wielding governmental powers, a core belief of our founding was that this natural inclination of man could only be immobilized by opposing centers of power (balance) with each power center possessing effective controls on all other power centers (checks). To an ever-increasing extent, this principle is being eroded with executive regulatory agencies that wield legislative and judicial powers, a judiciary that invades the domain of the other two branches, legislation that usurps state powers, executive orders with the force of law, to name only a few of the violations of this Founding Principle. If James Madison were alive today, he would probably tell everyone in government to return to their respective corners.

God and Government

Some cringe when the words *God* and *government* are spoken together. They believe it violates the separation of church and state. Actually, the phrase *separation of church and state* doesn't appear in the Constitution or any amendment. It comes from a letter written by Thomas Jefferson to the Danbury Baptists: "I contemplate with sovereign reverence that act of the whole American people which declared that their legislature should 'make no law respecting an establishment of religion, or prohibiting the free exercise thereof,' thus building a wall of separation between church and state."[67]

The First Amendment directed the national government (i.e., Congress) not to make any laws that prohibited the free exercise of religion. Conversely, the First Amendment prohibits the establishment of an official religion in the United States. This means the state is denied the use of religion as a lever to govern. It also means that a religion cannot use the government to impose its will on other Americans. It is yet another separation of power.

In 1835, Alexis de Tocqueville published the first volume of *Democracy in America*. He wrote, "Religion in America takes no direct part in the government of society, but it must nevertheless be regarded as the foremost of their political institutions."[68] Thomas Paine further wrote, "Were a man impressed as fully and strongly as he ought to be with the belief of a God, his moral life would be regulated by the force of belief; he would stand in awe of God and of himself, and would not do the thing that could not be concealed from either."[69] The Founders were obsessed with dispersing power and establishing checks and balances. It appears the First Amendment put another powerful check in place.

To assert that rights come from God is not to suggest that the United States should become a theocracy. It is only saying that true rights are not a social construct—in other words, they do not come from government. It should always be remembered that whoever grants a right could take it away. Would you rather this power be held by your government or your God?

Marcus Tullius Cicero (106 BC–46 BC) on Natural Rights

"True law is right reason in agreement with nature; it is of universal application, unchanging and everlasting; it summons to duty by its commands, and averts from wrong-doing by its prohibitions. ... We cannot be freed from its obligations by senate or people, and we need not look outside ourselves for an expounder or interpreter of it. And there will not be different laws at Rome and at Athens, or different laws now and in the future, but one eternal and unchangeable law will be valid for all nations and all times."

"The most foolish notion of all is the belief that everything is just which is found in the customs or laws of nations."

"But if the principles of Justice were founded on the decrees of peoples, the edicts of princes, or the decision of judges, then Justice would sanction robbery and adultery and forgery of wills, in case these acts were approved by the votes or decrees of the populace. But if so great a power belongs to the decision and decrees of fools that the laws of Nature can be changed by their votes, then why do they not ordain that what is bad and baneful shall be considered good and salutary? Or, if a law can make Justice injustice can it not also make good out of bad?"[70]

7

All Political Power Emanates from the People

"That to secure these rights, Governments are instituted among Men, deriving their just powers from the consent of the governed."

—*Declaration of Independence*

In 1776, upstart colonists penned the most revolutionary document in the history of man. The Declaration of Independence flipped the world upside down, and the Divine Right of Kings suddenly became the consent of the governed. The individual was now the one endowed by their Creator with certain unalienable rights. This was a world-shattering concept.

Like most revolutionary visions, this one didn't suddenly spring onto the world stage. Ironically, much of the philosophical basis for self-governance came from subjects of the British Crown. John Locke, David Hume, Adam Smith, and Thomas Paine were among many who advocated that consent of the governed was dictated by the *laws of nature and of nature's God*. Not everyone accepted this concept, of course—certainly not King George III or any of the English nobility. As John Locke wrote, "New opinions are always suspected, and usually opposed, without any other reason but because they are not already common."

The Founders, however, were steeped in this incendiary idea of self-governance. It didn't come to them only from philosophers. Self-governance had been part of their experience in the New World. The colonists were subjects of England, but a round-trip sail across the great Atlantic put three to four months between them and their king. To a great extent, they had no alternative but to learn how to rule themselves.

The Mayflower Compact

The Mayflower Compact was a rather strange dichotomy. It began by pledging loyalty to King James, but then went on to decree that the colonists would "combine together into a civil body politick, for our better ordering and preservation, and furtherance of the ends aforesaid: and by virtue hereof do enact, constitute, and frame, such just and equal laws, ordinances, acts, constitutions, and officers, from time to time, as shall be thought most meet and convenient for the general good of the colony." Basically, the Mayflower Compact was a written statement declaring self-government in colonial America.

Geography may have allowed the early colonists to govern themselves, but it was the writings of the Enlightenment philosophers that reminded them that self-rule was a natural right. This grand notion eventually led to the Declaration of Independence, which asserted that it was the right of the people "to institute a new government, laying its foundation on such principles and organizing its powers in such form, as to them shall seem most likely to effect their safety and happiness." This founding principle basically said that the people themselves held the power to form a new government at any time and in any shape that met their needs. It was a radical concept used to justify radical action.

The United States Constitution

The tradition of self-government continued to build until the colonists felt compelled to fight a war to secure their independence. In the Founders' minds, self-government meant representation in Parliament, which they were denied.

Despite the Founders' significant experience at the colony and state level, the initial exercise in self-government across all thirteen states did not work well. The first United Sates government operated under the Articles of Confederation, but the Articles were so weak, it became nearly impossible to govern. The fatal flaw in the Articles was that it formed a government that represented states instead of people, and any state could veto crucial collective action. In September of 1786, Alexander Hamilton and James Madison at the Annapolis convention called for a convention to meet in Philadelphia "for the sole and express purpose of revising the articles of confederation, and reporting to Congress and the several legislatures, such alterations and provisions therein as shall when agreed to in Congress, and confirmed by the States, render the federal constitution, adequate to the exigencies of government and the preservation of the union." While Congress was initially reluctant to endorse this call, they eventually did so, with only Rhode Island objecting.[71]

The instructions were clear. The convention was to recommend changes to the Articles of Confederation, and submit them to Congress and the state legislatures for approval. The delegates did not follow their instructions. Instead, they wrote an entirely new constitution—one that would dissolve the existing national government and take selected powers away from the states. How in the world would they get this thing approved? It threatened every entrenched political figure in the country. Congress and the state legislatures would never agree to being marginalized. (A trivia note: the convention delegates named the new legislature Congress in the hope that current members of Congress would assume that they would be elected to the new body.)

James Madison had an idea. All power emanates from the people, so neither Congress nor the state legislatures had the authority to approve a new government. In "Federalist No. 46," he wrote, "The ultimate authority, wherever the derivative may be found, resides in the people alone."[72] This principle dictated that the people were the sole authorizing force. To legitimatize their work, they needed to bypass Congress and the state legislatures and go directly to the people. This was the reason that the ratification conventions were independent of the state legislatures and Congress. It was a principled action that met only mild resistance because few were willing to challenge a basic precept of the revolution and founding.

A Most Audacious Letter

The convention decided that the best way to accomplish direct ratification by the people was to write a letter to Congress saying it was the convention's unanimous recommendation. The first draft was a convoluted rationalization for their actions and a long-winded pronouncement that their motives were pure. No one thought it was convincing, so in the end, they just told Congress what to do and how to do it. In less than three hundred words, the delegates wrote instructions on ratification and the mechanics for starting a new government from scratch. They simply directed Congress to submit the proposed Constitution to conventions of the people for ratification—without review or delay.

The national debate that ensued included opposing newspaper articles, sermons, competing pamphlets, and the ratification conventions. It wasn't the Constitutional Convention, Congress, or the state legislatures that made the Constitution a binding contract between the people and their government; it was ratification conventions and the surrounding debates that occurred in churches, taverns, and on street corners.

Supreme Law of the Land

The Constitution reads, "We the People ... do ordain and establish this Constitution for the United States of America." It is not a small matter that our United States Constitution starts with the words *We the People* in out-sized letters. The entire document is the people's document—a written contract wherein the people delegate specific authority to a national government. As is often stated in modern contracts, it was meant to be the sole agreement between the parties, and changed only by the process defined within the document.

United States Constitution, Article 6, Second Paragraph

This Constitution, and the Laws of the United States which shall be made in Pursuance thereof; and all Treaties made, or which shall be made, under the Authority of the United States, shall be the supreme Law of the Land; and the Judges in every State shall be bound thereby, any Thing in the Constitution or Laws of any State to the Contrary notwithstanding.

After nine states ratified the Constitution, the United States had a new government. It was a bloodless coup that abolished a defective system and replaced it with a government devised by reason and debate, and then subsequently approved by the ultimate authority—the people.

Today, some people think the Constitution made the national government the supreme authority. Others believe the national government is a creature of the states. Still others think national power depends on the circumstances, time frame, safety issues, or the greater good. The Founders were never confused. They devised a federal system with defined powers dispersed between the states and the various branches of the national government. Above all, they knew in their hearts that governments derived their just powers from the consent of the governed. Period.

This doesn't mean that people can choose when to obey the government. After all, President George Washington sent an army to quell the Whiskey Rebellion. Congress had imposed an unpopular tax on whiskey, and Washington believed this enforcement action was his duty because duly elected representatives had passed a law consistent with the enumerated powers in the Constitution.[73]

The crucial point is that the national government's authority comes solely from the Constitution—which is a social contract between Americans and their government. Exercising authority outside the bounds of the Constitution is not an exercise in just powers. This contract can be amended. In fact, it has been amended twenty-seven times—twelve in the last century. It's difficult to change, but not impossible. In fact, once a consensus develops that a change is needed, it has always proceeded with relative haste. It's the consensus building that takes time. Those impatient for change resisted by others use nefarious means to circumvent the Constitution, usually through a barrage of lawsuits until they get a decision that overturns an existing law or social practice. Government of the people, by the people, for the people mandates that changes be approved by elected representatives for legal issues or by the ratification process for constitutional issues.

People in government take an oath to preserve, protect, and defend the Constitution of the United States. This means they cannot ignore the Constitution, nor can they exercise authority beyond the enumerated powers. They are also obligated to call out others who violate the Constitution. Recent experience shows that this is not the common understanding in Washington, D.C. If some remain confused, perhaps words from the father of our country, George Washington, can help clarify what the Founders intended. "If in the opinion of the people the distribution or modification of the constitutional powers be in any particular wrong, let it be corrected by an amendment in the way which the Constitution designates. But let there be no change by usurpation."[74]

8

A Limited, Representative Republic Protects Liberty

"It is to be remembered that the general government is not to be charged with the whole power of making and administering laws. Its jurisdiction is limited to certain enumerated objects."

—*James Madison*[75]

The Founders distrusted strong governments. George Washington warned, "Government is not reason: It is not eloquence, it is force, like fire it is a dangerous servant and a fearful master." The Founders' own experience and history taught them that overly powerful governments always turned oppressive. But they understood that government was necessary; in fact, they knew they needed a stronger government than the one they had at the beginning of our nation. By the time the Constitutional Convention convened, a consensus had developed that the Articles of Confederation were severely flawed. Despite knowing they needed something different, there was enormous uncertainty about what kind of government could sustain a republic and give the people voice, while not threatening the liberty of its citizens. They knew it couldn't be too weak, but it also couldn't be too strong.

The Founders didn't seek a Goldilocks government. Instead, they did something far more complicated. The Founders listed only specific powers for the national government, balanced those powers, and then designed an elaborate set of checks to lessen the chance of abuse of those powers. They used a system of limited and checked powers so they could give the government enough authority to govern domestically and protect the nation from a dangerous world. In other words, they followed Thomas Jefferson's advice, "In questions of power, then, let no more be heard of confidence in man, but bind him down from mischief by the chains of the Constitution."[76] They built a stronger national government, but chained it down with the Constitution. It was an intricate formula, but they knew exactly what they were trying to achieve: a powerful national government, with "No Trespassing" signs where they did not want it to intrude.

A Republic, Not a Democracy

Our Constitution created a limited, representative republic. What is that? A republic is different from a democracy. In a democracy, the majority directly make laws, while in a republic, elected representatives make laws. Basically, in a pure democracy, the majority has unlimited power, whereas in a republic, a written constitution limits the majority and provides safeguards for individuals and minorities.

John Adams wrote that "there never was a democracy yet that did not commit suicide,"[77] and James Madison wrote in "Federalist No. 10" that "democracies ... have, in general, been as short in their lives as they have been violent in their deaths."[78] The reason democracies fail is that voters learn that they can legally take property or liberties away from others. Those subjected to abuse can be anyone outside the majority coalition, and their minority status can be based on race, religion, wealth, political affiliation, or even which state they reside in. This was not a new concept at the time. The Greek historian Polybius called it *cheirokratia*, loosely translated as *mob rule*, and the French political thinker Alexis de Tocqueville used the phrase *tyranny of the majority*. Demagogic leaders become adept at appealing to the emotions of jealousy, avarice, and entitlement. They also denigrate opponents in order to justify prejudicial actions taken by the majority. Soon, oppression of minority classes causes enough conflict to collapse the democratic process.

The slaveholding Madison argued the point dramatically during the Constitutional Convention. To illustrate the dangers of pure democracy, he said, "We have seen the mere distinction of color made in the most enlightened period of time, a ground of the most oppressive dominion ever exercised by man over man."[79] Many from the South were angry that he had made a direct reference to slavery. His comments may have been impolite for the day, but it was typical of Madison's irrefutable logic. He laid the evidence before them that rule by the majority in a pure democracy can be oppressive.

The word *democracy* is not mentioned in the Constitution. Some of the delegates had been frightened by Shays's Rebellion and equated democracy with mob rule. Others were convinced by Madison that different factions would come together until they formed a majority and then take advantage of those who were not members of their coalition. In fact, Madison showed that throughout history this phenomenon had destroyed every experiment in democracy.[80] The Founders wanted laws made by representatives in order to put a buffer between popular passions and legislation. This is the reason that we pledge allegiance to the flag of the United States of America, and to the Republic for which it stands.

The Founders may have avoided democracy at the national level, but our federal system of government reserves certain powers to the states, so we actually have both systems within the United States. There is no mechanism for Americans to directly enact legislation at the national level, but about half of the states allow ballot initiatives, which, if passed by a majority of the voters, have the force of law. Ballot initiatives are direct lawmaking by a majority of the general voting populace. An example would be California's Proposition 98, which mandates that about 40 percent of the state budget is allocated to K–14 education. Some complain that this proposition and others automate increased spending and hamstring the legislative budgeting process, but elected representatives cannot undo it.

How Do the People Exert Their Will in a Republic?

Without direct majority rule, how can people exert their authority over the government? Easy; whenever they're dissatisfied, they vote the rascals out. Alexander Hamilton wrote in "Federalist No. 21," "The natural cure for an ill-administration, in a popular or representative constitution, is a change of men."[81]

When the people's will is thwarted, regular elections give them the opportunity to dismiss their representatives. The delegates wanted the House of Representatives to be the most responsive to the will of the public so they gave them a relatively short two-year term. The Senate with a six-year term was designed to add stability to the system and provide a counterweight to runaway passions, but to also keep the Senate responsive to popular will, one third of them rotated out every two years.

The difference between a republic and a democracy is immediacy. In a democracy, decisions are made in the heat of the moment, while periodic elections in a republic provide a cooling-off period. To a great extent, democracies are ruled by feelings, while in a republic, the rule of law governs. In a republic, politicians can take principled actions that go against the will of many of their constituents with the knowledge that they will be judged by all the actions they take during their entire term in office. In a republic, political leaders are also given time to explain the reasons for their actions. Of course, if an elected official does something grievously offensive, then the voters can follow the advice of Hamilton.

A Limited Republic

The Founders set out to limit government powers at the national level. The rationale was explained by James Madison, "The essence of government is power; and power, lodged as it must be in human hands, will ever be liable to abuse."[82] The Founders limited the national government's power through six means:

1. Enumerated Powers
2. Balanced Power
3. Checks on Power
4. Two-Chamber Legislature
5. Temporary Terms of Different Lengths
6. Restricted Taxing Authority

In Article I, Section 8, the Framers enumerated the specific powers of the national government. The intent—made absolutely clear in the Tenth Amendment—was that all governmental powers not enumerated were retained by the states or by the people. The Founders believed that they had done such a good job of restricting national reach that a bill of rights was unnecessary because the national government had very limited power to reach down and affect an individual.

The next step was to balance power between the three branches and the states. This was difficult and they debated many alternatives. The most obvious illustration of this balancing act is that they gave Congress the power to declare war, and gave the president the authority to wage war. War, the most severe of government actions, was intended to be balanced between the legislative and executive branches. Another example was that the president had authority over government operations, but was without any means of raising the funds needed to run the executive branch. This was left in the hands of the legislature.

The Framers made sure that each of the three national branches had potent checks on the other two branches. For example, the president could make appointments to the Supreme Court or the executive branch, but the Senate had to consent to the appointee. Conversely, the president could veto bills passed by Congress, but Congress could override the veto with a two-thirds vote by each house of Congress. The intent was to give the national government only specified powers, and then each branch would have the authority to keep the actions of the other two branches within the confines of the Constitution.

Madison, among others, believed that the legislature could become dangerous. He wrote, "The legislative department is everywhere extending the sphere of its activity, and drawing all power into its impetuous vortex ... Its constitutional powers being at once more extensive, and less susceptible of precise limits, it can, with the greater facility, mask, under complicated and indirect measures, the encroachments which it makes on the co-ordinate departments ... The legislative department alone has access to the pockets of the people." The convention split the legislature into two houses to make it more difficult for the legislature to subjugate the other branches or the people.

During the Constitutional Convention, the delegates argued incessantly over the president's length of term and re-eligibility. They went back and forth between a long term without re-eligibility, and a short term with re-eligibility. They finally decided on a relatively short term of four years and unlimited re-eligibility. (The Twenty-Second Amendment put a two-term limit on the presidency.) It was determined that senators would serve six years, with one-third rotating out of office every two years. Members of the House of Representatives would serve for two years, and Supreme Court justices would serve for life. Originally, all of these various government officials were chosen differently, with representative elected by the people, senators elected by state legislatures, Supreme Court justices appointed by the president and confirmed by the Senate, and the president elected by an electoral college. (After the Seventeenth Amendment, Americans directly elected senators.) The varying terms, checks and balances, and different means of elections were all meant to work together to preclude a cabal from gaining control of the entire government.

When the Constitution was written, the national government had limited taxing authority, primarily restricted to imposts, duties, and excise taxes. Money equals power, and the Founders believed the best way to harness national power was to restrict revenue. The Sixteenth Amendment gave the national government the power to collect *taxes on incomes, from whatever source derived*, which is basically an unlimited taxing authority.

Is the United States Now an Unlimited Republic?

Today, many believe that the United States of America has become an unlimited republic. Through time, most of the power-limiting safeguards have been circumvented. James Madison said, "If Congress can do whatever in their discretion can be done by money, and will promote the *general welfare*, the government is no longer a limited one."[83] Many believe we have already reached that point. The enumerated powers have no force, power has gradually shifted to the executive, checks are frequently merely rhetorical, the Bill of Rights is misconstrued or ignored, and the national government has been collecting about one-fifth of the economy in taxes while spending nearly one-quarter of our entire national production. We remain a republic, however, and the ultimate authority of the people can still be exerted at the ballot box. If our representatives, whether in the House, the Senate, or the executive branch abuse the Constitution or the liberty of American citizens, we can still throw the incumbents out of office. It appears to be our last line of defense.

9

Consent of the Governed Requires a Written Constitution

"Our peculiar security is in possession of a written Constitution. Let us not make it a blank paper by construction."

—*Thomas Jefferson*[84]

The English have an unwritten constitution. The American colonies were part of the British Empire, and, for the most part, British immigrants populated the colonies. Why then did they depart from the English tradition of an unwritten constitution? The most obvious reason is that the English Constitution and common law evolved over centuries, while our forefathers were able to start with a blank slate. As Thomas Paine said in *Common Sense*, "We have it in our power to begin the world over again. A situation similar to the present, hath not happened since the days of Noah."[85]

From our earliest days, our national heritage was a written constitution that set the rules for governance between the people and their elected representatives. If you're given a fresh start to design a social contract where people hold political power, then you need to lay out the proposed system of government in writing so everyone has a chance to review it.

In Writing, Please

When the Pilgrims landed at Plymouth, Massachusetts, they almost immediately sat down and wrote the Mayflower Compact. In 1639, the Colony of Connecticut adopted the Fundamental Orders, which is considered the first constitution in North America. When our forefathers wanted independence, they felt obliged to express their grievances in a written Declaration of Independence. At the time of the Constitutional Convention, all thirteen states had a written constitution or charter, and nine of the thirteen states had formal declarations of rights.[86]

Only through the written word can everybody have an equal opportunity to read and understand the proposal so they can properly exercise their authority to approve or disapprove the substance of the document. With a written constitution, people can argue over the composition, hash out differences, make changes, distribute it for comment, approve or disapprove it, and then through the ensuing years, constantly refer back to it as a settled benchmark. James Madison wrote, "Law is defined to be a rule of action; but how can that be a rule, which is little known, and less fixed?"[87]

Some argue that an unwritten constitution, sometimes called an uncodified constitution, is stronger that a written constitution because tradition has a stronger hold on society than a document. There is more than a little truth in that assessment. Words do build a weak wall against tyrants. The old U.S.S.R. constitution, which guaranteed extensive rights and liberties, is often cited to buttress this argument.[88] This is not a particularly relevant argument in the United States, however, because in a very real sense, the entire ratification process created an instant American constitutional tradition. It takes time for an infant nation to develop traditions, but a structured approach can accelerate the process.

The formal ratification process worked, and now oppressive action is held at bay more by our traditions and faith in the Founding Principles than by the Constitution. It's in our genes. The Constitution is a written proclamation of acceptable behavior we can wave in front of politicians who wander off the approved path, but it's our American culture that makes us challenge politicians in the first place. We started as a rebellious lot, and we still get cantankerous when our authority is challenged.

Words Have Meaning

The United States Constitution didn't spring forth from some committee for a vote without anyone reading it. They read it over and over again and debated every word. Our Founders were serious men with a serious purpose. During the convention, there were three iterations of the constitution, each one highly scrutinized. As a result, there were many changes and refinements between versions. Finally, the Committee of Style polished the text until it shined. After they got their work the way they wanted, they sent it out to the nation to be analyzed, debated, and ratified.

Our Founders wouldn't have spent so much time on the wording if they had intended the Constitution to be open to interpretation by whoever happened to hold office or be on the court at any particular time. They wanted it written down because words have meaning, and they chose their words carefully. The meaning of the Constitution should be derived from the Constitutional Convention and the ratification process. Every nuance of the wording was argued by an entire nation for over two years. At the time, there was less disagreement about meaning than there was about the ramifications of this new design. The consistent theme of the debates was the likelihood of this or that feature eventually leading to tyranny. Opinion articles like the *Federalist Papers* and *Anti-Federalist Papers* fueled popular debate that then highly influenced the formal debates inside the ratification conventions. At the end of the deliberations, the nation approved the Constitution and it became the supreme law of the land.

No lawyer in America believes in a living contract between two businesses. That would mean that on any particular day, one party could interpret the contract in a way that best served its interests. Why even bother to write a contract? But for some reason, many who are trained in law find acceptable a *living* supreme law of the land. James Madison wrote, "Can it be of less consequence that the meaning of a Constitution should be fixed and known, than a meaning of a law should be so?"[89]

When something in a contract isn't working properly, then the contract must be amended, and contracts are amended every day all over this country. The Constitution was never deemed to be perfect and included provisions for amendment. In fact, the United States Constitution has been amended twenty-seven times. The Founders believed a constitution was a compact between the people and their government. If the compact needed to be changed, then the changes needed to be approved by the representatives of the people in the prescribed manner.

On occasion, the Supreme Court needs to provide further clarification of the Constitution, but it should never use current opinion, political preferences, foreign rulings, or feel-good sentiments to make its decision. That would violate the people's compact with their government by putting another authority above the American people. Supreme Court precedents can also be misleading. No one would want the *Dred Scott v. Sandford* decision to influence any other cases. The Constitution itself, the Constitutional Convention debates, the ratification process, and responsible Supreme Court precedents should provide sufficient guidance to the court.

A Living Constitution Would Be Abhorrent to the Framers

Some believe that a document over two hundred years old cannot provide guidance in a diverse world of speedy travel, instant communication, deadly weapons, skewed wealth, and other modernity. This is a huge misconception—a misconception propagated by those who don't want to be hemmed in by constraints on their exercise of power. Our Constitution isn't a list of laws that can become obsolete as technology or social norms change. The United States Constitution defines government powers to make, execute, and adjudicate laws, and it's these laws that are supposed to respond to modern needs. The governmental form itself does not need to change.

In 1791, Jefferson told Washington that "to take a single step beyond the text would be to take possession of a boundless field of power."[90] Madison then recommended in a speech before Congress that the government "keep close to our chartered authorities."[91]

The Three Clauses That Have Caused Much Mischief

The Founders wanted to bequeath to posterity a straightforward government that inhibited the abuse of power. Their written words remain clear. Certain politicians and judges have skewed their meaning to do what they want, but most of the harm can be attributed to three clauses:

1. The necessary and proper clause,
2. The commerce clause,
3. And the general welfare clause.

It is nonsensical to assert that the Founders meant for any of these clauses to license general national authority. The necessary and proper clause came at the end of Article I, Section 8. It reads, "To make all Laws which shall be necessary and proper for carrying into Execution the foregoing Powers." The operative word of the clause was *foregoing*. It was clearly meant to be restricted to the enumerated powers listed just prior to the clause.

To regulate commerce meant the regulation of trade, not the regulation of all economic activity.

The relevant general welfare clause introduces the enumerated powers (Article I, Section 8) and reads, "The Congress shall have Power To lay and collect Taxes, Duties, Imposts and Excises, to pay the Debts and provide for the common Defence and general Welfare of the United States." This clause is meant to define the national government's taxing authority. The use of the words *general welfare* precluded repeating all of the enumerated powers that immediately follow. If the Founders wanted to give Congress unlimited general authority, they would have ended Section 8 right there. (The term *general welfare* can also be found in the preamble, but the preamble does not bestow powers.)

Joseph Story, who served on the Supreme Court from 1811 to 1845, wrote the following about the necessary and proper clause.

"The plain import of the clause is, that congress shall have all the incidental and instrumental powers, necessary and proper to carry into execution all the express powers. It neither enlarges any power specifically granted; nor is it a grant of any new power to congress."[92]

In "Federalist No. 22," Alexander Hamilton wrote that national supervision of commerce was needed because "the want of it has already operated as a bar to the formation of beneficial treaties with foreign powers, and has given occasions of dissatisfaction between the States."[93] The dissatisfaction between the states was caused by state taxes imposed on trade. The commerce clause was meant to give the national government authority over trade treaties with foreign powers and taxes associated with interstate trade. It was never intended to give the national government authority over every aspect of our lives that required the expenditure of money.

As for the general welfare clause, James Madison, the Father of the Constitution, wrote, "With respect to the words general welfare, I have always regarded them as qualified by the details of power connected with them. To take them in a literal and unlimited sense would be a metamorphosis of the Constitution ... not contemplated by the creators."[94]

Do Ordain and Establish

The Founders did not intend for a few clauses to negate their life's work. These three clauses taken in context are crystal clear. The elasticity has been applied by persons who wanted to do something prohibited by the Constitution. They violated the agreement between the governed and the governors. Actually, to uphold a contract in a legal sense, the offended party must enforce the terms. That means *we the people* must raise up in one voice whenever our Constitution is abridged.

Thomas Jefferson advised, "On every question of construction carry ourselves back to the time when the Constitution was adopted, recollect the spirit manifested in the debates and instead of trying what meaning may be squeezed out of the text or invented against it, conform to the probable one in which it was passed."[95]

A written constitution has meaning only if words have meaning.

Otherwise, a constitution—or any law for that matter—is simply ink on a page. Our forefathers spent blood, treasure, and decades of their lives to break away from an empire so they could create the kind of republic that would last and protect individual liberty. It worked so well that Americans took a raw wilderness and built the strongest, freest, wealthiest, and most noble nation in world history. Yes, the Constitution is constrictive, but not to American citizens. The United States Constitution only constricts its political leaders—and rightly so.

10

Liberty Depends on Private Property Rights

"The pillars of our prosperity are the most thriving when left most free to individual enterprise."
—*Thomas Jefferson*[96]

In the Founders' minds, private property rights and liberty were intertwined. Does this interrelationship make sense? Let's go back to the mindset in 1776. At the time, Americans revolted against more than the British; they also revolted against the divine right of kings. In their recent past, only nobility had owned property and the great mass of humanity were serfs. As this system withered, the common man developed property rights, and with property, gained political voice. By the second half of the eighteenth century, most British subjects, in England and throughout the rest of the empire, equated property rights with liberty because they had witnessed that one followed the other.

Only a few generations earlier, the common man had experienced the worst kind of oppression propagated by those anointed with a right to own property. Those fortunate individuals were the nobility, and those nobles had controlled every aspect of their lives. This was firmly ingrained in the collective memory of the common man and, consequently, the Founders. They understood that property rights have enormous consequences for individual liberty. For example, women didn't start to make significant progress toward equal stature in society until primogeniture laws were rescinded or the practice started to be ignored. The Enlightenment preached that every person possessed God-given rights, which included the right to own property.[97]

Small Businessmen or Self-Employed

Early Americans were highly entrepreneurial. Immigrants to the new world were in search of opportunity, freedom, or adventure. They were ambitious and industrious. Most of them ran a small trade or farm, and a considerable number were self-employed as lawyers, doctors, bookkeepers, or clergy. A few relatively large businesses existed in shipping, publishing, brewing, and planting. There were employees, to be sure, but apprentices, farmhands, clerks, and merchant fleet officers all worked toward the day when they could own their own shop, farm, counting house, or ship.

The American colonists, or their forebears, had sailed to the New World with little more than they could carry in their arms, and in less than two hundred years they had turned a raw wilderness into one of the most prosperous places on earth. Philadelphia was the grandest city in North America with a busy harbor and myriad industries, New England ships plied all seven seas, southern planters grew rich on tobacco, trades flourished throughout the colonies, and anyone with determination could own land. Even if some never saw fulfillment of all they desired, the American Dream was already firmly entrenched in peoples' minds. This was the Founders' world, and they understood that property rights made it all possible.

Government's Rightful Role in Property

In the Founders' view, prosperity and a broad distribution of wealth depended on the government's protection of private property. Even before the Declaration of Independence, the Virginia Declaration of Rights led off with, "All men are by nature equally free and independent and have certain inherent rights, of which ... namely, the enjoyment of life and liberty, with the means of acquiring and possessing property."

James Madison went even further, writing, "Government is instituted to protect property of every sort ... This being the end of government, that alone is a just government which impartially secures to every man whatever is his own."[98]

Some argue that a benevolent government should control property, because only the government can distribute the fruits of ownership fairly. This sounds good, except that these proponents can't point to a single good example—not in the world today, nor in history. Concentrated property ownership, whether by individuals or a government, has always inflicted oppression. Individual liberty and prosperity depend on the freedom to retain the proceeds of one's own labor, capital, or ideas. When this freedom is protected, individuals strive to build material comfort, and as a result, property becomes distributed broadly throughout the populace. This doesn't mean property is distributed evenly, but protecting property rights will distribute property more evenly than any system based on redistribution of wealth.

The relationship between liberty and private property is not black and white. It's a sliding scale. The more private property is protected, the freer the economic system and the more the citizenry enjoy personal liberty. The more property and planning are centralized, whether by the state or another institution, the more liberty is eroded. It doesn't matter if it's feudalism, fascism, communism, theocracy, socialism, or even crony capitalism. To one degree or another, liberty is eroded in all these systems.

Government Confiscation

Wealth is coveted, and unless the government impartially protects property rights, the ruthless will take what they want. The Founders believed government should protect private property, but they were also aware that government could become the greatest threat to property. In recent decades, property owners have been given good reason to fear government confiscation of property. Presently, governments within the United States use four primary methods to take control of private property: eminent domain, civil forfeiture, regulatory takings, and redistributive taxes and fees.

In *Kelo v. City of New London* (2005), the United States Supreme Court said government could take property from one private owner and give it to another private owner if it was for the public good, which included such a simple objective as higher tax revenue. Prior to *Kelo*, courts had restricted property acquired under eminent domain to public use.[99] True liberty never allows the government to take a person's property. James Madison said, "It is not a just government, nor is property secure under it, where arbitrary restrictions deny to part of its citizens that free use of their faculties."[100]

Another flawed Supreme Court property case was *Bennis v. Michigan*[101] (1996). Police caught the husband of Mrs. Bennis in his car participating in an illegal sex act. Under "civil forfeiture," the state confiscated the car, claiming that it had been used in the commission of a crime. Mrs. Bennis spent seven years in court trying to get back the $300 for her half of the car's value. Mrs. Bennis claimed that she was an innocent co-owner, and the car was not *used* in the crime. The case made it all the way to the Supreme Court, which upheld the Michigan statute. The Supreme Court's endorsement of the confiscation of property peripherally associated with a crime started a wave of similar statutes. Soon, local governments all over the nation were trying to plug revenue shortfalls with property confiscated in the process of investigating a crime.

Property confiscation can come in the form of regulations that diminish value for a supposed public good. With eminent domain, the government must at least maintain the pretense of just compensation, but regulatory takings that end up requiring some amount of compensation are limited to very extreme cases. In *Penn Central Transport v. New York* (1978), the Supreme Court ruled that the government was under no obligation to compensate Penn Central for a $150 million regulatory taking.[102] Regulatory takings have become a favorite tool of activist groups, and it seems that every law passed by Congress provides yet another avenue for special interests to attack private property through regulatory takings.

Money is also property. When it is earned, it is taxed at progressive rates that penalize accomplishment. If a person eventually succeeds in accumulating some money after faithfully paying their income taxes, they might believe their life savings are safe from confiscation. They would be wrong. Beyond government pickpocketing through inflation,[103] there are many other ways the government can grab a share of a person's accumulated wealth. The tax code gives the government a priority claim when a person invests (capital gains) or merely spends their money for life's essentials (local sales tax). If a person buys real property, like a home, a car, or a boat, the government extracts substantial annual fees to retain legal ownership. Even if the money is just husbanded away in a bank, the government wants their cut of any earnings, no matter how slight. Finally, when a person dies, the government has first call on an arbitrarily set share of the estate.

There is another aspect of government confiscation of property that has yet to be codified. During the financial crisis of 2008, the government engaged in a number of shocking and possibly precedent-setting actions. With a complete absence of restraint, the government violated long-standing bankruptcy law and proceeded to redistribute the remnants of Chrysler and General Motors any way they felt fit. The government also overrode contractual relationships that took value away from disfavored parties without compensation. Since the financial debacle, there have been a number of other governmental actions that have made people with assets restive.

Why Redistribution Destroys Liberty

Redistribution of wealth always harms liberty. Again, it's a sliding scale, with reasonable acquisition through public domain laws on one end to a pure form of socialism on the other end. The difference is whether an individual or an entire society is harmed. It doesn't matter if the property is confiscated by bullies, warlords, or government. Contrary to the opinion of some, it is not beneficial for government to own vast amounts of property because over time bureaucrats learn how to gather up for themselves the benefits of controlling property. We've seen this time and again throughout history all over the world. Government never remains a benevolent redistributor of wealth or a benign custodian of property. Here's why:

- People who have property taken away fight back, politically or physically. Those resisting the confiscation of their property must be suppressed.

- Government control requires bureaucratic judgment instead of reliance on the marketplace. Bureaucrats always fail at this Herculean task, but they won't give up, so the government ends up dictating more and more aspects of everyday life.
- Miscalculations result in scarcities. This leads to complaints and criticisms that must be suppressed. Additionally, corrupting black markets and underground economies are overlooked to provide a relief valve for outrage caused by the shortages.
- When events don't go as planned, the government uses indoctrination—and worse—to create a common mindset. Leaders come to believe that if everyone has the greater good in mind, then everything would work as planned.

Concentrate property, and you concentrate power. It doesn't matter if that concentration is with a few individuals, a few corporations, or the government. The bottom line is that concentration of power corrupts—every single time without fail. It was Lord Acton who first wrote, "Power tends to corrupt, and absolute power corrupts absolutely."[104]

It doesn't matter how property rights are violated. If government allows bullies to take what they want, then anarchy reigns. If government gathers up property unto itself, then tyranny reigns. Either way, liberty suffers. Spain provides a modern example. Until 2004, Spain was an "economic miracle" of Europe, with huge job growth, surpluses, and declining debt. Then the Socialist Workers Party gained power. After only six years of progressive leadership, Spain was experiencing negative growth and unemployment was at 20 percent (43 percent for youths). The government increased taxes, arbitrarily interfered in business, attempted to control production, and blithely disregarded EU regulations. As is the norm for aggressive redistribution programs, basic freedoms have been impaired.[105]

Private Property and Free Markets

If private property enhances liberty, then wouldn't equal distribution of property be even better? No, the world doesn't work that way. Private property and free markets go hand in hand. Whenever you have free markets, some will build wealth faster than others. The only alternative is to restrain the industrious, the inventive, and the entrepreneurial. The result might be a more even distribution of wealth, but there would also be less wealth for everyone, including the government, due to decreased tax receipts.

Thomas Jefferson said, "To take from one because it is thought that his own productivity has acquired too much, in order to give to others who have not exercised equal industry and skill is to violate arbitrarily the first principle of association: the guarantee to everyone of a free exercise of his hard work and the profits acquired by it."[106]

Private Property Is a Right

Property may not be distributed equally, but rights are. All men are created equal. James Madison said, "As a man is said to have a right to his property, he may be equally said to have a property in his rights."[107] He meant that even if a person owns nothing else, he still owns his rights, which are the most valuable property of all. One of those rights is a right to secure ownership of property, which means that every American should feel confident that no one will confiscate the fruits of their labor.

Look around and examine history. The wealthiest countries have limited interference by government. They enjoy free markets, private property rights, a large middle class, societal improvement, and cleaner environments, and the residents enjoy life, liberty, and the pursuit of happiness.

The Founders were right; private property rights and liberty are intertwined. John Adams, in *A Defence of the Constitution of Government of the United States of America*, wrote, "The moment the idea is admitted into society that property is not as sacred as the laws of God, and that there is not a force of law and public justice to protect it, anarchy and tyranny commence. If *Thou shalt not covet* and *Thou shalt not steal* were not commandments of Heaven, they must be made inviolable precepts in every society before it can be civilized or made free."[108]

11

Power Must Be Balanced and Checked

"The powers of government should be so divided and balanced among several bodies of magistracy, as that no one could transcend their legal limits, without being effectually checked and restrained by the others."

—*Thomas Jefferson*[109]

When you study the political formation of the United Sates, one is struck by the recurrence of the checks and balances theme—in Madison's convention notes, the Constitution itself, the Federalist Papers, the minutes of the ratification conventions, and even the Anti-Federalist papers. There can be no doubt that the Founders believed that liberty depended on each part of the government acting as an effective check on all the other parts of the government, and that meant not only between the three national branches, but also between the states and the national government.

The phrase *checks and balances* has become so commonplace that it is often spoken as if it were a single word, but in the eighteen century, it was two distinctly different concepts. John Adams may have been the first to put the words together in his 1787 publication, *A Defense of the Constitutions of Government of the United States of America*, but *balances and checks* is the phrase used in *The Federalist*, and that is the sequence Madison would have thought appropriate.

First balance powers between the branches of government, and then place checks on those powers so they are not abused.[110]

The Sixth Principle

The five principles reviewed in prior chapters would have found concurrence among all the delegates at the start of the Constitutional Convention. Many, however, would have disagreed with balanced power. Under the Articles of Confederation, the president was chosen from the members of Congress, similar to a parliamentarian system. Most of the states also had a similar system. There was not only a prejudice against a strong executive, there was a common belief that a legislature-driven government was far more responsive to the people. The delegates were familiar with Montesquieu, Hume, Locke, and even John Adams, who all advocated balanced and/or separated powers, but they still feared that a runaway executive would trample the legislature unless the legislature was given superior power. History was a continuous stream of kings and rulers supplanting legislative bodies. Despite these initial misgivings, through the course of the debates, Madison had so convinced the delegates that balanced power with effective checks was the best way to secure liberty that the idea became the foremost concern in designing a new government.

Power Corrupts, Absolute Power Corrupts Absolutely

The design of the government under the Constitution was not haphazard. Our Founding Fathers understood that governments can oppress people. They knew it from their own experience—and they knew it from their extensive scrutiny of governmental forms throughout history. Concentrated power was more than dangerous... it was life-threatening.

That's why:

1. They balanced power between the three branches.
2. They gave each branch robust checks on the other two.
3. They gave the national government only enumerated powers,

and retained all other power in the hands of either the people or the states.

4. The members of each branch were chosen by a different method.
5. The term of office varied by government position.
6. They used the states to check the central government.

Concentrated political power frightened the Founders. They believed that only by limiting government could liberty survive the natural tendency of man to dictate the habits of other men. The balanced separation of power with checks was designed to prevent a majority coalition from taking control of the government. Each branch was given delineated powers, and then each of these powers was limited and checked by another branch or entity. The system was purposely designed to slow governmental actions enough to allow due deliberation. This frustrates those who want the government to always "do something" about every problem, but it also hampers the government from doing something grievous that affects our life, liberty, and pursuit of happiness.

Balancing Act

The Constitutional Convention looked at two different ways of defining national powers. They debated long and hard about whether to call out each power individually or, alternately, to list restrictions on general powers. Simply put, they had to decide whether to write down what the federal government could do or what the federal government could not do.

Because they feared they might forget some crucial restrictions, the delegates decided it was safer to define the powers instead of the limitations. Besides, monarchies had general power, and since they had just escaped a monarchy, they would give their national government only delineated powers. The Framers' intent remains clear: if a specific power was not expressly listed in the Constitution, then that power remained with the States or with the people. They decided this was the safer route because if they made an error, it would leave the authority closer to the people.

The assignment of powers to the three branches was not perfunctory. The delegates argued incessantly about this for more than four months. For example, once the Great Compromise altered the composition and selection of the Senate, the delegates revisited every branch and rebalanced the powers between them. In fact, a stronger Senate allowed them to increase the powers of the executive.[111]

The delegates also decided to choose members of the national government by different means, so it would be difficult for one faction to gain control over the government. The House of Representatives would be elected directly by the people, the state legislatures elected senators, the president would be chosen by an Electoral College, and the Supreme Court would be appointed by the executive and confirmed by the Senate. As an additional safety measure, they set different terms for the president, senators, representatives, and the judiciary.

As mentioned previously, the separation of church and state is another check because it denies rulers the claim of divine guidance. By the late eighteenth century, a free press was also generally seen as a check on all governments, local and national. The Founders, however, intended the ultimate check on the national government to be the people.

The Constitution Is Amendable

The national government was not restricted for all time to the enumerated powers. Non-enumerated powers were retained by the states or the people, but the Founders included an amendment process, which the people could use to delegate additional powers to the national government. Some complain the amendment process is too difficult, but seven amendments were enacted within a year. If Americans are convinced of a need to change the Constitution, they can and will act with speed. Usurpation occurs when a majority of the people do not agree.

The Sixteenth Amendment is an illustrative example of an expansion of enumerated powers. Article I, Section 8, gave the national government the power to "lay and collect Taxes, Duties, Imposts and Excises," with the caveat that "all Duties, Imposts and Excises shall be uniform throughout the United States." The Sixteenth Amendment expanded national authority to "lay and collect taxes on incomes, from whatever source derived," which authorized the infamous income tax. The point is not whether this was a good or ill-conceived expansion of national powers. What matters is that it was done in the proscribed manner defined within the Constitution, and thus is a legitimate expansion of national power.

Another interesting example is the Eighteenth and Twenty-First Amendments. The Eighteenth Amendment could be said to have restricted liberty by enacting Prohibition, but the Twenty-First Amendment restored the right to legally consume alcohol. Regardless of the wisdom of Prohibition, the Constitution was legitimately altered by the supreme power of the people and then corrected using the amendment process when Americans decided they did not like the outcome.

Unfortunately, these are rare cases of the national government receiving legitimate expansions of power. In almost all other instances, Americans have witnessed authority being usurped by government.

Next, Install Speed Bumps

To a degree, each branch operates in slight fear that another branch will chastise or even overrule its actions. This was an intended consequence of the design. Madison wrote in "Federalist No. 51," "The great security against a gradual concentration of the several powers in the same department consists in giving to those who administer each department the necessary constitutional means and personal motives to resist encroachments of the others. The provision for defense must in this, as in all other cases, be made commensurate to the danger of attack. Ambition must be made to counteract ambition."[112] In Madison's opinion, liberty can only be protected by power restraining power. The Constitution doesn't contain any language preserving the boundaries of the three branches. It is up to the three branches to defend their independence with their assigned powers.

Congressional Checks

Let's take a look at the checks between the three branches, starting with Congress. The legislative branch's checks on the executive include the power of the purse; impeachment power; authority to declare war; a veto override provision; approval of appointment to fill a vice presidential vacancy; a required presidential State of the Union address to Congress; and Senate approval of appointments, treaties, and ambassadors. Although not quite as obvious of a check, Congress can also refuse to pass a bill the president wants passed.

The legislative branch's checks on the judiciary include impeachment power; authority to set the size of the Supreme Court; the power to establish courts inferior to the Supreme Court and to set their jurisdictions; and Senate approval of federal judges. If the Supreme Court declares a law unconstitutional, the legislature has the power to initiate a constitutional amendment.

Since Congress is bicameral, it is also self-checking because bills must pass both houses. Additionally, the House of Representatives must initiate all revenue bills, neither house can adjourn for more than three days without the consent of the other house, and journals of both houses must be published.

Executive Checks

The executive's checks on the legislature include veto power; recess appointments; the vice president is president of the Senate; and the president can call emergency sessions; or even force adjournment when both houses cannot agree on an adjournment date. The president is also commander in chief to balance the legislature's power to declare war.

The executive's checks on the judiciary include power to appoint judges and the authority to pardon.

Additionally, the authority of the vice president and cabinet to vote that the president is unable to discharge his or her duties is an executive self-check.

Judicial Checks

The judicial check on the legislature is judicial review. (Judicial review is not specifically called out in the Constitution but this power was probably assumed by most of the Constitutional delegates. In 1801, *Marbury v. Madison* confirmed this judiciary power.) On the defensive side, judges are assured independence because their compensation is protected, and they hold their seats through good behavior.

The judicial check on the executive is judicial review. The chief justice also sits as president of the Senate during presidential impeachment.

States as a Check on the National Government

The Founders did not restrict the checks and balances concept to the three Federal branches. The delegates to the Constitutional Convention intended the states to be a potent check on the national government. They included five provisions for this purpose:

1. Enumerated powers, later reconfirmed by the Tenth amendment
2. Equal state representation in the Senate
3. Senators elected by state legislatures
4. Limited national taxing authority
5. An Electoral College

Unfortunately, few in Washington consider the enumerated powers a constraint; as a result of the Seventeenth Amendment, senators are now popularly elected; the Sixteenth Amendment allows Congress to collect taxes on *incomes, from whatever source derived*; and the Electoral College is under attack.

These provisions have severely weakened the states as a check on a growing national government, so the states have turned to lawsuits as their primary weapon. State lawsuits have proliferated against the Patient Protection and Affordable Care Act, commonly called ObamaCare. Texas and several other states have sued the national government over EPA regulations, and Utah has filed suit over seizure of public lands. States have also passed laws reasserting the Tenth Amendment, limiting ObamaCare, and pushing back against the growing tide of illegal immigration. It is yet to be seen whether lawsuits and state laws can provide an effective check against the growth in the national government.[113]

Bursting Free of Restraint

The Founders harnessed their new government with Lilliputian ropes that would hopefully restrain it from trampling the little people. From our high school civics class, we all learned about the checks and balances between the three branches, but teachers seldom mentioned the intended check of the national government by the states. Nor were we taught that the Founders wanted our national leaders selected and elected by different means for different terms as yet another check on a runaway government. The entire design was devised to prevent our government from gaining enough power to become oppressive.

Except, like Gulliver, our behemoth national government has shrugged off one constraint after another until there are no practical limits to its power. All three branches regularly overstep their boundaries as if each were given unchecked authority. The states are currently struggling to reassert their rightful place in a federal system. The general welfare, commerce, and necessary and proper clauses have all been used to circumvent enumerated powers. As a result, the national government has few acknowledged constraints except for the ballot box.

The ballot box, however, is still a mighty potent check on the abuse of power. Granted, purposely staggered terms means it takes several election cycles to turn the ship of state, but that is a safety mechanism that has served the nation well for several centuries. If Americans get riled enough to express their dissatisfaction repeatedly over a number of election cycles, it means that a course correction was desperately needed. The Founders trusted the people, and so can we.

PART IV

୧ଡ଼ୗୡ

The Founding Issues

12

Defying Congress

"The example of changing a constitution by assembling the wise men of the state, instead of assembling armies, will be worth as much to the world as the former examples we had given them."

—*Thomas Jefferson*[114]

It's been called a miracle. The Federal Convention of 1787, which we now call the Constitutional Convention, was an astonishing accomplishment. There were several moments during the convention when it looked certain to fail. Tempers often grew hotter than the stifling room. It was an unusually hot summer for Philadelphia, and for a few weeks there was an infestation of big black flies that buzzed around the delegates' eyes. To facilitate deliberation, the delegates voted for closed proceedings, but secrecy also meant that the windows were nailed shut and the doors remained closed. The stench of stale sweat and absence of any air circulation made the chamber extremely unpleasant, but despite discomforts and quarrels, they refused to leave until they could present to their nation a new government consistent with the principles they held dear.

Thomas Jefferson called the delegates "an assembly of demigods." That was an exaggeration, but they were certainly bright and learned. These were patriots who had already committed their lives and fortunes to an ideal they saw slipping away. They knew that this convention was the last chance to save the American experiment in self-government. They were determined not to fail, but good enough for the moment was not acceptable. They were committed to principled action.

A Sanctioned Insurrection?

In July of 1776, the thirteen North American colonies declared their independence from Great Britain. It took seven more war years until, on September 3, 1783, the Treaty of Paris legitimized the sovereignty claims of the United States of America.

At that time, the thirteen former colonies considered themselves independent states loosely federated for self-defense. The Articles of Confederation, the first United States Constitution, allowed one vote per state, did not provide for an executive branch or national judiciary, and only allowed requests to the states for money, which the states frequently ignored with impunity. More significant, revisions to the Articles required unanimous agreement by all thirteen states.

A convention at Annapolis in the summer of 1786 collapsed due to a lack of a quorum of seven states. James Madison and Alexander Hamilton attended the aborted Annapolis Convention and made a pact to promote another national conference the following summer. The following February, Congress authorized a convention in Philadelphia to recommend revisions to the Articles of Confederation. Acceptance of any proposals from this convention would have required unanimous consent of the states. Some of the most powerful states arrived with a plan to dissolve the existing confederation and replace it with a much stronger national government. The scheme was called the Virginia Plan, and it had the backing of the Deep South, Virginia, Pennsylvania, Massachusetts, and a somewhat shaky Maryland.[115] If this plan had been adopted, the convention probably would have been over in less than a month. But the small states fought to retain a stronger position for the states. The Great Compromise, which assigned two senators per state, resolved the impasse and the convention went forward on a different path that resulted in the United States Constitution.[116]

Much has been made of this bloodless coup. A sitting government was overthrown without their permission—except that this narrative is not entirely true. Congress had sanctioned the convention, and knew it might go beyond its instructions. Some probably hoped the convention would go beyond their charter because it was obvious the country would not survive under the Articles. Many of the delegates were current or former congressmen, and unlike the convention itself, there was no secrecy proviso when the Virginia Plan was constructed or these elaborate alliances were built. The replacement of the Articles of Confederation is still the greatest bloodless coup in history, but to some extent, the established government was complicit in the intrigue.[117]

Secrecy

One of the first acts of the Federal Convention was a vote to conduct their proceedings in secret. The intent was to promote open debate and allow the delegates to change their minds. There was a fear that once a position was taken and publicized, delegates would be reluctant to reconsider that position. Secrecy also served the Virginians' strategy because they knew their plan would be controversial, and they wanted some time shielded from public scrutiny to convince other states to go along with it. The convention also didn't want to excite Congress or the public before they could put forward a complete, agreed-upon plan. Historians have not discovered a single leak from even one delegate during the four months of debate, which is surprising, since many vehemently disagreed with one issue or another. In modern politics, politicians often leak secret proceedings to put public pressure on negotiations. It speaks well of the character of the delegates that they took their oath of silence seriously.

Despite the secrecy, we know exactly what happened during the proceedings. The official minutes were, for the most part, terse recordings of the votes, but several delegates took notes, and James Madison's notes were excruciatingly comprehensive. His records of the proceedings were published after his death in 1836.

With secrecy in place, the first hurdle was getting agreement to go beyond their instructions from Congress. With a little parliamentary maneuvering, the delegates decided, "a national government ought to be established, consisting of a supreme legislative, a supreme executive, and a supreme judiciary."[118] This word *supreme* in this motion meant that the national government would be superior to the states, and the three branches were a major departure from the Articles. In one audacious move, they voted to unshackle themselves from the Articles of Confederation.

Practice Makes Perfect

The debates were long, and at times acrimonious. Worse, they had to do everything twice. At the start, they convened as a Committee of the Whole. This meant the entire assembly was declared a committee. This was like a dress rehearsal because committees cannot adopt measures, only make recommendations. During the Founding, this was a common parliamentary maneuver for controversial issues. It allowed opponents to vent, and gave the weaker side time to prepare a stronger argument. This parliamentary exercise helped to build unity after everything was said and done.[119]

During these dual deliberations, the convention had to choose between competing plans. The Virginia Plan had the support of the large states, while small states pushed for approval of the New Jersey Plan. Alexander Hamilton proposed yet another plan that approximated the mixed system of Great Britain, and Charles Pinckney of South Carolina proposed a shockingly democratic plan. Going into the convention, the Virginia Plan looked to have insurmountable momentum behind it. The two largest and richest states, Virginia and Pennsylvania, met daily to plot the passage of this plan, which could legitimately be called the James Madison Plan. The small states believed the Virginia Plan would be a death knell for the states, so they fought furiously, first with delaying tactics, and then with the New Jersey Plan. (Roger Sherman, a leader of the small states, once said, "When you are in the minority, talk; when you are in the majority, vote.")[120]

A deadlock was finally broken with the Great Compromise. Initially proposed by Roger Sherman of Connecticut, this compromise gave each state an equal number of senators. The South liked it because they could use the Senate to stop any anti-slavery legislation, and the small states in the north liked it because an equal voice in the upper house would protect state sovereignty.[121]

Miles to Go before I Sleep

The Great Compromise did not settle everything. In fact it only resolved the large state/small state issue. Once the Senate had been restructured, the convention had to revisit all three branches and make adjustments to retain the philosophy of checks and balances. Presidential powers consumed weeks because the delegates wanted to preclude an elected king. Slavery was an ongoing issue. Many in the North wanted to put slavery on the path to extinction. After a lot of arguing, the anti-slavery forces succeeded in getting a ten-dollar per person tax on imported slaves and an opportunity to completely stop the slave trade after 1808. One of the last issues was the nation's capital. The delegates wanted a national government independent of the states, so they added a stipulation that a new ten-square-mile capital district would be carved out of somewhere.[122]

None of this was easy. The newspapers of the time were full of opinion pieces that suggested the convention should propose two or three different nations: a slave nation, a non-slave nation, and possibly a separate nation for the New England states.[123] Some inside the chamber agreed, but Washington, Madison, Franklin, and Hamilton continued to fight for a single nation built on first principles.

Does the Constitution Adhere to the Founding Principles?

We'll leave the principle that rights come from God to the chapter on the Bill of Rights (page 151).

All Power Emanates from the People

Did the people have voice in the new government as first ratified? They did. Members of the House of Representatives were elected directly by the people, and the term was set short so people could frequently express their judgment. Senators were originally elected by the state legislatures, but most people at the time believed that the thirteen state legislatures were the closest politicians to the people. In fact, in early America, state legislators were often neighbors. If state legislators appointed a bad senator, they would hear about it at church or their local tavern.

The longest debate was about the presidential election. In the final days, the delegates decided that the states could determine how delegates to the Electoral College were chosen. They knew that given the choice, states would provide for the popular election of presidential electors. When Washington was elected the first time, state legislators picked the electors in all thirteen states, but within a few election cycles, all the states allowed popular election to the Electoral College.[124]

The greatest test of adherence to this principle was ratification. The instructions from Congress said that Congress and the state legislatures would approve their work. Instead, the convention sent a letter to Congress ordering them to immediately pass the Constitution on to the states for ratification by conventions of the people, which they did. Although some delegates to the ratification conventions were state officials or elected representatives, there was no official connection between the ratification Conventions and Congress or the state legislatures. Each of the ratification conventions was independent, with their own parliamentary rules.

A Limited, Representative Republic

The original Constitution as ratified was a representative republic with enumerated powers. The Framers balanced power between the three branches, and crafted checks on the abuse of power. As ratified, the states were a potent check on the national government, and people had ample opportunity to express their opinions at the ballot box. Since ratification, the Constitution has been amended twenty-seven times. Some of these amendments legitimately altered the original design, but the major erosion of the limited government concept has come through the courts, where American citizens have little influence.

Written Constitution

The Constitution was written in clear language that most people have no trouble understanding. Those who insinuate that the language is vague usually want to do something the Constitution prohibits, or the designated responsible parties refuse to take some action they desire. The intellectually honest have no difficulty discerning the intent of the necessary and proper, commerce, and general welfare clauses.

What does the Constitution mean? During the convention and ratification, there was plenty of disagreement, but it wasn't the arguments that define original intent, it was the conclusions drawn from these arguments. What counts is what they decided after thorough deliberation. The Constitutional language is clear, and following the flow of the debates to their conclusions provides additional clues as to the original intent. Should original intent guide constitutional interpretation? The alternative is to rely on an unaccountable tribunal.

Private Property Rights

All rights, not just property rights, appear to have received scant attention during the Constitutional Convention. Most of the delegates believed that if the national powers were held in check, then common law and state declarations of rights provided sufficient safeguards to protect rights. There were a couple provisos in the base document that protected property rights. States were prohibited from impairing the obligation of contracts, and intellectual property was protected, giving "authors and inventors the exclusive right to their respective writings and discoveries."[125]

Surely the Bill of Rights rectified this absence of protection for private property, right? Not entirely. The *takings clause* in the Fifth Amendment is one of the few outright protections of property. It reads, "Nor shall private property be taken for public use without just compensation." It would appear that this clause protects property owners from government confiscation, but cities, states, and the federal government have become increasingly brazen about taking property for public domain purposes. *Kelo v. City of New London* and the innovation of regulatory takings have shunted aside the takings clause like it was piece of flotsam in the way of a great ocean liner. The dismissal of the *takings* clause is an illuminating object lesson that proves the Founders were right—unchecked power trumps protections written on a piece of parchment. The clause is clear, yet it has been a weak shield against the abusive exercise of determined power.

In 1996, President Bill Clinton—with no Congressional action— declared 1.9 million acres in Utah the Grand Staircase-Escalante National Monument. President Obama designated an additional 2 million acres as national monuments and is considering restricting another 13 million acres. During the government-directed Chrysler bankruptcy, bondholders were unlawfully shoved to the back of the line so union demands could be given priority. When an American dies, the government feels it has a stronger claim on the deceased's property than that person's heirs. No wonder many Americans have come to fear their government as a real risk to owning property.

The Founders believed that protecting property rights was not an issue. It was assumed to be a natural function of government. Property rights may not have been an issue in 1787, but restoring these rights is certainly an issue today.

Checks and Balances

Limiting national government powers was the primary concern of the Framers. Although they did a magnificent job of balancing power and applying checks, through the years, politicos have found ways to break through one constraint after another. If there is a lesson here, it is that once a power is breached or a check set aside, there is no easy way to go back to the founding intent.

A Republic for the Ages

Though the Founders endured that nasty summer indoors, repeatedly arguing the same issues, they never gave up despite the hardships and disagreements. George Mason told the convention, "It cannot be more inconvenient to any gentleman to remain absent from his private affairs, than it is for me; but I will bury my bones in this city rather than expose my country to the consequences of a dissolution of the convention without any thing being done."[126] The Founders felt an obligation to their fellow citizens ... and to posterity. They insisted on taking principled action to build a republic for the ages.

It was important to them, and it should always remain important to us.

13

State Rights

"Who would convert our (government) into one either wholly federal or wholly consolidated—in neither of which forms have individual rights, public order, and external safety, been all duly maintained—they aim a deadly blow at the last hope of true liberty on the face of the Earth."

—*James Madison*[127]

The Great Compromise resolved the impasse between small and large states. It had been a long and hostile clash, but after the states gained equal representation in the Senate, the convention moved to other issues. Today, the concept of states' rights is one of the most misunderstood parts of the Constitution.

A few still contend that the Constitution is a creature of the states. At the other extreme, some say the purpose of the Constitution was to create a powerful national government and thus the national government is superior to the states. Those who believe in state nullification or think that states have a right to secede are examples of people who fall into the first camp. People who believe states are subordinate to the national government usually hold that the commerce clause has no practical limit and any other level of government should never interfere with any law passed by Congress.

Both of these interpretations are very wrong.

A System Partly Federal and Partly Consolidated

The United States of America is a federal system. A federal system is one where a lower level of government cedes a portion of its authority to a higher level. In the United States, we have a national government, state governments, county governments, and city governments. Each of these government levels was intended to operate within their own sphere of authority. Madison wrote in "Federalist No. 46," "The federal and state governments are in fact but different agents and trustees of the people, constituted with different powers, and designed for different purposes."[128]

When Madison writes about a system wholly federal or wholly consolidated, he is referring to a loose confederation like we had under the Articles versus a system where the national government is always superior. Madison and the remaining Framers believed they had devised a system between these two extremes.

A key Founding Principle was that all political power emanates from the people. The Framers intended that the people would delegate to each of these government entities certain powers and certain powers only. Although there might be some overlap, each level would be the ultimate authority within its respective sphere. This is a very different arrangement than a hierarchical system, where each level is subordinate to the level above.

Not a Creature of the States

Our governmental system is not a creature of the states. This was a contention of the South prior to the Civil War and it has never fully gone away. True, the states were equally represented at the Constitutional Convention, but it was not the convention that made the Constitution the law of the land, it was the ratification process. The convention delegates purposefully and officially decided that the people of the states, not the state legislatures, would ratify the Constitution. The philosophical basis for this directive was that only the people could delegate powers to a national government because enlarging these powers was outside the purview of the states. There was a practical reason, as well. The Framers wanted ratification by the people so states could not claim jurisdiction over nationally enumerated powers.

As a result, our national government derives its just powers directly from the people, not the states. This means that when the Constitution was adopted, we ceased to be a confederation. Although the United States of America gained a true national government, it was not a national government completely independent of the states. The states have constitutionally sanctioned influence at the national level: equal state representation in the Senate, a state-weighted Electoral College, and, most important, a national government limited by enumerated powers. These provisions were incorporated into the Constitution to provide a check on an overreaching national government. The national government is not a creature of the states, but our Constitution gives the states direct and indirect influence inside the national government.

The Superior Political Authority

The American system is not hierarchical. At least, it was not supposed to be hierarchical. It was never intended that the national government would have final authority across every aspect of state operations or American lives. The national government was supposed to stay within its delegated powers, with the states retaining authority in other matters.

There is a superior political force in this nation, and that force is the American people. To a large degree, that force is exercised at the ballot box, but not exclusively. The First Amendment protects the rights of Americans to peaceably assemble, to express opinions, or petition the government for redress of grievances—at any time. Other constitutional amendments expanded political power so *consent of the governed* applied to all Americans. The ordinary American is the ultimate superior political power in the United States.

A balanced federal system is far from the way we operate today, but it was clearly the intent of the Framers. In "Federalist No. 14," James Madison wrote, "It is to be remembered that the general government is not to be charged with the whole power of making and administering laws. Its jurisdiction is limited to certain enumerated objects."[129] On the other side of the aisle—metaphorically speaking—Madison's convention opponent, Roger Sherman, said, "The state and general government ought to have separate and distinct jurisdictions, but they ought to have a mutual interest in supporting each other."[130]

Were the Framers Right?

No other government in the world uses a federal model as explicit as ours. In fact, it can be argued that the United States itself no longer operates under a federal model. If we have abandoned this model, was it sensible in the first place? We could discuss government theory and the Founders' reasoning, but practical examples often makes understanding a philosophical issue easier. Let's use K–12 education to evaluate whether the Framers were right to distribute power, or if it's better to apply leadership consistently across the entire country from the nation's capital.

The Department of Education and K–12

The Department of Education came into existence in 1980 as the result of a campaign promise by President Carter. The act separated education from the Department of Health, Education, and Welfare, and elevated education to cabinet level. (The National Defense Education Act of 1957 actually started national spending and intrusion into education, but we'll focus on the past thirty years.)[131]

According to the Department of Education website, the average expenditure per student in 1980 was about $5,000, and according to the latest government report, we now spend $12,922 per student. Since 1980, the Department of Education discretionary budget has grown from $11 billion to $69 billion. K–12 student enrollment is declining nationally, but the *Wall Street Journal* reports that the "National Center for Educational Statistics forecasts that the number of teachers will rise anyway—from 3.66 million in 2011 to 3.7 million in 2012, and to 3.75 million in the fall of 2013."[132]

Spending on education has soared since the creation of the

Department of Education. Putting aside constitutional issues, did the increased spending at least get us better education for our children? The Cato Institute, using government sources, reports that since 1980, national government spending per student has increased about 170 percent, but performance scores in reading and math have remained stubbornly flat, and the scores in science have actually declined. Normalized SAT scores for college-bound students show no improvement in reading and a statistically insignificant improvement in math.[133]

No Child Left Behind testing is too new to judge trends, but we are starting to get data on how we compare against other counties through the Programme for International Student Assessment scores. These tests started in 2000 and occur every three years. The first three tests show the United States trending down in science and math in comparison to other countries. The proliferation of college remedial classes is another indicator that our schools have failed under increasingly strident national leadership.[134]

No Harm, No Foul?

The best than can be said is that Department of Education spending has not harmed students. But every parent knows that is not true—28 percent of our youth do not graduate high school in four years. Since the overall dropout rate is 8.1 percent, this means the education system is focused on keeping students in school, but delivering such miserable quality that about one-fifth of all students need more than four years to graduate.[135]

American parents and grandparents have witnessed K–12 education deteriorate in their lifetimes. The movie *Mr. Holland's Opus* actually presents a good visual history of the deterioration of public schools. The biggest problem for the education bureaucrats is that there are people alive who can remember when public schools in the United States were the envy of the world.

The baby boomer generation went to school in an era of dramatically lower education spending (and much lower local taxes) and they were provided with books and supplies, healthful meals for a stipend, choice between all kinds of fully equipped shop and home economics classes, music and art programs, driver education, language labs, and extensive physical education programs. Almost all of these programs were made available to students at no extra charge. Classrooms produced literate young adults that could do general math without a calculator. High school graduates understood the basics of science, civics, and American history, and they had a reasonable understanding of geography.

Solid statistics on student performance are so rare, it makes one suspect that there is an ulterior motive. Although the available numbers generally reflect flat performance over the last thirty years, K–12 has gotten so bad that parents no longer need numbers. Instead of seeking measurement, they are seeking alternatives: private schools, vouchers, charter schools, and even taking on the duties themselves through homeschooling. Any alternative that can be accessed is being used. Parents are taking their children out of public schools in droves because they have lost faith in the system of education. Instead of taking responsibility and responsible action, public schools fight parents at the ballot box and in Washington, D.C. What they don't understand is that no industry has ever survived by fighting its customers.

Is the Department of Education Constitutional?

There seems to be no question that national government exercise of authority over education is unconstitutional. Even the Department of Education website states, "The responsibility for K–12 education rests with the states under the Constitution. There is also a compelling national interest in the quality of the nation's public schools. Therefore, the federal government, through the legislative process, provides assistance to the states and schools in an effort to supplement, not supplant, state support."[136] The national government intrusion is justified by a *compelling national interest in the quality of the nation's public schools*, and the constitutionality question is circumvented by simply defining national involvement as *assistance*. Yet, any educator will tell you that every federal dollar comes loaded with policy directives.

In 1962, the Arizona Legislature directed the (then) Office of the Post Auditor to make recommendations as to the effect of federal grant-in-aid programs on the state of Arizona. This was fifty years ago, but the Post Auditor responded with such clarity, it is worth repeating. In the summary, the report said, "As our investigation progressed; it became increasingly apparent that the State of Arizona possesses very little discretionary authority regarding Federal aid programs. In large measure the state is merely a field office administering programs whose purposes, limits, and other essential features have been set by the Federal government and are not subject to change by the State. States are given a single choice either to reject a proffered program or accept with conditions attached. Even here there is no real alternative. State lawmakers are faced with the fact that the citizens of their own state are being taxed and indebted to finance every Federal program. The inducement to provide the citizens of their own state with *their fair share* of the aid being doled out is overpowering and prevails over considerations which would otherwise prohibit adoption of the program."

The current question, however, is not the constitutionality of the national government being engaged in education. Education is only an example to assess whether the Framers were right to design a federal system where different levels of government had clear authority over different delegated areas.

The Framers Were Right

For the most part, the baby boom generation had good schools and great teachers that prepared young people to handle life and become good citizens. Teachers were not paid well, class sizes were large, and the support structure behind a teacher usually consisted of less than a half dozen people—all of which were right down the hall.

What made the difference? The difference was local control. Local government administered the school system and principals managed the schools. Parents were tightly connected to their child's education. The baby boom generation dreaded parent/teacher conferences because they were about performance, not self-esteem. Each school had a Parent Teacher Association (PTA) that wielded real influence.

PTA meetings were packed with parents, schools gave out real information, and every question was either answered in the meeting, or the parent got a follow-up phone call with the answer.

Today, school teachers and administrators constantly lament the lack of parental involvement. The educational establishment is being slyly equivocal because they know the Department of Education is the actual guilty party. It was the nationalization of education that ripped away local control and separated the parent from the school. After creation of the Department of Education, everything went national: curriculum, unions, and PTA were all centered in Washington, D.C., and spending priorities increasingly came from the nation's capital.

The slogan for the PTA—headquartered, of course, in Alexandria—is *everychild. onevoice.* It used to be that every parent had a distinct voice; now it is a collective voice shouted from on high. The PTA home page encourages parents to "start making an impact—for your child and for all children across the nation."[137] Parents used to make an impact for their child and the children in their neighborhood. There is a huge difference between sending an e-mail note to some opaque bureaucracy in Washington, D.C., and walking to a local PTA meeting with friends and neighbors. Today, the PTA is not an effective tool for parents to help their children because the PTA has become the de facto publicity arm for teacher unions. There are still a few effective parent-teacher organizations, but they are highly localized and usually go by a different name.

Local Control Gives Voice

The Framers did not want a homogenized citizenry. The big things, the ones with national scope, were enumerated as responsibilities of the national government. All the rest was meant to stay local. Nondelegated powers were to remain local for two reasons: Americans could better manage those in power when they were near at hand, and a true federal system protects liberty.

The people are the source of political power, so they have a right to monitor all government functions and hold incumbents and civil servants accountable. This is much easier to do when you can go see a government official by foot or car, rather than by airplane. When government is close, it is also less expensive—far less expensive. Nationalized services invariably drive costs through the roof. There are no economies of scale coming from Washington, D.C. This is because the government's boss, American citizens, are nowhere within sight. What is within sight are lobbyists whose only purpose in life is to encourage additional spending.

Liberty depends on being left alone to make your own decisions or having a voice in decisions that need to be made collectively. Keeping governmental powers local, or at least within the state, increases liberty. Centralizing power in the nation's capital makes the citizenry helpless. Personal liberty and effective services depend on government being close at hand, carefully watched by those paying the bill. The Framers understood this key principle because they had been subjected to rule from afar.

Restoring Our Federal System

The term *states' rights* is a misnomer. A more accurate term would be *state powers*. The Tenth Amendment reads, "The powers not delegated to the United States by the Constitution, nor prohibited by it to the States, are reserved to the States respectively, or to the people." As the amendment wording makes clear, the states do not own *all* powers not enumerated in the Constitution—the people do, which they may retain or delegate to their state, city, or other local government.

Another problem with the term *states' rights* is that the concept has been abused in a grievous way. The concept has been used to fight slavery, as when Northern states objected to the Fugitive Slave Act of 1850, but the notion is more closely associated in the popular mind with protecting slavery, justifying secession, and defending segregation. This taint is real, but unassociated with the concept as envisioned by the Founders. *States' rights* was not a common term in their vocabulary; they preferred to use the term *state sovereignty*—which has connotations of autonomy rather than privilege. Independent of terminology, the principle of distributed, non-overlapping powers is the best system to preserve liberty and deliver effective government services at the lowest cost to taxpayers. We have moved away from this original model. The result is soaring debt, massive bureaucracies, and government intrusion into more and more aspects of Americans' daily lives. We need to relearn and reapply the lessons from the origins of the American Republic.

In "Federalist No. 46," Madison wrote, "Ambitious encroachments of the federal government, on the authority of the State governments, would not excite the opposition of a single State, or of a few States only. They would be signals of general alarm. Every government would espouse the common cause. A correspondence would be opened. Plans of resistance would be concerted."[138] Madison was again prophetic. The attorneys general of the states are banding together as never before to challenge the national government. State legislatures are taking coordinated actions as well to thwart overreach by the national government.

The Framers designed safeguards into the system because they knew that government officials could not restrain themselves from gathering up power and trying to control everything. The career bureaucrats and politicians have trampled one safeguard after another until there is nothing left to inhibit their limitless ambitions—nothing but Americans themselves. We must band together to reenact constitutional checks and balances so our children and grandchildren can enjoy their lives without being crushed by overwhelming debt, confiscatory taxes, and oafish bureaucracies that believe that only they can direct the lives and livelihoods of more than three hundred million people.

We need to put the genie back in the bottle.

14

Slavery

"To contend for our own liberty, and to deny that blessing to others, involves an inconsistency not to be excused."

—*John Jay*[139]

Slavery is reprehensible. If Founders believed in the Founding Principles, then they knew in their heart that slavery was the epitome of oppression. Slavery denied other humans the exercise of their liberty, which the Founders understood to be precious. Yet it was a slaveholder who wrote, "All men are created equal, that they are endowed by their Creator with certain unalienable rights."

Slavery is a difficult issue in our nation's history. The Founders, especially the Constitutional Framers, have received censure for not taking greater action against slavery. Some of the more prominent Founders are denigrated because they owned slaves. Jefferson, who wrote that "all men are created equal," professed to abhor slavery, while working his property from "no see to no see"—meaning from dawn to dusk. How can the Founders' comments be reconciled with their actions? The answer to that question is not simple, but it helps to understand the country in 1787.

Slavery at the Founding

At the time of the Constitutional Convention, slavery was illegal only in Massachusetts; more than two hundred slave ships regularly sailed out of New England; and over half of the wealth in the South comprised slaves. Both England and the North held a large amount of loans collateralized by slaves. In 1787, slavery was widespread, and a major element of the economy in both the South and the North.[140]

Despite the position of slavery in 1787, many of the Founders believed slavery was already on its way to extinction. The slave trade had been made illegal in ten of the thirteen states. All thirteen states were seeing an increase in free blacks, especially in the North and the frontier areas of the South. Between 1775 and 1800, the number of free blacks in the nation increased from fourteen thousand to one hundred thousand. Virginia had passed legislation that freed slaves who served in the army or navy. In 1780, Quakers in Pennsylvania pressured the state legislature to pass a law declaring all children of slaves free. With the importation of additional slaves prohibited in most of the country, declining slave labor economics, and growing pressure to declare the newborn of slaves free, most of the Founders didn't want to jeopardize the union over an institution that was already dying. For this reason, even staunch abolitionists like Benjamin Franklin only made peripheral swipes at slavery during the Constitutional Convention.[141]

The Founders did not anticipate King Cotton. Cotton, and Eli Whitney's new technology to process the fiber, made slaveholding so lucrative that only war could eventually end the travesty. (Cotton production expanded a thousandfold from 1790 to 1860.[142]) The trail of blood and money from cotton was not restricted to the South. It was a worldwide phenomenon, where New York bankers financed both slaveholdings and the cotton trade, New England shipping depended on cotton cargos, and cotton provided the essential raw material for the huge textile industries of England and France. By the mid-nineteenth century, instead of gradual extinction, slavery had come to be viewed as indispensable to the paramount special interests of the day, and the South had powerful allies with a common cause to perpetuate slavery.[143] This worldwide development, however, was beyond the view of the Founders, who were grappling with a difficult choice.

A Hobson's Choice in Philadelphia

During the Constitutional Convention, many in the North and a few in the South wanted abolition—or at least severe restrictions on slavery. All the delegates, however, wanted union. The South insisted that if any restrictions were placed on slavery, they would bolt the convention and remain under the Articles of Confederation or form a separate nation. If the Framers wanted a single country with a stronger national system, the South presented them with no choice. Anti-slavery delegates were limited to nibbling around the edges of slavery, which they did—in the belief that they were accelerating its demise.

The Constitution held a provision that the slave trade could be made illegal in all of the states after 1808. In the meantime, a ten-dollar tax could be imposed on each imported slave. It was hoped that these measures would keep slavery moving toward extinction. The fact that the word *slave* never appears in the Constitution indicates awareness that slavery was tainting the founding. Were these measures significant? The importance of these slave trade limitations can be gauged by the unyielding resistance to them by the Deep South.

On the other side of the ledger, the Constitution required that fugitive slaves be returned to their owner. There were many abolitionist movements. For example, immediately after the convention, Benjamin Franklin became President of the Pennsylvania Society for Promoting the Abolition of Slavery.[144] Many of these societies hid runaway slaves. Some in the South equated this with theft, and got this clause inserted in the Constitution and the Northwest Ordinance of 1787. Beyond the fugitive slave clause, there was the infamous 3/5 rule.

Slaves as Less Than a Full Person

People who wish to malign the Constitution often refer to the 3/5 clause as so despicable that the founding and the Founders can be dismissed. These detractors claim that the Founders sanctioned slavery in our most precious document. This is untrue. The Founders can be justly criticized for not ending slavery, but there is nothing in the Constitution that sanctions slavery, especially not the 3/5 rule.

The South wanted their slaves counted as full persons for the purpose of determining the number of representatives they would get for their state. The North knew they would use the added clout in the House of Representatives to protect slavery, so they didn't want slaves counted at all. As a negotiating strategy, the North insisted that if slaves were counted as a full person for representation, then they would also be counted as a full person for taxation purposes. The North didn't want the South to have the representation, and the South did not want to pay the extra taxes, so a compromise was needed.

When no one will give an inch in a legislative body, the compromise that is struck is often nonsensical. (Actually, this 3/5 rule was borrowed from Congress, who had established the rule as a basis for tax allocations under the Articles of Confederation.) The 3/5 rule may have been an ugly compromise, but it was not a judgment on the worth of an African-American. Not one of the delegates believed that a slave was three-fifths of a person. The North counted a free black as a full person, and the South did not accept a slave as even being a partial person. The 3/5 rule was nothing more than a grab for as much political power as the other side was willing to cede. In the end, the rule was inconsequential because the Senate became the South's great bastion against any infringement on slavery.[145]

Slavery as an Issue at the Constitutional Convention

Detractors like to paint the Founders as all supporting slavery and further claim that the Constitution endorsed slavery. An equally inane argument is that anyone who wants to abide by the Constitution wants to reinstitute slavery and deny women the right to vote. This is ridiculous because people who argue to restore the Constitution to the Founding Principles mean the entire Constitution, including amendments.

The truth is that most of the Founders did not support slavery, but some fought aggressively to protect slavery. A few slaveholding Southerners wanted slavery ended, but were unwilling to take the actions necessary to make it happen. George Washington, Thomas Jefferson, and James Madison arguably fell into this category. Some, especially those from the Deep South, would take any action necessary to protect slavery and structure a government that would give them enough power to extend slavery into perpetuity. Many in the North fought for abolition, complete and final. Benjamin Franklin and John Adams are prominent members of this category. Unfortunately, others from the North were ambivalent, accepting slavery as something odd that was generally restricted to the South.

Slavery was the most contentious issue at the Constitutional Convention. The proceedings started with quarrels between small and large states and ended with arguments about presidential powers, but slavery not only dominated the middle of the convention, it underscored every other issue. Slavery was omnipresent: a tug of war between those wishing to terminate slavery and those fighting to preserve it. Essayist John Jay Chapman (1862–1933) wrote that "There was never a moment when the slavery issue was not a sleeping serpent. That issue lay coiled up under the table during the deliberations of the Constitutional Convention of 1787 ... Thereafter slavery was on everyone's mind, though not always on his tongue."[146]

The word *slavery* may never appear in the Constitution, but in Madison's convention notes, the words *slave, slavery, Negro, blacks*, and *bondage* were used fifty-three times during the debates, meaning delegates brought the subject up in debate numerous times. Antonyms, like *free white inhabitants* were used countless times, and euphemisms would increase the count multifold. So if the delegates talked and argued about slavery, who won—those who wanted to accelerate the supposed demise of slavery or those committed to its preservation?

At the close of the proceedings, most of the delegates probably thought that slavery had been put on a road to extinction, especially when Congress simultaneously passed the Northwest Ordinance, which excluded slavery from any state carved out of the Northwest Territories.[147] The exclusion of slavery from the Northwest Territories would eventually cause the Senate to tip toward emancipation and the demise of slavery would be certain. At least that would have been the majority thinking on September 17, 1787.

Nearly all the delegates left Philadelphia convinced that they got as much as they could. It had been hard and bitter bargaining. Oliver Ellsworth wrote, "The only possible step that could be taken towards it by the convention was to fix a period after which they should not be imported."[148] (He failed to mention the hefty interim import tax, or the slavery exclusion in the Northwest Ordinance.)

Another delegate, James Wilson, said, "If there was no other lovely feature in the Constitution but this one, it would diffuse a beauty over its whole countenance. Yet the lapse of a few years, and Congress will have power to exterminate slavery from within our borders."[149] Sadly, Congress did have the power, but not the will.

Slavery Is Part of Our History

During our nation's founding, slavery was real, cruel, and pervasive. It was a blemish on the principles of the founding. This doesn't make the Founding Principles wrong. It means they were not always adhered to. Despite all the bickering and maneuvering during the convention, slavery had no lasting impact on the design of our governmental system—a design thoroughly imbued with principles from the European Enlightenment, where they had resolved or exported their slavery issues.

Benjamin Franklin wrote, "Slavery is such an atrocious debasement of human nature, that its very extirpation, if not performed with solicitous care, may sometimes open a source of serious evils."[150] Unfortunately, Dr. Franklin was right. After the Civil War, and despite adoption of the Thirteenth, Fourteenth, and Fifteenth amendments, subjugation of blacks continued, assisted by a Supreme Court that turned a blind eye (as reflected in the Slaughterhouse Cases).[151]

Many slaveholding Founders were conflicted about owning human beings, and they can be criticized for leaving the tough work to their descendants, but the ideals that they so eloquently espoused set a lofty standard for America and Americans. Frederick Douglass said, "Interpreted, as it ought to be interpreted, the Constitution is a glorious liberty document ... Take the Constitution according to its plain reading, and I defy the presentation of a single pro-slavery clause in it. On the other hand it will be found to contain principles and purposes, entirely hostile to the existence of slavery."

It took us a long time to right some serious wrongs, but the Declaration of Independence's phrase "All men are created equal, that they are endowed by their Creator with certain unalienable rights" has resonated with freedom-loving people all over the world. It remains a daily struggle to bring this Founding Principle home to every American.

15

Congress

"If the present Congress errs in too much talking, how can it be otherwise in a body to which the people send one hundred and fifty lawyers, whose trade it is to question everything, yield nothing, and talk by the hour?"

—*Thomas Jefferson*[152]

At the start of the Constitutional Convention, the legislative branch was considered noncontroversial. For one thing, the delegates had a prejudice in favor of the legislature and distrusted the executive and the judiciary. Part of that distrust, of course, was because prior to independence, the crown appointed the executive and judiciary, while early Americans voted for representatives in the colonial legislatures.

"No taxation without representation" had a broader meaning than the exact words. The Founders believed that just governance required that representatives of the governed made all laws. This is what they meant by *consent of the governed* in the Declaration of Independence. Since an elected legislature fulfilled this basic principle, few expected to spend much time on the branch until Connecticut proposed that the Senate represent states instead of people.

The Constitutional Convention ended up arguing about every detail of the legislative branch. The congress that they finally settled on was far different than the congress under the Articles of Confederation.

A Congress by Any Other Name...

Under the Articles, Congress had one house, congressmen served for one year and were appointed by state legislatures, state delegations could be between two and seven members, the president was elected from the membership for one year, the judiciary was a committee of Congress, each state had one vote, there was a term limit of serving for only three out of six years, congressmen were paid by their home state, and amendments to the Articles of Confederation had to be agreed upon by each and every state.[153]

Under the Constitution, Congress was different in almost every aspect. It was bicameral (two houses), with a House of Representatives and a Senate. Senators served for six years and representatives served for two years. Representatives were elected directly by the people and state legislatures originally appointed senators. The leader of the Senate was the nation's vice president, and he served for four years and was re-eligible. Although not specifically called out in the Constitution, the House of Representatives have traditionally chosen their leader from their membership. The House of Representatives was proportional to population, but each state had two senators who voted independently. There were no term limits on either house. All members of Congress were paid by the national government. The Constitution amendment process can be started by a two-third majority of both houses.

Since the convention was knowledgeable about the current Congress—many were current or past members—why did they make so many changes to this branch? After all, they could have added a separate judiciary and executive to what they already had and been done. Obviously they thought they were making corrections to a flawed system. A review of the convention debates shows why they made so many dramatic changes.

A Bicameral Legislature

Benjamin Franklin wanted a single-house legislature like Pennsylvania.[154] He did not have much company. Almost all of the other delegates accepted the Virginia Plan proposal for a bicameral legislature. Two houses slow down legislation. Since the job of a legislature is to make laws, why would the delegates want to hinder the body's purpose in being? As in everything else, safety-conscious delegates wanted to disperse power. Good lawmaking required reasoned deliberation, and two houses would force increased consideration prior to the passage of a law.

The Senate was supposed to temper the passions of a House designed to be much closer to the people. The requirements for office in the two chambers provide a good indicator of their thought process. Compared to a representative, a senator must be five years older (thirty years of age) and have been a citizen two years longer (nine years). A senator also served six years, compared to a relatively short two years. The delegates wanted senators that were more mature, had a longer tenure as citizens, and were not as worried about constantly running for re-election. The difference in structure between the two houses was meant to make legislative deliberation more expansive.

Another concern about Congress was corruption. The delegates had witnessed bribery of officials, favors handed out in exchange for legislation, and outrageous conflicts of interests. Delegates believed that larger legislative bodies and additional chambers would make it harder to corrupt Congress. The Founders were highly practical men. They did not trust in the goodness of man. Safety depended on a greater number of members and dispersing those numbers into two separate power centers. The theory was that they couldn't stop the corruption of an occasional representative, but if each representative was only a cog in a bigger apparatus, then they couldn't do irreversible damage.

Who Should Make Up the Senate

For the first two months, most of the controversy centered on the Senate. From the beginning, everyone accepted that the House of Representatives would be directly elected by the people and represent their interest in the national government. But what interest should the Senate serve? A few wanted an ignoble equivalent of a House of Lords. Madison and other like-minded delegates argued that the Senate should represent people in general instead of the landed and wealthy. The small states, however, demanded that the Senate represent states.[155]

As a result of the Great Compromise, it was decided that the Senate would be made up of two senators per state. At first, there were going to be an odd number of senators for each state and each state would have a single vote. This would have been close to the organization of the then current Congress and the Constitutional Convention. Toward the end of the convention, there was a movement to dilute state influence, so a final adjustment gave each state two senators who were allowed to vote independently. Although the state legislatures would appoint senators, they would be paid by the national treasury to further dilute state influence. They also expected a relatively long term of six years to increase the independences of senators. They wanted the Senate to be a stabilizing force, but not disconnected to the public mood, so they rotated out one-third of the members every two years.[156]

When the Great Compromise was first agreed upon, the Senate literally represented the states, but adjustments through the ensuing months made senators more independent and attuned to the people. After the Seventeenth Amendment in 1913, senators became popularly elected, and this further increased their independence. Senators still remain the greatest voice for the states in the national government.

Term limits—what the Founders called re-eligibility—were debated at length. More accurately, they were debated sporadically over many weeks. The final decision was that there would be no limitations on terms for either house, but contrary to the existing Congress under the Articles, no member of Congress could serve in any executive position. Although simultaneous service in the executive and legislature had been a common practice, this restriction advanced the goal of separation of power by denying patronage that could be used by a president to influence legislation.

The Constitutional Convention designed the House to be highly responsive to the people and gave the states strong influence in the Senate, but no direct authority. In the end, they avoided an elite upper house like British Parliament or a Senate that mirrored the lower house. They made the two houses very different so they could be effective checks on each other.

Indecision over the Veto Override

It was never highly contentious, but the convention flip-flopped on legislative override of an executive veto. They vacillated between a three-quarters versus two-thirds requirement. The delegates finally decided on a two-thirds veto override because it would be difficult to garner that many votes in two houses. Besides, by the end of the conference they were ready to shave some power from the executive.[157]

Franklin Causes a Small Row

Benjamin Franklin disliked a Senate intended to represent states. He made it very clear that his support of the Great Compromise depended on money bills originating in the House of Representatives with no amendment capability by the Senate. He insisted, "It is always of importance that the people should know who has disposed of their money, and how it has been disposed of."[158] Other delegates wondered what difference it made where a bill started if both houses eventually had to agree on it anyway. In the end, they stipulated that money bills had to arise on the House side, but allowed amendments in the Senate.

The Last Great Convention Battle

The House of Representatives was not a major issue until the end of the convention. In retrospect, they made a mountain out of a molehill. Since no constitutionally required census had been taken, the initial number of representatives had to be arbitrarily set by a committee. The South insisted on a larger number of representatives than their population warranted. After a lot of haggling, they finally settled on the exact same split that an initial committee had come up with, but shifted a few southern representatives from the Deep South to Virginia and Maryland. The 1790 census made this a pointless squabble because the South received a very short-term benefit.

Final Touches

The Constitutional Convention delegates were not the only ones with a bias in favor of the legislature. The general public also held this opinion. When Gouverneur Morris took home the draft of the Constitution for editing, he returned with a cleanly worded document that included a breathtaking preamble. His fellow committee members were full of praise ... except for one reservation. The Morris document started with the executive branch. The committeemen were afraid that when they released the document to the public, they might think the convention had placed priority on the executive. This would feed into the greatest fear of these early Americans—an elected king. That would never do. The solution was simple. Morris reversed the first two articles, and that is why the Constitution starts with Article I—The Legislative Branch. This revision illustrates how the delegates had already shifted from designing the government to promoting the acceptance of their work outside the doors of the Pennsylvania State House.

Rules of Its Proceedings

The Constitution gave a bicameral legislature checks on the other two branches and the authority to set its own rules. Unfortunately, the bicameral nature has tended to focus the attention of each house on its opposite number. The Founders envisioned representatives that were generally equal in power, but committee chairs have created minor fiefdoms, so rule-making authority contributed to an inward-looking Congress. As a result of jockeying for preeminence within each house and intermural squabbling between houses, Congress has not fully protected its assigned powers from encroachment by the other branches.

The authority to establish law was intended to be held solely by Congress. Unfortunately, we have seen the executive and the judiciary intrude on this obvious congressional power. The country needs three co-equal branches. To get back to where the Founders intended, Congress will need to exert its external checks as well as its internal prerogatives.

The Distinction between the Constitution and a Law

In "Federalist No. 53," James Madison wrote, "The important distinction so well understood in America, between a Constitution established by the people and unalterable by the government, and a law established by the government and alterable by the government, seems to have been little understood and less observed in any other country. Wherever the supreme power of legislation has resided, has been supposed to reside also a full power to change the form of the government."[159]

There are several remarkable points made in these two sentences. First, the Constitution was *established by the people* and thus is *unalterable by the government*. On the other hand, a law is established *by the government,* so it may be *alterable by government*. The quote also makes the point that the United States is unique. These concepts are another repetition of Founding Principles. It's amazing how consistent the Founders remained. They stood on solid principles and seldom wavered.

This brings up another remarkable element of this extract from "Federalist No. 53." Madison says this principle is "so well understood in America." During the founding, the American citizenry were very well versed in the Constitution and "the form of the government." Regrettably, this is not as true today. We have a lot of work to do to ensure that every American again understands that their heritage is based on principle and the Constitution is a priceless birthright available only in this great nation.

16

The Executive

"Writers against the Constitution seem to have taken pains to signalize their talent of misrepresentation. Calculating upon the aversion of the people to monarchy, they have endeavored to enlist all their jealousies and apprehensions in opposition to the intended President of the United States; not merely as the embryo, but as the full-grown progeny, of that detested parent."
—*Alexander Hamilton*[160]

The greatest fear of early Americans was an elected king. The history of the world had been the story of strong men who bludgeoned their way to power. Kings, emperors, tsars, maharajahs, potentates, sultans, chieftains, and warlords were perceived as tyrants one and all. These men, and a few women, took what they wanted and ruled with a stern hand. Americans hated King George III and continued to retain deep reserves of bitterness toward nobles and court sycophants. The Founders knew the country needed an effective executive with enough authority to govern, but they also knew they had to tread carefully, or their fellow citizens might tar and feather them.

Alexander Hamilton wrote in "Federalist No. 70," "Energy in the executive is a leading character in the definition of good government. It is essential to the protection of the community against foreign attacks; it is not less essential to the steady administration of the laws; to the protection of property against those irregular and high-handed combinations which sometimes interrupt the ordinary course of justice; to the security of liberty against the enterprises and assaults of ambition, of faction, and of anarchy."[161]

How could they give the president adequate powers, but preclude a tyrant from gathering up even more power in order to oppress Americans and possibly even resist ouster from office? A stronger Senate provided part of the answer. The primary constraint on dictatorial powers would have to come from distributing power, and then imposing checks by another branch of the government. As James Madison said, "Ambition must be made to counteract ambition." It was determined that another piece of the puzzle was limiting the amount of time an executive remained in office, or forcing that executive to occasionally seek public approval to remain in office.

Nobody Knows What Sort May Come Afterwards

When Benjamin Franklin argued against making the president too powerful, he said, "The first man put at the helm will be a good one, but nobody knows what sort may come afterwards. The Executive will be always increasing here, as elsewhere, till it ends in a monarchy."[162] Franklin did not explain his reference to "the first man put at the helm," but everybody in the chamber knew he meant the man sitting stoically on a low dais at the front of the room. It was assumed by all that George Washington would be the first executive and he would be a *good one*—a principled man, a man that could be trusted with power. After all, he had held power before and had willingly relinquished it. This was Franklin's subtle way of prodding the delegates to assume the worst sort of man might one day follow and to design the office with this less stellar individual in mind. Like most of the Founders, Franklin did not put his trust in the goodness of man.

One Quarrelsome Delegate

George Mason insisted on an executive council of three co-equals. Few agreed with him and when he was absent from the chamber, the convention voted for a single executive. This infuriated Mason. In the end, he refused to sign the Constitution, and despite his expressed complaint about the absence of a Bill of Rights, a single executive may have contributed to him becoming a leading Anti-Federalist during ratification.

On June 4, after the vote for a single executive, Mason told the convention, "We are, Mr. Chairman, going very far in this business. We are not indeed constituting a British government, but a dangerous monarchy, an elective one...Do gentlemen mean to pave the way to hereditary monarchy? Do they flatter themselves that the people will ever consent to such an innovation? If they do I venture to tell them, they are mistaken. The people will never consent!"[163]

The Re-eligibility Debate

The design of the executive was not so much controversial as perplexing. They debated many alternatives, but it was more deliberative than quarrelsome. How could they constrain this position so the president couldn't threaten liberty? They decided that since strong men had a knack for amassing power, the initial focus should be on tenure. (What we call term limits, the Founders called re-eligibility.) The convention argued about whether it was safer to give the president a long term in office and not permit him another term, or give the executive a short term and allow him to run for office again? This was a major issue during the last month or so of the convention.

One school of thought said that a re-eligible president would use patronage, political favors, and even graft to remain in office, so it was safer to give the executive a longer term and then dispatch him home.

The danger, of course, was that a longer term would give an unscrupulous individual more time to bypass constitutional restrictions, or an ex-president could simply put a crony in place and dictate affairs from the sideline. Some further argued that limiting re-eligibility would deny the nation the continued services of a competent executive.[164]

Alexander Hamilton, "Federalist No. 72"

"Exclusion (from additional terms) would be the temptation to sordid views, to peculation, and, in some instances, to usurpation ... A third ill effect of the exclusion would be the depriving the community of the experience gained by chief magistrate in the exercise of his office. That experience is the parent of wisdom is an adage the truth of which is recognized by the wisest as well as the simplest of mankind."[165]

The other alternative would be a relatively short presidential term with the freedom to run for additional terms. The danger was that an adept or unscrupulous politician might find ways to retain the office for life. An argument for this option was that a strong executive would not be tempted to circumvent the Constitution to stay in office because he could run for re-election. The Founders believed maintaining the integrity of the Constitution was important. A shorter term might also give the public voice by allowing reconfirmation of their approval of the president.[166]

In the end, they decided on a four-year term and unlimited re-eligibility. (In 1947, the Twenty-Second Amendment limited the president to two terms.) Madison's notes do not record any suddenly convincing argument or grand revelation. The same arguments seemed to be repeated over and over again. The delegates ended up weighing the two options and then went with the one that the majority believed would result in the best government.

The Civil War Tested the Delegates' Wisdom

Were they right? When the slaveholding states seceded from the union prior to the Civil War, they created a Constitution for the new Confederate States of America that was very similar to the United States Constitution...with two big exceptions. First, the Confederate Constitution directly protected slavery, and second, the president served for six years with no re-eligibility.[167] Abraham Lincoln had to run for re-election in the middle of an awful war, while Jefferson Davis served comfortably in the knowledge that he would never run again. Some historians claim that this is one of the reasons that Davis was considered irascible and uncommunicative with his Congress. Could this have hurt the South's war effort? Lincoln, on the other hand, had to work with his cabinet, Congress, local officials, and the people because his tenure was comparatively short. We'll never know for sure, but it appears that the Founders again made the correct choice.[168]

The Election of the President

The delegates argued over more than term and re-eligibility. They also argued over how to elect the president. They voted repeatedly on different notions, but they all failed. They finally landed on a solution that most delegates could accept. The president would be chosen by electors, and electors would be chosen however the states decided. Why did they finally decide on an Electoral College? First, they knew most of the states would decide to popularly elect the electors. Why not have the people vote directly for the president? The key is in the number of electors assigned to each state. Each state received an elector for each representative and each senator. Since population determines the number of representatives, but every state gets two senators, this was a compromise between those who wanted a popular election and those who felt the states should collectively pick the president.[169]

The practical result of the Electoral College is that presidential candidates cannot ignore the great expanses of this country that don't have a large population. Generally, this would be the middle of the country because the large population centers are on the periphery of the nation. The Electoral College and Senate help insure that the rural sections of the country are not ignored; otherwise the United States would be like most of the other capital-centric nations of the world, with government, business, education, and culture all centralized in the capital city. Paris, London, Moscow, Buenos Aires, and Cairo are examples of how everything gravitates to the capital city when the head of state is chosen by any method that doesn't give the hinterlands an outsized voice. This phenomenon is visible in the United States. For example, Phoenix and Salt Lake City dominate Arizona and Utah politics to the disadvantage of the rural areas of the states.

Presidential Powers

On first impression, presidential powers are vaguer than the powers of Congress. Article I, Section 8, is a tidy list of congressional enumerated powers, whereas presidential powers are dispersed throughout Article II and seem imprecise. It is wrong to evaluate the articles of the Constitution in isolation from the remainder of the document. The Founders designed a balanced system with interwoven checks on the exercise of power. The Constitution is an all-inclusive, closed system. The *checks and balances* model dictates that the Constitution must be read and analyzed as a whole. The Constitution gives the president *executive power* and several other very specific powers. The Founders believed that executive power was limited to foreign affairs, and the administration and enforcement of laws passed by Congress, which made the president as constrained by Article I, Section 8 as Congress. In other words, the president had no just powers to administer and enforce activities that were beyond enacted legislation. At least, that was the thinking in 1787.

The Constitution gives the president the following powers. This list has been extracted from Article II, and slightly rearranged to put similar powers together. (Capitalization has been modernized.)

- The executive power shall be vested in a president ... he shall take care that the laws be faithfully executed ... he may require the opinion, in writing, of the principal officer in each of the executive departments.
- The president shall be commander in chief ... and shall commission all the officers of the United States.
- He shall have power to grant reprieves and pardons.
- He shall have power, by and with the advice and consent of the Senate, to make treaties, provided two-thirds of the senators present concur.
- He shall nominate, and by and with the advice and consent of the Senate, shall appoint ambassadors, other public ministers and consuls, judges of the Supreme Court, and all other officers of the United States.
- He shall from time to time give to the Congress information of the State of the Union, and recommend to their consideration such measures as he shall judge necessary and expedient.
- He may, on extraordinary occasions, convene both Houses, or either of them, and in case of disagreement between them, with respect to the time of adjournment, he may adjourn them to such time as he shall think proper.

Note: Although Article II uses the male pronoun in defining powers, the neutral *person* is used in Section I when defining the qualifications and election procedures for the president. No amendment is necessary for a woman to serve as president.

Defining the Presidency

Section II of the Constitution defines the executive role in government and it is only 1,025 words. This is shorter than most job descriptions for a frontline supervisor. Yet the way a United States president works and behaves across a plethora of duties is well established. How did this happen?

The Constitution defined the parameters of the presidency, Supreme Court decisions settled some uncertainties, and two hundred-plus years of wars, foreign affairs, economic issues, and government expansion and have all played a part, but to this day, George Washington had more to do with defining the presidency than all the rest of this combined.

Washington started setting precedents within a second of taking office. He followed the constitutionally mandated oath of office with the words, "So help me God." He institutionalized civilian control of the military. Prior to election, Washington made a habit of wearing suits with a military flair. After his election, he never again wore any clothing with the slightest hint of the military. He started the tradition of the president being accessible to people. It was Washington who instituted the practice of using the cabinet as advisors. He famously set a 143-year tradition of presidents serving only two terms. When Franklin Roosevelt violated this tradition, the country quickly ratified an amendment to make the tradition a law.[170]

Washington's greatest precedent was the restrained exercise of power. He could have been emperor. Many wanted to call him "His Excellency," but he insisted on the pedestrian "Mr. President."[171] George Washington gave the country more than eight years as president; he gave the country a revered model for the presidency that has survived to this day.

How Did the President Become So Powerful?

The president of the United States of America is often called the most powerful person in the world. Over the centuries, presidential power has increased enormously, both domestically and internationally. This was not the intent of the Founders. The president was supposed to be a co-equal partner in a three-party government focused on the needs of Americans. Today, the executive is arguably more powerful than the other two branches.

Domestic Power

The moniker of the most powerful person in the world starts at home. Granted, the president is one individual versus a larger number of people in the other two branches, but this singularity isn't the reason a modern executive wields such enormous power.

The greatest increase in presidential power came from the growth in government. As the national government grew, from around 4 percent of gross domestic product (GDP) in the 1920s to 25 percent in 2010,[172] presidential power grew exponentially because all but a smidgeon of that money ended up in the executive branch. The executive branch is by far the largest employer in the world with at least 5.2 million employees, counting the Department of Defense but excluding the semi-private Post Office.[173] The bigger the national government grows, the more powerful the executive is as an individual.

To a large degree, the tilting of power toward the executive has come from Congress passing laws with only general guidance and then allowing the executive branch to write rules that have the force of law. (An exception to this trend is earmarks, which are very explicit.) This was a congressional delegation of lawmaking authority to the executive branch.

When Congress broke the restraints of the enumerated powers, it likewise enlarged executive authority to regulate more and more aspects of Americans' lives.

Another growth in domestic presidential powers came from the Budget and Accounting Act of 1921, which formally put the president in the lead for government budgets and expenditures.[174] (Revenue is the purview of Congress, but the Constitution is silent on budgeting.)

Presidential power also expanded through what are called inherent powers and special prerogatives. These are basically powers not specifically called out in the Constitution, but claimed by the president. Inherited powers are inferred from executive authority. These are powers used by previous presidents without challenge, or powers supported by Supreme Court decisions. An example of an inherited power would be executive orders. Special prerogatives, on the other hand, go back to English law and are rights possessed by an official by virtue of the office. An example of a special prerogative would be the use of executive privilege to withhold information from another branch.[175]

Inherent powers and special prerogatives slowly evolve over time in a tug of war between the three branches. The Founders would have been proud of this tripartite sumo-like wrestling match between the branches.

International Power

In *United States v. Curtiss-Wright Export Corp* (1936),[176] the Supreme Court ruled that the president has almost unrestricted powers in international affairs. The Court said that this singular authority over foreign affairs is "the very delicate, plenary and exclusive power of the President as sole organ of the federal government in the field of international relations—a power which does not require as a basis for its exercise an act of Congress." One of the few exceptions to this *exclusive* power is Senate approval of treaties.

This ruling by itself did not make the president the most powerful person on the world stage. Three other developments made that happen.

The first development was that the American free enterprise system built the largest, most robust economy in the world. The United States is the biggest market for goods and services, which means that every other country wants to export their products to us. Historically, the ever-increasing productivity of American workers and companies has meant that we could also sell our goods and services overseas, while maintaining the highest per capita income in the world. (The twenty-first century has not matched the twentieth century's productivity gains, but this can be righted by a return to sound economic policies.)

The second development was the vacuum of power after World War II. The Soviets were dangerous, and their ambitions for empire threatened the world. Someone had to step into the breach. The rest of the world may have publicly complained about American hegemony, but they always changed their tune when the United States discussed withdrawing from some unpleasant or expensive part of the world.

The third development was the global reach of modern weaponry. The incentive for building an immense American arsenal was worldwide competition in weapons development and manufacturing, but the indisputable supremacy of the United States was a direct result of the American capitalist system—in funding, innovation, and inventiveness.

Is It Time to Reduce the Power of the Presidency?

The Founders did not intend for the president to be the most powerful person in the world. Does that mean presidential powers should be reduced? Yes and no.

On the domestic front, the size of government must be reduced. This would simultaneously reduce executive power. In fact, presidential powers cannot be significantly affected without dramatic cuts in spending. Spending equals power: power over people because governments govern. Re-instilling at least some level of discipline on the enumerated powers would not only shrink government, but also have the added benefit of enlarging personal liberty for Americans.

There is a movement afoot to require new executive branch regulations to be submitted to a congressional committee for review prior to enactment. This may not be an ideal solution, but it would be a major improvement that has the potential of putting Congress back into the driver's seat on legislation.

Internationally, the easiest way to diminish presidential powers would be to slow down the economic growth of the United States. If we were no longer so successful, our leadership position would necessarily be weakened. Nobody would want that. Also, we can't completely abandon safeguarding the world from bullies and despots, nor would unilaterally disarming make sense. All of this means that we will continue to be a major player in world affairs. But we need a well-articulated foreign policy that can be debated as a nation. That way, popular opinion will keep the president relatively compliant with a strategy that has been publicly determined to be in the interests of the United States.

The president of the United States will probably continue to be the most powerful person in the world. Domestically, steps need to be taken to once again make the president a co-equal with Congress and the Supreme Court. That will require a return to the principles embedded in the Constitution. Internationally, we ought to establish simple, prime principles the United States abides by in foreign affairs.

For example, if we steadfastly stood for the principle of free trade, the world might mute their criticism about our size and commercial leadership. Speaking of principles, perhaps our number one export ought to be our Founding Principles.

17

The Judiciary

"There is not a syllable in the plan [Constitution] which directly empowers the national courts to construe the laws according to the spirit of the Constitution."
—*Alexander Hamilton*[177]

During the Constitutional Convention and state ratification conventions, the judiciary was the least discussed branch of the national government. From a design perspective, almost all of the debate and alarm seemed to have been focused on the executive and the legislature. The simplest explanation is that the judiciary was familiar and noncontroversial. Hamilton wrote in "Federalist No. 78," "The judiciary, from the nature of its functions, will always be the least dangerous to the political rights of the Constitution; because it will be least in a capacity to annoy or injure them."[178] Every delegate knew what a judge did, and understood their role in the government, and their only concern was insuring their independence. A few anticipated that judges might legislate from the bench, but most of the delegates were more concerned about politicians or outsiders putting undue pressure on judges. The Founders' solution to this threat was to give justices life tenure.

For nearly one hundred and fifty years, the Supreme Court restricted itself to evaluating laws based on what today would be called an originalist perspective. For the most part, the Commerce, General Welfare, and Necessary and Proper clauses, as well as the Bill of Rights, were interpreted on a generally narrow basis; the court took the enumerated powers seriously, showed deference to state authority, and restricted interference with contracts by the states.

During these first years, the Court did not go out of its way to discover new rights, but enforced rights specifically called out in the Constitution—with one tragic exception. That exception, of course, was the rights of black Americans. The Supreme Court never ruled slavery unconstitutional and after the Civil War, the Court permitted (and later endorsed with *Plessy v. Ferguson*) racial segregation to deny rights to Americans that were unequivocally full citizens as declared by the Fourteenth and Fifteenth Amendments.[179] This shameful behavior by the court was the first serious occurrence of the Supreme Court kowtowing to public opinion and political pressure. The country should have taken greater notice because the court's turning of a blind eye toward violations of the Constitution was a harbinger of things to come.

Something Went Awry

The Supreme Court abandoned self-control during Franklin Roosevelt's terms in office. In a 1935 letter to a Congressional committee chairman, Roosevelt wrote, "I hope your committee will not permit doubts as to the constitutionality, however reasonable, to block the suggested legislation."[180] At first, the court resisted constitutionally expansive programs of the New Deal, but later became collaborators with Roosevelt by acquiescing to his desire to ignore Constitutional limits.

Robert A. Levy and William Mellor, in *The Dirty Dozen: How Twelve Supreme Court Cases Radically Expanded Government and Eroded Freedom*, made clear that one decade of court decisions gutted the limits that the Framers had carefully crafted into the Constitution. Worse, the Roosevelt court gave license to courts that followed that they, too, were free to rule based on justices' assessment of what was right or popular sentiment, rather than on the written Constitution. Here are some of the major cases between 1934 and 1944.

- 1934, *Home Building & Loan Association v. Blaisdell* negated the Contracts Clause, allowing states and eventually the federal government to ignore private contract obligations when it suited their needs.

- 1937, *Helvering v. Davis* untied the General Welfare Clause from enumerated powers, effectively giving the Federal government general, rather than enumerated powers.

- 1938, *United States v. Carolene Products Co.* delegated the Ninth Amendment rights "retained by the people" to second-class status, with special implications for economic liberty.

- 1939, *United States v. Miller* conditioned the *right of the people to keep and bear arms* to the militia clause, thus giving the government the authority to restrict individual Second Amendment rights.

- 1942, *Wickard v. Filburn* unlocked the Commerce Clause from any restraint whatsoever, allowing the national government unprecedented authority over states and individuals.

- 1943, *National Broadcasting Co. v. United States* excised the nondelegation doctrine from the Constitution, allowing administrative agencies to simultaneously exercise legislative, executive, and judicial powers.

- 1944, *Korematsu v. United States* overruled the Due Process Clause during times of emergency.

From that ignominious decade forward, the Supreme Court has supplanted the Constitution as the ultimate arbiter of what our government can and cannot do ... and even how it may do it. With these decisions—and others that followed—the plain English of the Constitution was no longer a barrier to concentrating immeasurable power in Washington, D.C.

Home Building & Loan Association v. Blaisdell

Since *Home Building & Loan Association v. Blaisdell* was the first of these cases, and it has relevance to the current housing crisis, we'll examine it a little more carefully. As Levy and Mellor point out in *The Dirty Dozen*, it's actually seldom that a Constitutional issue that reaches the Supreme Court is black and white. *The Home Building & Loan Association v. Blaisdell* was one of those rare cases. In an attempt to stem home and farm foreclosures, Minnesota passed a law that allowed a mortgagor to temporarily pay court-determined rent that was set well below the contractual mortgage amount. The mortgage holder could take no foreclosure action while the reduced rent was being paid. The decision by the Supreme Court to uphold this Minnesota law was in direct violation of the Constitution, which reads, "No State shall ... pass any ... Law impairing the Obligation of Contracts."

During the Constitutional Convention in 1787, foreclosures were rampant, and several states had passed laws that *impaired* contracts by forcing debtors to accept purposely inflated state-generated paper money as legal tender. These laws put a stranglehold on credit markets, deepening difficult economic times. The Founders didn't want this to happen again. Their intent—and the wording could not be clearer—was to preclude the exact type of action taken by Minnesota.

Minnesota's violation of the contracts clause could not be more blatant, yet the Supreme Court arbitrarily overrode the Constitution and gave the states permission to violate private contracts. The result of this sanctioned contract interference chilled the nation's credit markets. Lenders could no longer rely on loan collateral. The Supreme Court's action was heartless because its sympathetic treatment of a few borrowers helped to deepen and elongate the Great Depression, which caused enormous suffering for a great swath of the population.

There is another aspect of *Blaisdell* that makes it a monumental decision: it started the modern trend of looking at the Constitution as a living force that could be molded to meet popular passions. The Constitution had certainly been violated in the past, but the basic meaning had not been irrevocably altered. Once the floodgates had been pried open, the judiciary progressively stretched their political powers. When the Supreme Court overruled clear constitutional clauses, they suffered few complaints, while on the other side, so many cheered that the courts grew to feel comfortable in the role of *Supreme Law of the Land*. The FDR courts and those that followed now had license to ignore the actual wording and intent of the Constitution. From that point forward, the Constitution could no longer be relied upon. It was in flux, subject to the whims of a tribunal.

Artful Apologists

On July 6, 2005, the *New York Times* published an op-ed piece titled, "So Who Are the Activists," by Paul Gewirtz and Chad Golder.[181] The intent of the editorial was to turn the table on those who used *activist* as a pejorative term. They started by claiming that there was no definition of a so-called activist ruling—except that the person using the term simply disagreed with a decision. In their minds, this left the field wide open for Gewirtz and Golder to invent their own definition. Their definition was based on how many times a justice voted to strike down a law passed by Congress. The premise was that judges that overruled democratically enacted laws were the true activists.

With this definition in hand, Gewirtz and Golder ran some numbers and reversed the generally perceived order of sitting activist justices, with Clarence Thomas now being tagged as the supreme activist, and Stephen Breyer celebrated as a paragon of judicial restraint. This was the same Stephen Breyer who believes the Constitution provides "a structural flexibility sufficient to adapt substantive laws and institutions to rapidly changing social, economic, and technological conditions."[182] In other words, the Constitution can mean what Breyer needs or wants it to mean.

Flawed Analysis

Did Gewirtz's and Golder's analysis make sense? First, there already existed a generally accepted definition of an activist judge. The term was used for justices who ventured into the legislative or executive realm. But this was not the biggest problem with this *New York Times* opinion piece. The fatal error was that the basic premise was wrong.

Gewirtz and Golder opened by writing, "Congress, as an elected legislative body representing the entire nation, makes decisions that can be presumed to possess a high degree of democratic legitimacy," and conclude their editorial by claiming that their analysis "clearly illustrates the varying degrees to which justices would actually intervene in the democratic work of Congress." Everything the authors conclude is derived from this premise—the Supreme Court has no right to overrule democratically enacted laws. To accept their definition would mean that democracy is sacrosanct, not the Constitution.

As a philosophical dispute, this might be hard to follow, but fortunately Paul Gewirtz provides us a practical example. In another *New York Times* op-ed piece published almost exactly five years later, on July 2, 2010,[183] Gewirtz writes, "It is no secret that the current Supreme Court is an activist one in striking down congressional legislation—just look at the prominent cases from the court's just-completed term, most notably *Citizens United v. Federal Election Commission*, in which a 5–4 majority of the court's more conservative justices struck down key provisions of Congress's bipartisan campaign finance laws." In this editorial, Gewirtz ups the ante by bolstering unassailable *democratically enacted laws* with the ever-alluring *bipartisan* stamp of approval.

The Supreme Court's job is to evaluate laws based upon constitutionality, not congressional desire or popular will. The United States is not a democracy. It is a republic. All three branches are supposed to operate under the auspices of the Constitution. If the judiciary felt obligated to rubber stamp every law passed by Congress, then there is no restraint on government, and we have no need for a Constitution—or a judiciary for that matter. In point of fact, we have already traveled far down this road.

The Founders relied on a few good principles. So should we. That will require restoring the Constitution to an approximation of original intent. Some recent Supreme Court decisions have shown progress in this regard, while others have continued to wear away the fabric of our national heritage. Fresh decisions have reasserted an individual's right to bear arms, and there has been some progress in viewing campaign contributions as protected political speech. On the other side of the ledger, the Takings Clause has been sorely diminished, and the Supreme Court has yet to rein in the capacious view of the Commerce Clause.

Thomas Jefferson Writes a Letter

In 1819, Thomas Jefferson forewarned a friend against treating the Constitution like "a mere thing of wax." Here is a section of the letter. Parenthetical comments have been added by the authors.

"If this opinion be sound, then indeed is our constitution a complete felo de se. (Felo-de-se is an archaic term for suicide.) For intending to establish three departments, co-ordinate and independent, that they might check and balance one another, it has given, according to this opinion, to one of them alone, the right to prescribe rules for the government of the others, and to that one too, which is unelected by, and independent of the nation. For experience has already shown that the impeachment it has provided is not even a scarecrow; that such opinions as the one you combat, sent cautiously out, as you observe also, by detachment, not belonging to the case often, but sought for out of it, as if to rally the public opinion beforehand to their views, and to indicate the line they are to walk in, have been so quietly passed over as never to have excited animadversion (criticism), even in a speech of any one of the body entrusted with impeachment. The constitution, on this hypothesis, is a mere thing of wax in the hands of the judiciary, which they may twist, and shape into any form they please."[184]

An Ideal World

In an ideal world, a justice would hold up a law against the Constitution, and rule if it is in compliance or not with a simple up or down vote. This ruling should be based on the clear wording of the Constitution, with perhaps a look at the debates and ratification process to discover the intent of a document meant to bind the government to strict rules of behavior. Another consideration might be precedent rulings by prior courts, but these rulings should be secondary to the Constitution—after all, both conservatives and liberals can point to dreadful decisions by the Supreme Court.

Unfortunately, the United States does not live in this ideal world. Today, activist judges revise laws by using inventive interpretations of the Constitution. (In his later years, Rexford Tugwell, a Roosevelt advisor, called the Court's actions during Roosevelt's era "tortured interpretation.") Unsanctioned revisions have expanded national authority over people, states, corporations, and organizations.

Liberty depends on the rule of law, not the whim of a tribunal. The Supreme Court is supposed to be the steady hand on the tiller. The Supreme Court's highest regard is supposed to be for the law. The Supreme Court is supposed to be the guardian of our Constitution. It's past time for the Court to reassume its proper duties.

Madison's Rare Error

Most of the delegates to the Constitutional Convention saw the judiciary as a great check against the abuse of power by the national government. In a speech proposing the Bill of Rights to the House of Representatives, Madison said, "If they [rights] are incorporated into the Constitution, independent tribunals of justice will consider themselves in a peculiar manner the guardians of those rights; they will be an impenetrable bulwark against every assumption of power in the legislative or executive; they will be naturally led to resist every encroachment upon rights expressly stipulated for in the Constitution by the declaration of rights."[185]

Madison was wrong. The Supreme Court has been an accomplice, not an *impenetrable bulwark* against assumptions of power by the legislature or the executive. Neither has the court resisted "every encroachment upon rights expressly stipulated for in the Constitution."[186] Instead, the court has denied stipulated rights, and went out of its way to protect unstipulated rights.

Getting Back to Basics

Restoring the Constitution won't be easy … or quick. For one thing, the selection of a Supreme Court Justice has become a big media event charged with emotion and politics. It's instructive that political movements hyperventilate when fighting a nominee they dislike, and spend an inordinate amount of resources influencing Supreme Court nominations they do like. Everyone knows these are enormously powerful people—with life tenure. But everyone also pretends their candidate is an impassive judge that measures every decision by the law, but if that were so, no one would care so much about who sat on the bench.

The only way to repair our Constitution is with justices that have a deep-seated loyalty to the Founding Principles. Since presidents typically appoint based on political leanings, it will be up to the Senate to *advise* the president on acceptable candidates, and then *consent* only to candidates that can show a life's work of being faithful to the Constitution. If Constitutional integrity is going to be restored, the weight of the task will be on the Senate.

18

The Bill of Rights

"The Sacred Rights of mankind are not to be rummaged for among old parchments or musty records. They are written, as with a sunbeam, in the whole volume of human nature, by the Hand of the Divinity itself, and can never be erased or obscured by mortal power."
—*Alexander Hamilton*[187]

Individual rights were not a significant issue during the Constitutional Convention, but a Bill of Rights certainly became a major issue during ratification. The Founders believed they had restricted national powers to such an extent that a bill of rights wasn't necessary because the national government couldn't reach down and touch an individual. The ratification debates exposed the country's deep desire for a Bill of Rights. In fact, due to the ratification process and rapid adoption of the first ten amendments, the Bill of Rights can almost be thought of as part of the base document. Americans agreed to this new government form, but only as long as that government's first order of business was to prepare a statement of rights.

Those who fought for a Bill of Rights weren't looking for a government warranty of rights. The Anti-Federalists also believed that rights came from God, not the government. These Constitutional dissenters were demanding that government be restricted from interfering with their rights. Madison said in his speech to Congress that introduced the Bill of Rights, "The great mass of people who opposed [the Constitution], disliked it because it did not contain effectual provisions against encroachments on particular rights."[188] Madison, a person ever careful with words, did not say that those who opposed the Constitution wanted a guarantee of rights from the national government; he said, "It did not contain effective *provisions against encroachment.*" In other words, the *great mass of people* wanted it made crystal clear where the government dare not tread.

Rights in the Constitution Prior to the Bill of Rights

The base document included a few rights interspersed throughout the text. Writ of habeas corpus could not be suspended—unless the country was under attack; no bill of attainder or ex post facto law could be passed at the national or state level; Americans were guaranteed a jury trial for criminal cases; there could be no religious test for federal office; no state law could impair the obligation of contracts; and the citizens of each state were entitled to the privileges and immunities of the citizens of every other state.

Federalists Resist

Despite the clamor for a Bill of Rights, the Federalists continued to insist that one was not needed because the national government's powers were restricted, and most state constitutions already possessed declarations of rights. As Hamilton explained in "Federalist No. 84," "I go further, and affirm that bills of rights, in the sense and to the extent in which they are contended for, are not only unnecessary in the proposed Constitution, but would even be dangerous. They would contain various exceptions to powers not granted; and on this very account, would afford a colorable pretext to claim more than were granted. For why declare that things shall not be done which there is no power to do?"[189]

We have a Bill of Rights today because Anti-Federalists vehemently disagreed.

The impasse was finally overcome by the Massachusetts Compromise. Massachusetts secured ratification by getting some Anti-Federalists to vote yes through a pledge to add a Bill of Rights in the First Congress. Four additional states raised similar demands.[190]

Bill of Rights: A Short History

Bills of rights were not new at the time of the Founding. The 1215 Magna Carta forced King John to respect specified rights, the English Bill of Rights of 1689 guaranteed rights, and many states had previously enacted declarations of rights into their state constitutions.[191]

The call for a Bill of Rights was the Anti-Federalists' most powerful political weapon against ratification. For many Anti-Federalists, the real objection was a national government far too strong for their taste, but this argument floundered, while a bill of rights gained enormous traction with people. Influential Founders made vocal and repeated demands for a Bill of Rights. Thomas Jefferson called the omission a major mistake, writing, "A bill of rights is what the people are entitled to against every government on earth." Richard Henry Lee objected to the lack of protection for "those essential rights of mankind without which liberty cannot exist." At first, the Federalists argued that the Constitution's checks and balances constrained the government so it couldn't abridge individual rights. But in the Virginia convention, Patrick Henry denounced the Constitution's checks and balances, calling them "specious, imaginary balances" and "ridiculous ideal checks and contrivances."[192]

Madison's support for a bill of rights became crucial. At first he objected, then he was unsure, and finally he fully turned to become a forceful advocate. He came to believe that a Bill of Rights had become a political necessity. He even promised to seek a Bill of Rights in his campaign for Congress in his strongly Anti-Federalist district in Virginia.[193]

As usual, once he made up his mind, Madison applied all of his efforts to achieve his goal. To speed up the process, Madison studied state declaration of rights and the proposals by the state ratification conventions and used all of this information to compile a list of rights that were broadly popular. As a member of the First Congress, he worked tirelessly to enact these amendments. In his speech on June 8, 1789, when he first proposed a Bill of Rights, he said, "It may be thought all paper barriers against the power of the community are too weak to be worthy of attention... yet, as they have a tendency to impress some... it may be one mean to control the majority from those acts to which they might be otherwise inclined."[194] Politically, Madison became a strong advocate for these amendments, but as these words reflect, he may have remained ambivalent philosophically.

On September 25, 1789, the First Congress of the United States sent the proposed amendments to the states. The three-fourths Constitutional requirement meant that eleven of the fourteen states had to ratify each article for them to become law. (Vermont was admitted as the fourteenth state on March 4, 1791.) Seventeen amendments were approved by the House, the Senate trimmed the list to twelve, and ten ended up ratified by the states. With Virginia's ratification on December 15, 1791, amendments one through ten became our revered Bill of Rights.

Restricting the Prerogatives of Government

The ten amendments were perceived at the time as restrictions on the national government. A reading of the Bill of Rights from the Founders' perspective clearly shows that these were not meant to guarantee certain rights. In the first eight amendments, the people are telling the national government that these are some of the rights endowed by their Creator, and the government has no authority of any kind to interfere with the free expression of these rights.

Most people have forgotten that there is a preamble to the Bill of Rights, which among other things reads, "The Conventions of a number of the States, having at the time of their adopting the Constitution, expressed a desire, in order to prevent misconstruction or abuse of its powers, that further declaratory and restrictive clauses should be added." Here are some of the *declaratory and restrictive clauses* used in the first eight amendments.

Congress shall make no law
shall not be infringed
without the consent
shall not be violated
nor shall be compelled
the accused shall enjoy
nor be deprived
no fact tried by a jury, shall be otherwise re-examined
shall not be required

Despite a modern perception that the Constitution bestows and protects rights, it is clear that the Bill of Rights is really a list of government prohibitions. The Founders did not believe in government benevolence, and would never have accepted the government—including the Supreme Court—as the arbiter of rights. If additional rights needed protection from the government, they believed they had an adequate insurance policy in the Ninth and Tenth Amendments.

The Ninth and Tenth Amendments

Because the Founders feared that a Bill of Rights might impede liberty due to sins of omission, the Ninth Amendment provided that "the enumeration in the Constitution of certain rights, shall not be construed to deny or disparage other rights retained by the people." The Tenth Amendment further stated that "the powers not delegated to the United States by the Constitution, nor prohibited by it to the States, are reserved to the States respectively, or to the people." These unassuming fifty words encapsulated the political philosophy of the Founders. Rights are not bestowed by the government; they are "endowed by their Creator" and reside with the people, and liberty depends on government operating within the restriction of enumerated powers delegated by a sovereign people.

This simple but effective philosophy has been diminished. Americans seem to turn to their government to validate and protect real and presumed rights, and increasingly rely on government to guarantee the substance of life. The Founders feared overly powerful government, while today many Americans embrace national authority and fight to enlarge governmental powers.

Mr. Madison Writes a Letter to Mr. Jefferson

Prior to championing a Bill of Rights in the First Congress, James Madison wrote a revealing letter to Thomas Jefferson in October of 1788. Interestingly, much of the letter was written in a secret code only the two of them shared. The following extract from the letter gives insight into Madison's mindset and the thinking of many of the Founders.

It is true nevertheless that not a few, particularly in Virginia have contended for the proposed alterations from the most honorable and patriotic motives; and that among the advocates for the Constitution, there are some who wish for further guards to public liberty and individual rights. As far as these may consist of a constitutional declaration of the most essential rights, it is probable they will be added; though there are many who think such addition unnecessary, and not a few who think it misplaced in such a Constitution. There is scarce any point on which the party in opposition is so much divided as to its importance and its propriety. My own opinion has always been in favor of a bill of rights; provided it be so framed as not to imply powers not meant to be included in the enumeration. At the same time I have never thought the omission a material defect, nor been anxious to supply it even by subsequent amendment, for any other reason than that it is anxiously desired by others.

Wherever the real power in a government lies, there is the danger of oppression. In our governments the real power lies in the majority of the community, and the invasion of private rights is chiefly to be apprehended, not from acts of government contrary to the sense of its constituents, but from acts in which the government is the mere instrument of the major number of the constituents. Wherever there is an interest and power to do wrong, wrong will generally be done.

The restrictions however strongly marked on paper will never be regarded when opposed to the decided sense of the public; and after repeated violations in extraordinary cases, they will lose even their ordinary efficacy.[195]

This is an incredibly prescient letter. A good example of Madison's wisdom would be the Kansas-Nebraska Act (1854). The Missouri Compromise (1820) prohibited slavery above Parallel 36°30', and pro-slavery forces used the Kansas-Nebraska Act to repeal the Missouri Compromise and allow new states to decide the slavery issue by popular vote. Senator Stephen A. Douglas of Illinois was the strongest proponent of the bill, saying, "The great principle of self-government is at stake, and surely the people of this country are never going to decide that the principle upon which our whole republican system rests is vicious and wrong." Douglas appealed to egalitarian impulses to expand slavery—a tactic that cloaked malevolence in a pretext of democracy.

Fortunately, Senator Douglas's crass appeal to the South for a planned presidential run energized an embryonic Republican Party. The party unsuccessfully pitted Abraham Lincoln against Douglas in his next Senate race, but Lincoln defeated Douglas for president in 1859.

The point is that Madison was right: "the real power lies in the majority of the community" and "restrictions however strongly marked on paper will never be regarded when opposed to the decided sense of the public." Douglas said, "The great principle of self-government is at stake." This was a manipulation of the truth. The Founders fervently believed in self-governance, but they created representative self-government, not democracy. There are many other examples in American history, but the Kansas-Nebraska Act is a textbook illustration showing why the Founders avoided egalitarianism. They knew that minority rights were not safe in a pure democracy.

Judicial Enlargement

Until the early 1900s, there were several commonly held beliefs about the Bill of Rights. Most of these were turned upside down in the twentieth century.

- The Bill of Rights did not grant rights; it restricted government actions.
- The Bill of Rights restricted only the national government.
- Rights not specified were retained by the people and could be delineated, altered, controlled, or protected only through amendments or actions by the people's representatives in the legislature.
- The Bill of Rights listed rights that applied to individuals.

Most of these concepts have become passé. (Recent Supreme Court decisions have revived the precept that all ten amendments were meant to protect individual rights—including the "right of the people to keep and bear arms."[196]) Nowadays, social justice is the province of government, except most social issues are not decided by the peoples' representatives in state legislatures or Congress, but by the Supreme Court. Over the years, the Supreme Court has succeeded in setting itself up as the arbiter of rights. So much so, many people have come to view government—specifically the Supreme Court—as the grantor and guarantor of rights.

A few examples are in order. The Supreme Court started interpreting the due process clause of the Fourteenth Amendment as prohibiting state governments from abridging all rights. These decisions injected the Supreme Court as never before into issues that had previously been exclusive to the states. Then in *Griswold v. Connecticut,* the Supreme Court ruled that enumerated rights cast shadows that included unspecified rights—in this case privacy. Later, the Supreme Court extended this already extended right to justify a right to abortion.[197] In neither case, privacy nor abortion, did the justices base their prime argument on the Ninth Amendment. If they had, they would have had to acknowledge that they did not have the power to enlarge rights because the American people had retained that power.

Like any government entity, the Supreme Court is not inclined to diminish its exercise of power.

The Bill of Rights as a Mallet

Most Americans revere the Constitution. Constitutional devotees generally fall into two categories: those who primarily focus on the basic document with its powers and checks and balances, and those who see the Constitution as a mere vehicle to carry a Bill of Rights.

Either perspective would have disappointed the Founders. When the Bill of Rights was ratified in 1791, almost all of the Founders were still alive. They had fought, argued, and spent a good deal of their personal wealth to make the Constitution and the first ten amendments the supreme law of the land. What made the Constitution the supreme law of the land was not the Constitutional Convention, but the ratification process. Since the ratification process led immediately to the adoption of a Bill of Rights, they saw the Constitution and first ten amendments as a unified whole. If called on, they would fight again to preserve the ideas embraced by the entire document.

Many social activists focus only on the first ten amendments. They ignore the original intent of these amendments and use a proven strategy to enlarge rights. These activists start by getting some personal issue popularly perceived as a right, then they harangue the general populous, state legislatures, the courts, and Congress until the Supreme Court officially declares their passion a right—generally one that has been loitering for several hundred years in the shadow of an existing right. As the Ninth Amendment states, rights exist that are not included in the first eight amendments, but the proper way to protect these rights from government interference is through laws at the state level or through the constitutional amendment process.

The Founders anticipated minority factions using the Constitution as a bludgeon. Hamilton wrote in "Federalist No. 1," "A dangerous ambition more often lurks behind the specious mask of zeal for the rights of the people than under the forbidding appearance of zeal for the firmness and efficiency of government. History will teach us that the former has been found a much more certain road to the introduction of despotism than the latter, and that of those men who have overturned the liberties of republics, the greatest number have begun their career by paying an obsequious court to the people, commencing demagogues and ending tyrants."[198] Aristotle had a similar observation: "History shows that almost all tyrants have been demagogues who gained the favor of the people by their accusation of the notables."[199]

Today's Challenge

Previously, it was stated that rights granted by government can be taken away by government. An example would help illustrate the point. For a long period of time before June of 2010, restrictions on gun rights were ignored or actively supported by the judiciary. When the Supreme Court ruled in *McDonald v. Chicago* (2010), it reinstated a basic American right called out in the Second Amendment. In fact, the history of the Second Amendment demonstrates conclusively that rights supposedly granted by government are sustained at the will of government. Many people don't like guns, so they saw no problem with the infringement of this right. It didn't affect them personally, so they ignored the violation of others' rights. The problem with an attitude like this is that today it might be a right you abhor, but tomorrow it will be a right you embrace.

Today's challenge is to reinstate awareness in every American that "all men are created equal, that they are endowed by their Creator with certain unalienable rights, that among these are life, liberty and the pursuit of happiness. That to secure these rights, governments are instituted among men, deriving their just powers from the consent of the governed."

Bill of Rights Trivia

The Bill of Rights has lived almost as long as our Constitution. It has an extensive history with real people behind its creation, ratification, and legal challenges. Here are a few lesser-known facts about the Bill of Rights.

» Madison's proposal did not call for a list of rights as amendments, but rather for insertions, deletions, and revisions to be added right into the text of the Constitution. Congress decided to add them as a list at the end.[200]

» Washington had copies made and sent to the fourteen states. Where are the original copies of the Bill of Rights? Three copies are preserved at the National Archives. Eight states still have their copies, and another copy is in a New York library. Two copies are missing.[201]

» Massachusetts, Connecticut, and Georgia did not ratify the Bill of Rights until 1939 on the 150th anniversary of ratification by eleven of the fourteen states.[202]

» Two of twelve proposed amendments were not ratified by the states. One of the rejected amendments put restrictions on Congress setting its own salary. More than two hundred years later, this amendment was ratified and became the twenty-seventh amendment.[203]

PART V

Lessons for Today

19

Lessons from the Founding of the American Republic

"It can be lost, and it will be, if the time ever comes when these documents are regarded not as the supreme expression of our profound belief, but merely as curiosities in glass cases."[204]

—*Harry Truman*

Liberty is fragile. Every generation has its challenges, but the twentieth century has been particularly hard on our Founding Principles. Two world wars, the Cold War, many smaller wars, a Great Depression, and the emergence of worldwide -isms have all eroded the Constitution. Then on the dawn of the twenty-first century, the United States suffered a surprise attack on September 11, 2001, and the Constitution was arguably eroded further. As the first decade wore on, governments all over the world suddenly realized they had lost fiscal control. The entire world was awash in debt and addicted to spending beyond their means.

When Americans searched for answers, many discovered wisdom in the founding. Word spread, and soon more and more Americans felt a need to return to their nation's roots. They wanted a government far more like the one the Founders intended. Getting back to constitutional government will be a long, arduous trek, but a trek that a growing number of Americans have committed to undertake for the benefit of themselves and their children. There are grand lessons from the origins of the American Republic. The question is how do we implement those lessons in our modern world?

There are four actions necessary for a rebirth of the founding spirit:

1. Become fiscally responsible.
2. Re-instill the Founders' fear of powerful government.
3. Return to the Founding Principles.
4. Restore constitutional government.

Become Fiscally Responsible

Before we can address cultural issues, the country must resolve its financial dilemma. A bankrupt United States cannot deliver the American Dream or anything else to the next generation. We need to not only eliminate the annual deficit, we need to make the national debt a much smaller percentage of the gross domestic product. Anyone who has done the math knows that the only answer is reenergized economic growth. Economists and politicians seem befuddled on how to make this happen, but is this really such an insurmountable problem?

George Washington faced debt that looked almost as daunting. At the conclusion of World War II, our debt ratio was slightly higher than today. Ronald Reagan entered the White House with a financial crisis many believed would shortly destroy the nation. The country worked its way out way out of those predicaments, and it will work its way out of this one.[205]

Overcoming Revolutionary War Debt

Previously, this book described how Alexander Hamilton saved our financially shaky nation. Actually, he didn't do it by himself. Only George Washington had the political clout to overcome objections from powerful foes. Many people objected to Hamilton's plan, as is often the case when a nation is presented with the hard choices necessary to restore fiscal responsibility.[206]

Getting Out of the Great Depression

The Great Depression was horrific, and it was used as an excuse for government intrusion into every corner of the economy. Those government actions cost enormous amounts of money and they failed to pull the country out of an economic morass. World War II piled on even more debt. When peace came, the question on everyone's mind was, do we re-engage the New Deal with its massive deficits, or take a different path?

In 1946, Republicans ran against "big government, big labor, big regulation, and the New Deal's links to communism." The elections were a rout, with Republicans capturing the Senate and House for the first time since the start of the Depression. Republicans beat thirty-seven of sixty-nine liberal Democrats in Congress, which made the minority party more conservative as well. The Eightieth Congress passed the first balanced budget since the Great Crash, cut taxes, shred regulations, overrode Truman's veto of the Taft-Hartley Act, which restricted unfair labor practices, and shut down price controls.[207] Opponents screamed that Republicans were driving the nation back into the Great Depression. The naysayers were wrong. The country enjoyed more than two decades of prosperity.[208]

Getting Out of Stagflation

In January of 1981, the Misery Index was 19.33. This was a new measurement that added the unemployment rate to the inflation rate. The Misery Index had never been worse. Inflation was more than 10 percent, and a thirty-year fixed mortgage was 14.9 percent.[209] In mid-1979, President Carter declared a "Crisis of Confidence" in his famous so-called Malaise Speech. (Carter never actually used the word *malaise* in the speech.) Things were so bad that pundits were saying that the economy and world had become so complex that it was no longer possible for one man to manage the country's affairs. Perhaps they were right—it took two men. President Ronald Reagan and Federal Reserve Chairman Paul Volcker worked in tandem to put the economy back on track so fast that Reagan won re-election in 1984 in a landslide, winning forty-nine of fifty states.[210]

Reagan's Economic Principles

Ronald Reagan always led using a few easily understood principles. These principles were so powerful that he appeared to effortlessly manage a supposedly unmanageable situation. (Critics who had said the problems were so severe no one could resolve them were irritated that Reagan not only easily handled the crisis, but napped during boring meetings.)

There were four bedrock principles that drove Reagan's economic plan, commonly referred to as Reaganomics or supply-side economics.

» Reduce the growth of government spending

» Reduce income tax and capital gains tax

» Reduce government regulation

» Control the money supply to reduce inflation[211]

Getting Out of the Current Economic Crisis

All three of these financial crises had one common characteristic: we worked our way out of them by returning to a sound fiscal and monetary policy that supported a strong dollar and re-inspired confidence. Confidence drove high rates of growth in the private sector, thereby reducing the proportion of government activity in the economy.

We are now in another economically dangerous situation. The good news is that our current predicament is no worse than these historic crises. To put things right, we need to restore confidence in the private sector by adopting sound fiscal and monetary policy. The right actions are not hard to find. They're right there in our own history. Those who repeat history are not always condemned.

Re-instill the Founders' Fear of Powerful Government

Limited government advocates are accused by their opponents of wanting no government at all. It's a straw man argument that in essence says we must keep every little piece of government or nothing at all. Next, they claim that any government cuts will discontinue high-visibility government services that are very popular.

This whole argument is a deflection away from the real issue. Limited government advocates do not want to eliminate all government, they just want to put government back in its rightful place. Reductions in government can be made, even to vital services. Opponents to limited government act as if there are no excess costs in the delivery of these services. To them, it doesn't matter that the Washington, D.C., metropolitan area has the highest per capita income in the nation, and it's insignificant that the capital is the only part of the nation to escape the housing crisis. All of that money being spent isn't getting to seniors, the needy, or being used for vital services. Much of it remains inside the Beltway.

The Founders didn't fear powerful government because they hated government; they feared powerful governments because they threaten liberty. This has been true throughout history. The more power government wields, the more it dictates the daily activities of its citizens. Big government doesn't sometimes oppress. Sooner or later, big government always oppresses.

Today, many people believe the government should take care of them. The government should right every wrong and insure a fair distribution of necessities. The sad truth is that making sure everyone has shelter, food, health care, training or education, protection against disability or unemployment, and a risk-free retirement is expensive. Government services in excess of national income can work for a long time—decades even. Basically, it's a sly way of buying votes with the next generation's money. Unfortunately, it can't last. Once the interest on the borrowed money starts claiming a big piece of the current budget, the responsibly can no longer be foisted onto the next generation, and the fiscal charade begins to crumble. That day has arrived. The adage is true—there is no such thing as a free lunch.

Why are people not only unafraid of government, but enamored with government? This is partly because proponents of an ever-bigger government have deftly deflected people's fears toward corporations, religion, unseen contaminants, and even the weather. Big, bad corporations ruin people's lives, and religion wants to tell everyone how to behave. If the government doesn't take control, the seas will invade our homes. The statists are always bellowing that these are the real enemies, and only the government can protect people from abuse or worse.

The fear of corporate America is not rational because business power is relatively dispersed and transitory. The Fortune 500 companies represent much less than 40 percent of the private economy, and companies move onto and off the list all the time. Tens of thousands of other companies and small businesses make up the remainder of the private sector. That means that on average, each Fortune 500 corporation is involved in far less than 0.5 percent of GDP. The national government, on the other hand, controls 25 percent of the economy.[212]

An industrial company might have a capability to raise prices above what some see as appropriate, but the government can potentially threaten liberty. Corporations can touch your wallet; government will touch your life. People who fear corporate America tend to pick and choose which corporations are good and bad based on an emotional attachment. For example, few people believe their own employer or the purveyor of the latest technical gizmo is part of the problem. The Founders would be astounded. They believed any entity with outsized power would eventually be controlled by someone with nefarious intent. It is the concentration of power that should be feared, not whether the organization makes cool products or professes to do good.

George Washington said, "The people are not yet sufficiently mislead to retract from error [...] Evils, which oftentimes in republican governments must be sorely felt before they can be removed."[213] Have the problems of a bloated national government been *sorely felt* yet? It would appear so from the Tea Party movement. Compared to just a few years ago, it's startling how many people are aware of how our borrowing is jeopardizing the lives of our children and grandchildren. Everyone has not been convinced, however. There are still far too many people who staunchly believe the government is benevolent and can effect great change to make more and more people happy and comfortable in their chosen lifestyle.

Fear of an overly powerful government is healthy. The lesson from the origins of the American Republic is that if more government is deemed necessary by the people, then those government responsibilities should be dispersed to the national, state, and local levels so power is not concentrated in one place. We need to remind every American, and every generation, of this vital lesson from our Founders.

Is There a Tax on Wealth in the Wind?

Proponents of big government believe there is still plenty of money in this country to right social wrongs. Some are coming to the realization that tapping income won't provide enough money to finance all of their dreams, so they are propagating the idea that it's appropriate to tax accumulated wealth.

The sixteenth amendment basically gave the government authority to tax income, not wealth. That is why the United States has an estate tax. The government must wait until a person dies and the money is transferred to heirs as income for the government to claim an additional share. For technical reasons, a government that consumes more than 20 percent of the economy must borrow heavily, or tax consumption, or tax wealth, or do all three.

Return to the Founding Principles

Principles make behavior both easy and hard: *easy* because a person knows the right thing to do and *hard* because the right thing is often not easy or self-serving. Principles are the guardrails that keep us on the right path. The Constitution was based on solid principles, and we must restore these Founding Principles before we can restore the Constitution.

- Rights come from God
- All political power emanates from the people
- A limited, representative republic protects liberty
- Consent of the governed requires a written constitution

- Liberty depends on private property rights
- Power must be balanced and checked

Abraham Lincoln Has a Message for Us

Great leaders speak and act on principle. People will not only follow a principled leader, they will labor mightily in a principled cause. Abraham Lincoln gave a speech at the Cooper Union in New York City prior to being considered a serious candidate for the Republican nomination for president. He stood on principle and people followed—not everyone, but enough to change the course of the country. His words have relevance for today.

> Right and wrong is the precise fact upon which depends the whole controversy. Thinking it wrong, as we do, can we yield? Can we cast our votes with their view and against our own? In view of our moral, social, and political responsibilities, can we do this? Let us not grope for some middle ground between right and wrong. Let us not search in vain for a policy of don't care on a question about which we do care. Nor let us be frightened by threats of destruction to the government. Let us have faith that right makes might, and in that faith, let us, to the end, dare to do our duty as we understand it![214]

Lincoln was talking about slavery, but we should heed his words as we negotiate a path out of this fiscal quagmire. Principles matter. Action based on principles matter more. This is what is called character. It's time to send the half-measure people home, and send people with character to Washington, D.C. It's time to get back to basics.

Restore Constitutional Government

Politicos and talking heads are astounded by Americans' renewed interest in their Constitution. They thought that old musty document had been successfully sealed away under glass. These are troubling times. The public has rummaged around in our heritage for a solution and discovered a gem. They learned that the Founders had grappled with similar problems and, after considerable thought and debate, came to principle-based solutions. If the Constitution can facilitate the growth of a free nation from a raw wilderness into the world's greatest power, then it can lead us to a magnificent future: a magnificent future where the American Dream is available to all in the land of the free.

We are far from that path today. One indicator of national government overreach is that political activism is usually aimed at the national level. State and local government are seldom asked to solve thorny issues. Whether education, arbitration of social issues, health care, or the extension of rights, activists target their lobbying toward Washington, D. C. Soon a problem that started in one or a few states is a national issue. The cycle of issue elevation and then resolution at the national level has sucked more and more political power inside the Beltway. This trend must be reversed, or the people's voice will grow ever fainter.

How Do We Check Runaway National Power?

Government spending has gone ballistic, unaccountable bureaucrats intrude on every aspect of the economy, and increasingly more of our personal lives are being dictated from Washington, D.C. The citizenry keep voicing their objections, but nobody cares to listen. People have gone beyond frustration; they want to halt this runaway system and stop the nationalization of their neighborhoods and personal lives. Initiatives and organizations have arisen in every nook and cranny of the country to rein in a power-crazed government. Even in Washington, D.C., there has been a growing movement for a balanced budget amendment.[215]

What's going on here? All across our great nation, displeasure and discontent is building. The populous is distrustful because they see the three federal branches abrogating their Constitutional responsibilities. With no alternative inside the Beltway, they are looking to states to curb the national government's voracious appetite. This is not unreasonable. The delegates to the Constitutional Convention intended the states to be a potent check on the national government.

Is it really this bad? It is. The national debt is over $15 trillion, and increasing by $4.2 billion per day. That means every taxpayer owes nearly $130,000.[216] We need to stop this pell-mell charge toward insolvency. That means Americans must maintain counter-assaults on every front, but there is one overriding issue that must be addressed. The federal government has superior taxing authority and unlimited borrowing power. All of the states except Vermont are constitutionally required to balance their budgets and a grasping federal government is crowding out their tax revenue. The national government isn't overly greedy, just controlling. It sends a lot of money back to the states, but with hardwired strings and hefty handing fees attached. The result is that states are on the dole, and it's hard to challenge federal authority when you're begging for life-blood.

If Americans want to restore the Constitution, the first step is to restore the balance between the taxing authorities. Money is power. Curtail Washington's money, and its power will abate. The only way to achieve that goal is with a balanced budget amendment (BBA) to the United States Constitution. As long as the federal government is allowed to print and borrow money at will, the states are at a severe disadvantage. A balanced budget amendment will help restore our federal system by putting the national government under the same restrictions as the states.

Now for a couple of caveats. A balanced budget amendment isn't ironclad. Neither are the states' balanced budget requirements. There are plenty of shenanigans in state budgeting, and after ratification of the BBA, there will be mischief at the national level. But in both cases, a law requiring a balanced budget inhibits the worse offenses and gives the opposition the opportunity to expose shady bookkeeping. A second argument against a BBA is that it will result in increased taxes instead of curtailed spending. If Washington can't borrow or print money, the big government types will clamor for increased taxes. But they are doing that already. Taxes are much more visible to the average American, while borrowing and printing money can be hidden behind the curtain. Besides, printing money is really a form of taxation through inflation, and borrowing transfers cost to future generations. Of the three alternatives, taxes are the easiest to fight. Despite shortcomings, a balanced budget amendment will put the states and national government on a more equal footing, and cutting off faux money can help force the national government back to enumerated powers.

America cannot, however, focus on a balanced budget amendment as the sole solution. The situation is too dire to delay action until an amendment can be ratified. Americans must aggressively push forward simultaneously on every initiative. In addition, it is crucial that Congress repeals ObamaCare; freezes federal hiring and pay; requires spending cuts in excess of any new spending; eliminates nonessential government program(s)/agencies; and returns total expenditures to at least 2008 levels.

Our forefathers bequeathed to us a healthy republic making the American Dream attainable. Without fundamental change, we will leave our children a nightmare of debt and foreign ownership of our productive assets. We owe our kids more, and we owe our parents more. We owe our parents because they protected our liberty and our lives and passed a great republic to us. Now that we're responsible, we can do nothing less.

20

Every American's Obligation

"You are the light of the world. A city that is set on a hill cannot be hidden."

—Matt. 5:14, NKJV

Excerpt from Ronald Reagan's Farewell Address

I've spoken of the shining city all my political life, but I don't know if I ever quite communicated what I saw when I said it. But in my mind it was a tall, proud city built on rocks stronger than oceans, windswept, God-blessed, and teeming with people of all kinds living in harmony and peace; a city with free ports that hummed with commerce and creativity. And if there had to be city walls, the walls had doors and the doors were open to anyone with the will and the heart to get here. That's how I saw it, and see it still.[217]

In 1630 while still onboard ship, John Winthrop sermonized to his fellow Puritans that they were sailing to "a city upon a hill—the eyes of all people are upon us."[218] One hundred and fifty years later, the Founders believed this to their core. Although many politicians have used the idiom, the phrase "a shiny city on a hill" is most closely associated with Ronald Reagan. He used it many times in his political career, but never so poignantly as in his farewell address.

Our forefathers moved through the founding period knowing the world was watching. The Founders were good people guided by solid, well-thought-out principles. They set their sights high. They chose to do something great. They wanted to be the light of the world.

The United States of America is exceptional. We are not exceptional because we are a different kind of people. People are the same the world over. We are exceptional because of the uniqueness of our founding. The Declaration of Independence and United States Constitution were not events. They were processes that took many years to come to fruition. They both engaged an entire nation. They both were guided by clear principles. They both reflected timeless truths that inspired us to move ever closer to greatness. America is not the Constitution or the Declaration of Independence. America is a commonly held culture that emerged from writing and approving these documents.

Somewhere deep inside, we know it's important to preserve them as they were originally intended. They are our heritage. It hurts when someone assaults them. We often hear laments that our politicians no longer honor their pledge to preserve, protect, and defend the Constitution of the United States. This is backward. The Constitution was not written for politicians. Our political leaders have no motivation to abide by a two-hundred-year-old restraining order. Americans are the ones who must enforce the supreme law of the land.

The Constitution's first, outsized words are *We the People*. The people did "ordain and establish this Constitution for the United States of America." It's *our* document. It was always meant to be ours, not the government's. We should always treat it as our most prized possession because the Constitution is unique in all the world. The Founders didn't set out to build a run-of-the-mill nation fit for people to inhabit. Their aspirations were far higher. Early Americans worked for more than three decades to craft a republic that would harness the worst in people, while giving free rein to the best in people. The country didn't start out perfect, nor is it perfect today, but few other nations constantly strive to be nobler tomorrow than they were the day before.

The Constitution and our American culture were established using a few simple but amazing principles. These principles collectively preserve liberty. Because we have been fortunate, it's difficult for Americans to remember that liberty is a precious and highly unstable commodity. It takes the work of millions to protect liberty, not just a few politicians.

That's why each and every American has an obligation to preserve, protect, and defend the Constitution of the United States of America. Our children deserve nothing less.

Appendix
In Their Own Words

"We have it in our power to begin the world over again. A situation similar to the present, hath not happened since the days of Noah."

—Thomas Paine[219]

"In disquisitions of every kind there are certain primary truths, or *first principles*, upon which all subsequent reasoning must depend."

—Alexander Hamilton, "Federalist No. 31"[220]

"What is a Constitution? It is the form of government, delineated by the mighty hand of the people, in which certain first principles of fundamental law are established. The Constitution is certain and fixed; it contains the permanent will of the people, and is the supreme law of the land ... and can be revoked or altered only by the authority that made it."

William Paterson[221]

"On the distinctive principles of the government of our State, and of that of the United States, the best guides are to be found in, 1. The Declaration of Independence, as the fundamental act of union of these States. 2. The book known by the title of "The Federalist," being an authority to which appeal is habitually made by all, and rarely declined or denied by any as evidence of the general opinion of those who framed, and of those who accepted the Constitution of the United

States, on questions as to its genuine meaning. 3. The Resolutions of the General Assembly of Virginia in 1799 on the subject of the alien and sedition laws, which appeared to accord with the predominant sense of the people of the United States. 4. The valedictory address of President Washington, as conveying political lessons of peculiar value."

—*Thomas Jefferson, March 4, 1825*[222]

"It is, indeed, of little consequence who governs us, if they sincerely and zealously cherish the principles of union and republicanism."

—*Thomas Jefferson*[223]

"The deterioration of a government begins almost always by a decay of its principles."

—*Montesquieu*[224]

"A people that values its privileges above its principles soon loses both."

—*Dwight D. Eisenhower, President*[225]

"We've gone astray from first principles."

—*Ronald Reagan, President*[226]

"Liberty, once lost, is lost forever."

—*John Adams*[227]

"In Europe, charters of liberty have been granted by power. America has set the example... of charters of power granted by liberty. This revolution in the practice of the world, may, with an honest praise, be pronounced the most triumphant epoch of its history, and the most consoling presage of its happiness."

—*James Madison*[228]

"Safety from external danger is the most powerful director of national conduct. Even the ardent love of liberty will, after a time, give way to its dictates. To be more safe, they at length become willing to run the risk of being less free."

—*Alexander Hamilton, "Federalist No. 8"*[229]

"They who can give up essential liberty to obtain a little temporary safety, deserve neither liberty or safety."

—*Benjamin Franklin*[230]

"The accumulation of all powers, legislative, executive, and judiciary, in the same hands, whether of one, a few, or many, and whether hereditary, self-appointed, or elective, may justly be pronounced the very definition of tyranny."

—*James Madison, "Federalist No. 47"*[231]

"There are again two methods of removing the causes of faction: the one, by destroying the liberty which is essential to its existence; the other, by giving to every citizen the same opinions, the same passions, and the same interests."

—*James Madison, "Federalist No. 10"*[232]

"Objects of the most stupendous magnitude, and measure in which the lives and liberties of millions yet unborn are intimately interested, are now before us. We are in the very midst of a revolution the most complete, unexpected and remarkable of any in the history of nations."

—*John Adams*[233]

"We fight not to enslave, but to set a country free, and to make room upon the earth for honest men to live in."

—*Thomas Paine*[234]

"The Revolution was effected before the war commenced. The Revolution was in the minds and hearts of the people; a change in their religious sentiments of their duties and obligations.... This radical change in the principles, opinions, sentiments, and affections of the people, was the real American Revolution."

—*John Adams*[235]

"If ye love wealth greater than liberty, the tranquility of servitude greater than the animating contest for freedom, go home from us in peace. We seek not your counsel, nor your arms. Crouch down and lick the hand that feeds you; and posterity forget that ye were our countrymen."

—*Samuel Adams*[236]

"This was the object of the Declaration of Independence. Not to find out new principles, or new arguments, never before thought of, not merely to say things which had never been said before; but to place before mankind the common sense of the subject, in terms so plain and firm as to command their assent, and to justify ourselves in the independent stand we are compelled to take."

—*Thomas Jefferson*[237]

"The revolt from Great Britain and the formations of our new governments at that time, were nothing compared to the great business now before us; there was then a certain degree of enthusiasm, which inspired and supported the mind; but to view, through the calm, sedate medium of reason the influence which the establishment now proposed may have upon the happiness or misery of millions yet unborn, is the object of such magnitude, as absorbs, and in a manner suspends the operation of the human understanding."

—*George Mason*[238]

"It cannot be more inconvenient to any gentleman to remain absent from his private affairs, than it is for me; but I will bury my bones in this city rather than expose my country to the consequences of a dissolution of the convention without any thing being done."

—*George Mason*[239]

"What is government itself but the greatest of all reflections on human nature? If men were angels, no government would be necessary. If angels were to govern men, neither external nor internal controls on government would be necessary."

—*James Madison, "Federalist No. 51"*[240]

"It seems to have been reserved to the people of this country, by their conduct and example, to decide the important question, whether societies of men are really capable or not of establishing good government from reflection and choice, or whether they are forever destined to depend for their political constitutions on accident and force."

—*Alexander Hamilton, "Federalist No. 1"*[241]

"The ultimate authority, wherever the derivative may be found, resides in the people alone."

—*James Madison*[242]

"Sometimes it is said that man cannot be trusted with the government of himself. Can he, then, be trusted with the government of others?"

—*Thomas Jefferson*[243]

"There never was a democracy yet that did not commit suicide."

—*John Adams*[244]

"When a people shall have become incapable of governing themselves and fit for a master, it is of little consequence from what quarter he comes."

—*George Washington*[245]

"Government is instituted to protect property of every sort … This being the end of government, that alone is a just government which impartially secures to every man whatever is his own."

—*James Madison*[246]

"The excess of law-making seem to be the diseases to which our governments are most liable"

—*James Madison, "Federalist No. 62"*[247]

"It will be of little avail to the people, that the laws are made by men of their own choice, if the laws be so voluminous that they cannot be read, or so incoherent that they cannot be understood; if they be repealed or revised before they are promulgated, or undergo such incessant changes that no man, who knows what the law is to-day, can guess what it will be to-morrow. Law is defined to be a rule of action; but how can that be a rule, which is little known, and less fixed?"

—*James Madison, "Federalist No. 62"*[248]

"Has it not invariably been found that momentary passions, and immediate interest, have a more active and imperious control over human conduct than general or remote considerations of policy, utility or justice?"

—*Alexander Hamilton, "Federalist No. 6"*[249]

"If Congress can do whatever in their discretion can be done by money, and will promote the General Welfare, the Government is no longer a limited one."

—*James Madison*[250]

"The important distinction so well understood in America, between a Constitution established by the people and unalterable by the government, and a law established by the government and alterable by the government, seems to have been little understood and less observed in any other country."

—*James Madison, "Federalist No. 53"*[251]

"The apportionment of taxes on the various descriptions of property is an act which seems to require the most exact impartiality; yet there is, perhaps, no legislative act in which greater opportunity and temptation are given to a predominant party to trample on the rules of justice."

—*James Madison, "Federalist No. 10"*[252]

"In this world nothing can be said to be certain, except death and taxes."

—*Benjamin Franklin*[253]

"As parents, we can have no joy knowing that this government is not sufficiently lasting to ensure anything which we may bequeath to posterity. And by any plain method of argument, as we are running the next generation into debt, we ought to do the work of it, otherwise we use them meanly and pitifully."

—*Thomas Paine,* Common Sense[254]

"The essence of Government is power; and power, lodged as it must be in human hands, will ever be liable to abuse."

—*James Madison*[255]

"Government is not reason: It is not eloquence, it is Force, like fire it is a dangerous servant and a fearful master."

—*George Washington*[256]

"The example of changing a constitution by assembling the wise men of the state, instead of assembling armies, will be worth as much to the world as the former examples we had given them. The constitution, too, which was the result of our deliberation, is unquestionably the wisest ever yet presented to men."

—*Thomas Jefferson*[257]

"The greatest single effort of national deliberation that the world has ever seen."

—*John Adams*[258]

"The basis of our political systems is the right of the people to make and to alter their constitutions of government. But the Constitution, which at any time exists, 'till changed by an explicit and authentic act of the whole people, is sacredly obligatory upon all. ... If in the opinion of the people the distribution or modification of the constitutional powers be in any particular wrong, let it be corrected by an amendment in the way which the Constitution designates. But let there be no change by usurpation; for though this in one instance may be the instrument of good, it is the customary weapon by which free governments are destroyed."

—*George Washington*[259]

"An unwritten constitution is not a constitution at all."

—*Thomas Paine*[260]

"Our peculiar security is in possession of a written Constitution. Let us not make it a blank paper by construction. ... If it is, then we have no Constitution. ... To consider the judges as the ultimate arbiters of all constitutional questions ... would place us under the despotism of an oligarchy."

—*Thomas Jefferson*[261]

"The powers delegated by the proposed Constitution to the federal government are few and defined. Those which are to remain in the State governments are numerous and indefinite. The former will be exercised principally on external objects, as war, peace, negotiation, and foreign commerce; with which last the power of taxation will, for the most part, be connected. The powers reserved to the several states will extend to all the objects which, in the ordinary course of affairs, concern the lives, liberties, and properties of the people, and the internal order, improvement and prosperity of the State."

—*James Madison, "Federalist No. 45"*[262]

"With respect to the words general welfare, I have always regarded them as qualified by the details of power connected with them. To take them in a literal and unlimited sense would be a metamorphosis of the Constitution ... [that] was not contemplated by the creators."

—*James Madison*[263]

"It would reduce the whole instrument to a single phrase, that of instituting a Congress with power to do whatever would be for the good of the United States; and as they would be the sole judges of the good or evil, it would be also a power to do whatever evil they please. ... Certainly no such universal power was meant to be given them. It [the Constitution] was intended to lace them up straightly within the enumerated powers and those without which, as means, these powers could not be carried into effect."

—*Thomas Jefferson*[264]

"It is to be remembered that the general government is not to be charged with the whole power of making and administering laws. Its jurisdiction is limited to certain enumerated objects"

—*James Madison*[265]

"To take a single step beyond the text would be to take possession of a boundless field of power."

—Thomas Jefferson[266]

"The state and general government ought to have separate and distinct jurisdictions, but they ought to have a mutual interest in supporting each other."

—Roger Sherman[267]

"The plain import of the clause is, that congress shall have all the incidental and instrumental powers, necessary and proper to carry into execution all the express powers. It neither enlarges any power specifically granted; nor is it a grant of any new power to congress."

—Joseph Story[268]

"The federal and state governments are in fact but different agents and trustees of the people, constituted with different powers, and designed for different purposes."

—James Madison[269]

"For experience has already shown that the impeachment it has provided is not even a scarecrow."

—Thomas Jefferson[270]

"The legislative department is everywhere extending the sphere of its activity, and drawing all power into its impetuous vortex ... Its constitutional powers being at once more extensive, and less susceptible of precise limits, it can, with the greater facility, mask, under complicated and indirect measures, the encroachments which it makes on the co-ordinate departments ... The legislative department alone has access to the pockets of the people."

—James Madison, "Federalist No. 48"[271]

"In republican government, the legislative authority necessarily predominates. The remedy for this inconveniency is to divide the legislature into different branches; and to render them, by different modes of election and different principles of action, as little connected

with each other as the nature of their common functions and their common dependence on the society will admit."
—*James Madison, "Federalist No. 51"*[272]

"If the present Congress errs in too much talking, how can it be otherwise in a body to which the people send 150 lawyers, whose trade it is to question everything, yield nothing, & talk by the hour?"
—*Thomas Jefferson*[273]

"A mere demarcation on parchment of the constitutional limits of the several departments, is not a sufficient guard against those encroachments which lead to a tyrannical concentration of all the powers of government in the same hands."
—*James Madison, "Federalist No. 48"*[274]

"No wall of words, that no mound of parchment can be so formed as to stand against the sweeping torrent of boundless ambition on the one side, aided by the sapping current of corrupted morals on the other."
—*George Washington*[275]

"The powers of government should be so divided and balanced among several bodies of magistracy, as that no one could transcend their legal limits, without being effectually checked and restrained by the others."
—*Thomas Jefferson*[276]

"If the president alone was vested with the power of appointing all officers, and was left to select a council for himself, he would be liable to be deceived by flatterers and pretenders to patriotism."
—*Roger Sherman*[277]

"The great security against a gradual concentration of the several powers in the same department consists in giving to those who administer each department the necessary constitutional means and personal motives to resist encroachments of the others. The provision for defense must in this, as in all other cases, be made commensurate to the danger of attack. Ambition must be made to counteract ambition."

—*James Madison*[278]

"The authority of magistrates is taken from that mass of power which in rude societies and unbalanced democracies is wielded by the majority. Every separation of the executive and judicial authority from the legislature is a diminution of political and increase of civil liberty. Every check and balance of that legislature has a like effect."

—*Gouverneur Morris*[279]

"It is jealousy and not confidence which prescribes limited constitutions, to bind down those whom we are obliged to trust with power. ... In questions of power, then, let no more be heard of confidence in man, but bind him down from mischief by the chains of the Constitution."

—*Thomas Jefferson*[280]

"Ambitious encroachments of the federal government, on the authority of the State governments, would not excite the opposition of a single State, or of a few States only. They would be signals of general alarm. Every government would espouse the common cause. A correspondence would be opened. Plans of resistance would be concerted."

—*James Madison*[281]

"The first man put at the helm will be a good one, but nobody knows what sort may come afterwards. The Executive will be always increasing here, as elsewhere, till it ends in a monarchy."

—*Benjamin Franklin*[282]

"It only remains to know which power in the constitution has the most weight, for that will govern; and though the others, or a part of them, may clog, or as the phrase is, check the rapidity of its motion, yet so long as they cannot stop it, their endeavors will be ineffectual, the first moving power will at last have its way, and what it wants in speed is supplied in time."

—*Thomas Paine,* Common Sense[283]

"The natural cure for an ill-administration, in a popular or representative constitution, is a change of men."

—Alexander Hamilton, "Federalist No. 21"[284]

"A remedy must be obtained from the people who can, by the election of more faithful representatives, annul the acts of the usurpers."

—James Madison, "Federalist No. 44"[285]

"There is a simple sense in which at every election the electorate hold their representatives to account, and replace those who have failed to give satisfaction. This fundamental check is, we might say, the essence of the liberty to be found in representative government."

—John Adams[286]

"A bill of rights is what the people are entitled to against every government on earth."

—Thomas Jefferson[287]

"The majority may not sufficiently respect the rights of the minority."

—James Madison[288]

"The great mass of people who opposed [the Constitution], disliked it because it did not contain effectual provisions against encroachments on particular rights … It may be thought all paper barriers against the power of the community are too weak to be worthy of attention … yet, as they have a tendency to impress some … it may be one mean to control the majority from those acts to which they might be otherwise inclined."

—James Madison[289]

"In our governments the real power lies in the majority of the community, and the invasion of private rights is chiefly to be apprehended, not from acts of government contrary to the sense of its constituents, but from acts in which the government is the mere instrument of the major number of the constituents. Wherever there is an interest and power to do wrong, wrong will generally be done."

—James Madison[290]

"[A] dangerous ambition more often lurks behind the specious mask of zeal for the rights of the people than under the forbidding appearance of zeal for the firmness and efficiency of government. History will teach us that the former has been found a much more certain road to the introduction of despotism than the latter, and that of those men who have overturned the liberties of republics, the greatest number have begun their career by paying an obsequious court to the people, commencing demagogues and ending tyrants."

—*Alexander Hamilton*[291]

"I go further, and affirm that bills of rights, in the sense and to the extent in which they are contended for, are not only unnecessary in the proposed Constitution, but would even be dangerous. They would contain various exceptions to powers not granted; and on this very account, would afford a colorable pretext to claim more than were granted. For why declare that things shall not be done which there is no power to do?"

—*Alexander Hamilton*[292]

"In a just and free government … the rights both of property and of persons ought to be effectually guarded."

—*James Madison*[293]

"As a man is said to have a right to his property, he may be equally said to have a property in his rights."

—*James Madison*[294]

"Rightful liberty is unobstructed action according to our will within limits drawn around us by the equal rights of others. I do not add 'within the limits of the law,' because law is often but the tyrant's will, and always so when it violates the rights of the individual."

—*Thomas Jefferson*[295]

"The God who gave us life gave us liberty at the same time; the hand of force may destroy, but cannot disjoin them."

—*Thomas Jefferson*[296]

"The Sacred Rights of mankind are not to be rummaged for among old parchments or musty records. They are written, as with a sunbeam, in the whole volume of human nature, by the Hand of the Divinity itself, and can never be erased or obscured by mortal power."

—Alexander Hamilton[297]

"Rights come from God not the state. You have rights antecedent to any earthly governments rights that cannot be repealed or restrained by human laws. Rights derived from the great legislator: God."

—John Adams[298]

"And can the liberties of a nation be thought secure when we have removed their only firm basis, a conviction in the minds of the people that these liberties are the gift of God?"

—Thomas Jefferson[299]

"We need commonsense judges who understand that our rights were derived from God."

—George W. Bush, President[300]

"We have seen the mere distinction of color made in the most enlightened period of time, a ground of the most oppressive dominion ever exercised by man over man."

—James Madison[301]

"To contend for our own liberty, and to deny that blessing to others, involves an inconsistency not to be excused."

—John Jay[302]

"Nothing is more certainly written in the book of fate than that these people are to be free."

—Thomas Jefferson[303]

"There is not a man living who wishes more sincerely than I do, to see a plan adopted for the abolition of it [slavery]."

—George Washington[304]

"I will never concur in upholding domestic slavery. It is a nefarious institution. It is the curse of heaven on the states where it prevailed. Compare the free regions of the middle states, where a rich and noble cultivation marks the prosperity and happiness of the people, with the misery and poverty which overspread the barren wastes of Virginia, Maryland and the other states having slaves."

—Gouverneur Morris[305]

"All good men wish the entire abolition of slavery, as soon as it can take place with safety to the public, and for the lasting good of the present wretched race of slaves. The only possible step that could be taken towards it by the convention was to fix a period after which they should not be imported."

—Oliver Ellsworth[306]

"The abolition of slavery seems to be going on in the United States and the good sense of the several states will probably by degrees complete it."

—Roger Sherman, at the Constitutional Convention[307]

"Every master of slaves is born a petty tyrant. They bring the judgment of heaven on a country. As nations cannot be rewarded or punished in the next world they must be in this."

—George Mason, at the Constitutional Convention[308]

"If there was no other lovely feature in the Constitution but this one, it would diffuse a beauty over its whole countenance. Yet the lapse of a few years, and Congress will have power to exterminate slavery from within our borders."

—James Wilson[309]

"Every measure of prudence, therefore, ought to be assumed for the eventual total extirpation of slavery from the United States. ... I have, throughout my whole life, held the practice of slavery in ... abhorrence."

—John Adams[310]

"Slavery is such an atrocious debasement of human nature, that its very extirpation, if not performed with solicitous care, may sometimes open a source of serious evils."

—*Benjamin Franklin*[311]

"He has waged cruel war against human nature itself, violating its most sacred rights of life and liberty in the persons of a distant people who never offended him, captivating & carrying them into slavery in another hemisphere, or to incur miserable death in their transportation thither. This practical warfare, the opprobrium of INFIDEL powers, is the warfare of the CHRISTIAN king of Great Britain. Determined to keep open a market where MEN should be bought & sold, he has prostituted his negative for suppressing every legislative attempt to prohibit or to restrain this execrable commerce."

—*Thomas Jefferson, in draft of Declaration of Independence. Removed by Continental Congress.*[312]

"Abolish slavery tomorrow, and not a sentence or syllable of the Constitution need be altered. It was purposely so framed as to give no claim, no sanction to the claim, of property in man. If in its origin slavery had any relation to the government, it was only as the scaffolding to the magnificent structure, to be removed as soon as the building was completed."

—*Frederick Douglass*[313]

"Taxation and representation are strongly associated in the minds of the people, and they will not agree that any but their immediate representatives shall meddle with their purses. In short the acceptance of the plan will inevitably fail, if the Senate be not restrained from originating money bills."

—*Elbridge Gerry*[314]

"It is always of importance that the people should know who has disposed of their money, and how it has been disposed of. It was a maxim that those who feel, can best judge."

—*Benjamin Franklin*[315]

"If the system be established on basis of Income, and his just proportion on that scale has been already drawn from every one, to step into the field of consumption, and tax special articles in that, as broadcloth or homespun, wine or whiskey, a coach or a wagon, is doubly taxing the same article. For that portion of Income with which these articles are purchased, having already paid its tax as Income, to pay another tax on the thing it purchased, is paying twice for the same thing; it is an aggrievance on the citizens who use these articles in exoneration of those who do not, contrary to the most sacred of the duties of a government, to do equal and impartial justice to all its citizens."

—*Thomas Jefferson*[316]

"If we run into such [government] debts, as that we must be taxed in our meat and in our drink, in our necessaries and our comforts, in our labors and our amusements, for our callings and our creeds, as the people of England are, our people, like them, must come to labor sixteen hours in twenty-four, give the earnings of fifteen of these to the government for their debts and daily expenses, and the sixteenth being insufficient to afford us bread, we must live, as they now do, on oatmeal and potatoes, have no time to think, no means of calling the mismanagers to account; but be glad to obtain subsistence by hiring ourselves to rivet their chains on the necks of our fellow-suffers."

—*Thomas Jefferson*[317]

"If duties are too high, they lessen the consumption; the collection is eluded; and the product to the treasury is not so great as when they are confined within proper and moderate bounds."

—*Alexander Hamilton, "Federalist No. 21"*[318]

"The people of the U.S. owe their independence and their liberty, to the wisdom of descrying in the minute tax of 3 pence on tea, the magnitude of the evil comprized in the precedent. Let them exert the same wisdom, in watching against every evil lurking under plausible disguises, and growing up from small beginnings."

—*James Madison*[319]

"Excessive taxation ... will carry reason and reflection to every man's door, and particularly in the hour of election."

—*Thomas Jefferson*[320]

"On every question of construction carry ourselves back to the time when the Constitution was adopted, recollect the spirit manifested in the debates and instead of trying what meaning may be squeezed out of the text or invented against it, conform to the probable one in which it was passed."

—*Thomas Jefferson*[321]

"The constitution, on this hypothesis, is a mere thing of wax in the hands of the judiciary, which they may twist, and shape into any form they please."

—*Thomas Jefferson*[322]

"Can it be of less consequence that the meaning of a Constitution should be fixed and known, than a meaning of a law should be so?"

—*James Madison*[323]

"The first and governing maxim in the interpretation of a statute is to discover the meaning of those who made it."

—*James Wilson, in* Of the Study of Law in the United States[324]

"There is not a syllable in the plan [the Constitution] which directly empowers the national courts to construe the laws according to the spirit of the Constitution."

—*Alexander Hamilton*[325]

"If they [rights] are incorporated into the Constitution, independent tribunals of justice will consider themselves in a peculiar manner the guardians of those rights; they will be an impenetrable bulwark against every assumption of power in the legislative or executive; they will be naturally led to resist every encroachment upon rights expressly stipulated for in the Constitution by the declaration of rights."

—*James Madison*[326]

"Judges, therefore, should be always men of learning and experience in the laws, of exemplary morals, great patience, calmness, coolness, and attention. Their minds should not be distracted with jarring interests; they should not be dependent upon any man, or body of men."

—John Adams[327]

"The Judiciary ... has no influence over either the sword or the purse; no direction either of the strength or of the wealth of the society, and can take no active resolution whatever. It may truly be said to have neither force nor will."

—Alexander Hamilton, "Federalist No. 78"[328]

"The danger is not, that the judges will be too firm in resisting public opinion, and in defence of private rights or public liberties; but, that they will be ready to yield themselves to the passions, and politics, and prejudices of the day."

—Joseph Story, Commentaries on the Constitution of the United States[329]

"Our agenda is quite simple—to appoint judges ... who don't confuse the criminals with the victims; judges who don't invent new or fanciful constitutional rights for those criminals; judges who believe the courts should interpret the law, not make it; judges, in short, who understand judicial restraint. That starts with the Supreme Court. It takes leadership from the Supreme Court to help shape the attitudes of the courts in our land and to make sure that principles of law are based on the Constitution. This is the standard to judge those who seek to serve on the courts—qualifications, not distortions; judicial temperament, not campaign disinformation."

—Ronald Reagan, Remarks at Republican Governors Club Annual Dinner, October 15, 1987[330]

"It is of the nature of war to increase the executive at the expense of the legislative authority."

—Alexander Hamilton, "Federalist No. 8"[331]

"Men I find badly constructed, as they are more easily provoked than reconciled, more disposed to do mischief than to make reparation, more easily deceived than undeceived, and having more pride and pleasure in killing than in begetting one another, for without a blush they assemble great armies to destroy, and when they have killed as many as they can, they exaggerate the number, but they creep into corners or cover themselves with darkness when they mean to beget."

—*Benjamin Franklin*[332]

"To judge from the history of mankind, we shall be compelled to conclude that the fiery and destructive passions of war reign in the human breast with much more powerful sway than the mild and beneficent sentiments of peace; and that to model our political systems upon speculations of lasting tranquility would be to calculate on the weaker springs of human character."

—*Alexander Hamilton, "Federalist No. 34"*[333]

"Security against foreign danger is one of the primitive objects of civil society. It is an avowed and essential object of the American Union."

—*James Madison, "Federalist No. 41"*[334]

"No government could give us tranquility and happiness at home, which did not possess sufficient stability and strength to make us respectable abroad."

—*Alexander Hamilton*[335]

"As a very important source of strength and security, cherish public credit. One method of preserving it is to use it as sparingly as possible: avoiding occasions of expense by cultivating peace, but remembering also that timely disbursements to prepare for danger frequently prevent much greater disbursements to repel it; avoiding likewise the accumulation of debt, not only by shunning occasions of expense, but by vigorous exertions in time of peace to discharge the debts which unavoidable wars may have occasioned, not ungenerously throwing upon posterity the burthen which we ourselves ought to bear."

—*George Washington, Farewell Address*[336]

"Religion, which never intervenes directly in the government of American society, should therefore be considered as the first of their political institutions."

—*Alexis de Tocqueville*[337]

"Were a man impressed as fully and strongly as he ought to be with the belief of a God, his moral life would be regulated by the force of belief; he would stand in awe of God and of himself, and would not do the thing that could not be concealed from either."

—*Thomas Paine*[338]

"There is not a single instance in history in which civil liberty was lost, and religious liberty preserved entire. If therefore we yield up our temporal property, we at the same time deliver the conscience into bondage."

—*John Witherspoon,* The Dominion of Providence Over the Passions of Men[339]

"Believing with you that religion is a matter which lies solely between man and his God, that he owes account to none other for his faith or his worship, that the legislative powers of government reach actions only, and not opinions, I contemplate with sovereign reverence that act of the whole American people which declared that their legislature should 'make no law respecting an establishment of religion, or pro-hibiting the free exercise thereof, thus building a wall of separation between church and State."

—*Thomas Jefferson*[340]

"A native of America who cannot read or write is ... as rare as a comet or an earthquake."

—*John Adams*[341]

"We are more thoroughly an enlightened people, with respect to our political interests, than perhaps any other under heaven. Every man among us reads, and is so easy in his circumstances as to have leisure for conversations of improvement and for acquiring information."

—*Benjamin Franklin*[342]

"[A] good moral character is the first essential in a man, and that the habits contracted at your age are generally indelible, and your conduct here may stamp your character through life. It is therefore highly important that you should endeavor not only to be learned but virtuous."

—*George Washington*[343]

"Children should be educated and instructed in the principles of freedom."

—*John Adams*[344]

"The pillars of our prosperity are the most thriving when left most free to individual enterprise."

—*Thomas Jefferson*[345]

"To take from one because it is thought that his own productivity has acquired too much, in order to give to others who have not exercised equal industry and skill is to violate arbitrarily the first principle of association: the guarantee to everyone of a free exercise of his hard work and the profits acquired by it."

—*Thomas Jefferson*[346]

"In framing a system which we wish to last for ages, we should not lose sight of the changes which ages will produce. An increase of population will of necessity increase the proportion of those who will labor under all the hardships of life, and secretly sigh for a more equal distribution of its blessings. These may in time outnumber those who are placed above the feelings of indigence. According to the equal laws of suffrage, the power will slide into the hands of the former. No agrarian attempts have yet been made in this country, but symptoms of a leveling spirit, as we have understood, have sufficiently appeared in a certain quarters to give notice of the future danger."

—*James Madison, Federal Convention, June 26, 1787*[347]

"I have always thought that one man of tolerable abilities may work great changes, and accomplish great affairs among mankind, if he first forms a good plan, and, cutting off all amusements or other employments that would divert his attention, make the execution of that same plan his sole study and business."

—*Benjamin Franklin*[348]

"In transactions of trade it is not to be supposed that, as in gaming, what one party gains the other must necessarily lose. The gain to each may be equal. If A has more corn than he can consume, but wants cattle; and B has more cattle, but wants corn; exchange is gain to each; thereby the common stock of comforts in life is increased."

—*Benjamin Franklin*[349]

"I think the best way of doing good to the poor, is not making them easy in poverty, but leading or driving them out of it."

—*Benjamin Franklin*[350]

"That is not a just government, nor is property secure under it, where the property which a man has in his personal safety and personal liberty, is violated by arbitrary seizures of one class of citizens for the service of the rest."

—*James Madison*[351]

"A just security to property is not afforded by that government, under which unequal taxes oppress one species of property and reward another species."

—*James Madison*[352]

"Facts are stubborn things; and whatever may be our wishes, our inclinations, or the dictates of our passion, they cannot alter the state of facts and evidence."

—*John Adams*[353]

"To live under the American Constitution is the greatest political privilege that was ever accorded to the human race."

—*Calvin Coolidge, President*[354]

"Living political constitutions must be Darwinian in structure and in practice. Society is a living organism and must obey the laws of life, not of mechanics; it must develop. All that progressives ask or desire is permission—in an era when 'development,' 'evolution,' is the scientific word—to interpret the Constitution according to the Darwinian principle; all they ask is recognition of the fact that a nation is a living thing and not a machine."

—*Woodrow Wilson,* The New Freedom:
A Call for the Emancipation of the
Generous Energies of a People[355]

"The United States Constitution has proved itself the most marvelously elastic compilation of rules of government ever written."

—*Franklin Roosevelt, President*[356]

"It is the genius of our Constitution that under its shelter of enduring institutions and rooted principles there is ample room for the rich fertility of American political invention."

—*Lyndon B. Johnson, President*[357]

"The words of the Constitution ... are so unrestricted by their intrinsic meaning or by their history or by tradition or by prior decisions that they leave the individual Justice free, if indeed they do not compel him, to gather meaning not from reading the Constitution but from reading life."

—*Felix Frankfurter, Supreme Court Justice*[358]

"This understanding, underlying constitutional interpretation since the New Deal, reflects the Constitution's demands for structural flexibility sufficient to adapt substantive laws and institutions to rapidly changing social, economic, and technological conditions."

—*Stephen Breyer, Supreme Court Justice,* Federal Maritime
Commission v. South Carolina State Ports Authority[359]

"I cannot accept this invitation [to celebrate the bicentennial of the Constitution], for I do not believe that the meaning of the Constitution was forever 'fixed' at the Philadelphia Convention ... To the contrary, the government they devised was defective from the start."

—*Thurgood Marshall, Supreme Court Justice*[360]

"What must be done to defend the country must be done...The Constitution has never greatly bothered any wartime president."

—Francis Biddle, Attorney General under Franklin Roosevelt[361]

"It can be lost, and it will be, if the time ever comes when these documents are regarded not as the supreme expression of our profound belief, but merely as curiosities in glass cases."

—Harry Truman, President[362]

"If we're picking people to draw out of their own conscience and experience a 'new' Constitution, we should not look principally for good lawyers. We should look to people who agree with us. When we are in that mode, you realize we have rendered the Constitution useless."

—Antonin Scalia, Supreme Court Justice[363]

"Just talk to me as a father—not what the Constitution says. What do you feel?"

—Joe Biden, Vice President[364]

"No matter what anyone may say about making the rich and the corporations pay the taxes, in the end they come out of the people who toil. It is your fellow workers who are ordered to work for the Government, every time an appropriation bill is passed. The people pay the expense of government, often many times over, in the increased cost of living. I want taxes to be less, that the people may have more."

—Calvin Coolidge[365]

"Our constitution works. Our great republic is a government of laws, not of men."

—Gerald R. Ford, President[366]

"If you want total security, go to prison. There you're fed, clothed, given medical care and so on. The only thing lacking...is freedom."

—Dwight D. Eisenhower[367]

"There are severe limits to the good that the government can do for the economy, but there are almost no limits to the harm it can do."

—Milton Friedman, Nobel Laureate[368]

"If it were to be asked, 'What is the most sacred duty and the greatest source of our security in a Republic?' The answer would be, an inviolable respect for the Constitution and laws ... A sacred respect for the constitutional law is the vital principle, the sustaining energy of a free government ... The present Constitution is the standard to which we are to cling. Under its banners, bona fide must we combat our political foes—rejecting all changes but through the channel itself provides for amendments."

—Alexander Hamilton[369]

"The people may not yet be sufficiently mislead to retract from error. Evils must be sorely felt before they can be removed."

—George Washington[370]

"We might defy the little arts of the little politicians to control."

—Alexander Hamilton, "Federalist No. 11"[371]

"We can celebrate when we have a government that has earned back the trust of the people it serves ... when we have a government that honors our Constitution and stands up for the values that have made America, America: economic freedom, individual liberty, and personal responsibility."

—John Boehner, Speaker of the
United States House of Representatives[372]

Notes

Introduction

1   James Madison to Dr. William Eustis, 6 July 1819, *Letters and other writings of James Madison*, vol. 3 (J.B. Lippincott & Co., 1865), 140.

2   Benjamin Franklin qtd. in Stacy Schiff, *A Great Improvisation: Franklin, France, and the Birth of America* (New York: Henry, Holt, and Company, 2006), 350.

3   John Adams qtd. in Robert A. Gross, "Reading for an Extensive Republic," in *The History of the Book in America: An Extensive Republic: Print, Culture, and Society in the New Nation, 1790–1840*. Volume 2 of *History of the Book in America*. Edited by Robert A. Gross and Mary Kelley (Charlotte, North Carolina, University of North Carolina Press, 2010), 516.

Chapter 1

4   John Adams, letter to William Cushing, June 9, 1776, *Papers of John Adams: Volume 4-February–August 1776*. Edited by Robert J. Taylor, Gregg L.Lint, and Celeste Walker (Cambridge, Massachusetts: Harvard University Press, 1979), 245.

5   Joseph J. Ellis, *His Excellency: George Washington* (New York: Vintage Books, 2004), 19–39. Washington tried very hard to ingratiate himself with British officers and the Virginia elite, yet as Ellis notes, he was

"clumsy and ineffectual at playing the patronage game," as "it meant surrendering control to a purported superior, trusting his fate and future to someone else" (page 38). Washington resigned his commission in the British army in December of 1758.

6   Gordon S. Wood, *The Americanization of Benjamin Franklin* (New York: The Penguin Press, 2005), 147.

7   Robert Middlekauff, *The Glorious Cause: The American Revolution, 1763–1789*. The Oxford History of the United States, 2nd edition (Oxford: Oxford University Press, 2005), 118.

8   Thomas Hutchinson qtd. in Barry Friedman, *The Will of the People: How Public Opinion has Influenced the Supreme Court and Shaped the Meaning of the Constitution* (New York: Macmillan, 2009), 28.

9   Harlow Giles Unger, *Lion of Liberty: Patrick Henry and the Call to a New Nation* (Cambirdge, Massachusetts: Da Capo Press, 2010), 37–42.

10   Alfred H. Kelly, Winfred A. Harbison, and Herman Belz, *The American Constitution: Its Origins and Development*. Volume 1, 7th Edition (New York: W.W. Norton & Company, 1991), 7, 34; Robert Middlekauff, *The Glorious Cause: The American Revolution, 1763–1789*. The Oxford History of the United States, 2nd Edition (Oxford: Oxford University Press, 2005), 135.

11   Article One of the Constitution stated that "the Electors in each State shall have the Qualifications requisite for Electors of the most numerous Branch of the State Legislature."

12   Thomas Paine, "The American Crisis Number 4," in *Collected Writings: Common Sense, The Crisis, and Other Pamphlets, Articles, and Letters; The Rights of Man; The Age of Reason*. Edited by Eric Foner (New York: The Library of America, 1995), 150.

13   George Mason, letter to George Mason, Jr., June 1, 1787. *The Papers of George Mason, 1725–1792, Volume III 1787–1792*. Edited by Robert A. Rutland (Chapel Hill, North Carolina: University of North Carolina Press, 1970), 892–893.

14   The Roman Republic was to some extent an exception to the rule of self-governing societies dissolving into chaos, as it lasted over four hundred years before class conflict and powerful rival factions even-

tually created civil war and destroyed the Republic, ending with the dictator Julius Caesar and his heir, the first Roman emperor Caesar Augustus. For a detailed, but manageable history of the Republic, see Klaus Bringmann, *A History of the Roman Republic* (Malden, Massachusetts: Polity Press, 2007).

Chapter 2

15 William Paterson qtd. in William Mack and William Benjamin Hale, *Corpus juris: being a complete and systematic statement of the whole body of the law as embodied in and developed by all reported decisions,* vol. 12 (Cambridge, Massachusetts: Harvard University Press and the American Law Book Co., 1917, digitized 2007), 676.

16 James Madison, "Federalist No. 10," in Alexander Hamilton, James Madison, and John Jay, *The Federalist*, ed. J. R. Pole (Indianapolis, Indiana: Hacket Publishing Company, Inc., 2005), 48–54. Federlaist 10 is one of Madison's greatest writings, and perhaps the best explanation of how factions overwhelm pure democracies, and how a republican government is the only kind of government that can protect liberty and be just.

17 Thomas Paine qtd. in Matthew Spalding, *We Still Hold These Truths: Rediscovering Our Principles, Reclaiming Our Future.* The Heritage Foundation (Wilmington, Delaware: Intercollegiate Studies Institute, 2009), 89.

18 The Tenth Amendment to the Constitution makes it clear that states were to possess those powers not given to the federal government. James Madison and Thomas Jefferson also elaborated on the point that states could counteract an overactive government in the Kentucky and Virginia Resolutions of 1798. Madison furthered the argument on how states could counteract overreaching federal power in his Report on the Resolutions to the Virginia Legislature in 1799. The Kentucky and Virginia Resolutions and Madison's Report may all be found in Thomas Jefferson and James Madison, *The Kentucky-Virginia Resolutions and Mr. Madison's Report of 1799.* (Richmond, Virginia: Virginia Commission on Constitutional Government, 1960.)

19 John Mercer Patton and Conway Robinson, ed. *The code of Virginia: with the Declaration of Independence and Constitution of the United*

States; and the declaration of rights and constitution of Virginia, Vol. 2
(The Bavarian State Library: W.F. Ritchie, 1849, digitized 2010), 34.

Chapter 3

20   Theodore H. White, *In Search of History: A Personal Adventure* (New
York: Harper & Row, 1978), 333.

21   Pierce Butler qtd. in David C. Hendrickson, "In Our Own Image:
The Sources of American Conduct in World Affairs," in *The National
Interest,* No. 50 (Winter 1997).

22   For a good overview of women in the Revolution, see Carol Berkin,
Revolutionary Mothers: Women in the Struggle for America's Independence
(New York: Vintage Books, 2006.)

23   Middlekauff, 571–572. Pennsylvania was the only colony to abolish
slavery during the Revolutionary War. Other northern states began
emancipation after the war. Usually these laws were gradual, dictating
that slaves born after a certain date would be freed once they reached
the age of 18. The Northwest Ordinance of 1787 also banned slavery
from the Northwest Territories, what would become Ohio, Indiana,
Illinois, Wisconsin, and Michigan. By 1800, slavery was almost completely abolished in the northern states.

24   Aristotle's defense of slavery can be found in chapters four through
seven of Book I of *The Politics.* Aristotle, *The Politics,* translated by
T. A. Sinclair, revised by Trevor J. Saunders (London: Penguin Books,
1992) 63–73.

Chapter 4

25   George Washington, letter to Steptoe Washington, December 5, 1790,
The Writings of George Washington, Volume II, 1785–1790. Edited by
Worthington Chauncey Ford (New York: G.P. Putnam's Sons, 1891),
509.

26   Lucius Quinctius Cincinnatus (519 BC–430 BC) was twice handed
supreme authority in the Roman Republic and in both instances retired back to his farm after his work was complete.

27   Max Farrand, *The Framing of the Constitution of the United States* (New Haven, Connecticut: Yale University Press, 1962), 193–194.

28   Middlekauff, 683. Randolph's support for the Constitution was extremely influential at the Virginia Ratifying Convention, and may have helped the Constitution pass there.

29   Glenn A. Phelps, preface to *George Washington & American Constitutionalism* (Lawrence, Kansas: University of Kansas Press, 1994), viii.

30   Michael Klepper and Robert Gunther, *The Wealthy 100: From Benjamin Franklin to Bill Gates—A Ranking of the Richest Americans, Past and Present* (Secaucus, New Jersey: Citadel Press, 1996).

31   Esmond Wright, *Franklin of Philadelphia* (Cambridge: Harvard University Press, 1986), 55.

32   For a detailed biography on Franklin, see Walter Isaacson, *Benjamin Franklin: An American* Life (New York: Simon & Schuster, 2003). Electricity experiments: 137–144. Armonica, 266. Lightning rod, 141–143. Franklin stove, 130–131. Swim pads, 16, 47. Urinary catheter, 132 Bifocals, 2. Gulf Stream mapping, 129. On founding of the Junto—also called Leather Apron Society—see 55–60.

33   Walter Isaacson, *Benjamin Franklin,* 228–231. Franklin even testified before Parliament on how the colonies would respond to the Stamp Act. When asked what would happen if the British applied military force to the colonies, Franklin noted that if "They did not find a rebellion; they may indeed make one." 230.

34   Ibid., 445.

35   Diane Ravitch, *The American reader: words that moved a nation* (New York: HarperCollins, 2000), 42.

36   Isaacson, *Benjamin Franklin,* 312.

37   Joseph J. Ellis, *American Sphinx: The Character of Thomas Jefferson* (New York: Vintage Books, 1998), 60. Jefferson would complain to his friends that the delegates had "mangled … the Manuscript."

38   Isaacson, *Benjamin Franklin,* 313.

39   John Adams, *The works of John Adams, second president of the United States: with a life of the author, notes and illustrations*, vol. 2. Edited by

Charles Francis Adams (Berkeley, California: University of California Press, 1850, digitized 2009), 514.

40 Thomas Jefferson, Letter to Henry Lee, May 8, 1825 in *The Life and Selected Writings of Thomas Jefferson: Including the Autobiography, The Declaration of Independence & His Public and Private Letters*, ed. Adrienne Koch and William Peden (New York: The Modern Library, 2004), 656.

41 Harry Truman qtd. in Matthew Spalding, *We Still Hold These Truths*, 5.

42 James Madison qtd. in John R. Vile, *The Constitutional Convention of 1787: A Comprehensive Encyclopedia of America's Founding*, Volume 2 (Santa Barbara, California: ABC-CLIO, 2005), 263.

43 Joseph J. Ellis, *His Excellency: George Washington* (New York: Vintage Books, 2004)174–175.

44 John R. Vile, "James Madison and Constitutional Paternity," 37–62, in John R. Vile, William D. Pederson, Frank J. Williams, ed. *James Madison: Philosopher, Founder, and Statesman* (Athens, Ohio: Ohio University Press, 2008), 46. Morris spoke 173 times, and Wilson spoke 168 times.

45 Gordon Lloyd, "Committee Assignments Chart and Commentary." Ashbrook Center for Public Affairs at Ashland University. 2008. http://teachingamericanhistory.org/convention/delegates/committee_table.html (accessed October 22, 2011).

46 James Madison qtd. in John R. Vile, *The Constitutional Convention of 1787*, Volume 2, 108.

47 William Pierce, *Notes of Major William Pierce (Georgia) in the Federal Convention of 1787: Loose sketches and notes taken in the convention, May, 1787*. Yale Law School, The Avalon Project. http://avalon.law.yale.edu/18th_century/pierce.asp (accessed October 22, 2011).

48 John Vile, "James Madison and Constitutional Paternity," in Vile et al. 46.

49 Gouverneur Morris qtd. in John R. Vile, *The Constitutional Convention of 1787*, Volume 2, 283; Gouverneur Morris qtd. in James J. Kirschke, *Gouverneur Morris: Author, Statesman, and Man of the World* (New York: Macmillan, 2005), 176.

50 Alexander Hamilton, "The First Report on Public Credit," January

14, 1790, in *The Papers of Alexander Hamilton, Volume VI of December, 1789–August, 1790*, edited by Jacob Ernest Cooke (New York: Columbia University Press, 1962), 70.

51   Wood, *Empire of Liberty*, 95–98.

52   James Monroe qtd. in Joslyn T. Pine, *Wit and Wisdom of the American Presidents: A Book of Quotations* (New York: Courier Dover Publications Inc., 2000), 13.

53   Thomas Jefferson, letter to William P. Gardner, May, 1813. *The Jeffersonian Cyclopedia: A Comprehensive Collection of the Views of Thomas Jefferson Classified and Arranged in Alphabetical Order under Nine Thousand Titles Relating to Government, Politics, Law, Education, Political Economy, Finance, Science, Art, Literature, Religious Freedom, Morals, etc.* Edited by John P. Foley (Cambridge, Massachusetts: Harvard University Press and Funk & Wagnalls Company, 1900, digitized 2008), 7.

54   Samuel Adams letter to James Warren, November 4, 1775, *The Writings of Samuel Adams, Volume III: 1773–1777*. Edited by Harry Alonzo Cushy (New York: Octagon Books, Inc., 1968), 237.

Chapter 5

55   John Adams qtd. in Clinton Rossiter, ed., *1787: The Grand Convention* (New York: Macmillan, 1966), 11.

56   Robert Middlekauff, *The Glorious Cause: The American Revolution, 1763–1789*. The Oxford History of the United States, 2nd Edition (Oxford: Oxford University Press, 2005), 621. Daniel Shays led the infamous revolt known as Shays Rebellion in 1786–1787. Leading a band of discontented farmers, Shays and his ragtag rebels took over western Massachusetts and nearly marched on Boston before being dispersed by the armed militia of Massachusetts. This rebellion showed the weaknesses of the Articles, and may have helped spur the Founders to meet in Philadelphia and construct the new Constitution.

57   Farrand, *Framing of the Constitution*, 39. Jefferson was serving as Ambassador to France during the Convention. He characterized the Convention as an assembly of demigods in a letter to John Adams, who also could not be at the Convention as he was serving as Ambassador to Great Britain and was in London.

58   George Washington qtd. in Matthew Spalding and Patrick J. Garrity, *A Sacred Union of Citizens: George Washington's Farewell Address and the American Character* (Lanham, Maryland: Rowman & Littlefield), 76.

Chapter 6

59   Thomas Jefferson, "Notes on the State of Virginia," in *The Life and Selected Writings of Thomas Jefferson: Including the Autobiography, The Declaration of Independence & His Public and Private Letters*, ed. Adrienne Koch and William Peden (New York: The Modern Library, 2004), 258.

60   For Cicero's thoughts on Natural Law, see his work *The Laws*, Book Two. Cicero, *The Republic and The Laws*, translated and edited by Jonathan Powell and Niall Rudd (Oxford: Oxford University Press, 1998), 97–118.

61   John Locke, *The Second Treatise of Government and A Letter Concerning Toleration.* Dover Thrift Editions (New York: Dover Publications, Inc., 2002), 44.

62   Thomas Jefferson, "Summary View of the Rights of British America," in *The Life and Selected Writings of Thomas Jefferson: Including the Autobiography, The Declaration of Independence & His Public and Private Letters*, ed. Adrienne Koch and William Peden (New York: The Modern Library, 2004), 289.

63   John Adams qtd. in Bruce A. Findlay, *Your Rugged Constitution* (Stanford: Stanford University Press, 1969), 216.

64   For Montesquieu's views on separation of powers, see *The Spirit of the Laws,* Book 11. Montesquieu, *The Spirit of the Laws*, edited and translated by David Wallace Carrithers (Berkeley, California: University of California Press, 1977), 196–214; Hume's concept of separation of powers permeate his work, and can be best seen in David Hume, *Political writings*, edited by Stuart D. Warner and Donald W. Livingston (Indianapolis, Indiana: Hackett Publishing Company, Inc., 1994.)

65   Middlekauff, *The Glorious Cause*, 625–641; Alfred H. Kelly, Winfred A. Harbison, and Herman Belz, *The American Constitution: Its Origins and Development*. Volume 1, 7th Edition (New York: W.W. Norton & Company, 1991), 68–74. The states took many varying methods

in their state constitutions. Rhode Island and Connecticut retained their corporate charters and used them as state constitutions; New Jersey also retained its colonial government structure as a state. Virginia's constitution was the first drafted of the new states, with three separate branches and a bicameral legislature that would have the most power. This was a model adopted by five other states. Pennsylvania and Maryland provided the extreme ends of the spectrum, with Pennsylvania having a unicameral legislature which stood for election annually and a very weak plural executive with almost no power; Maryland had more aristocratic control, with a bicameral legislature, the Senate indirectly elected, and the relatively powerful governor elected by the legislature and not by the people.

66   Thomas Jefferson qtd in Luigi Marco Bassani, *Liberty, State, & Union: The Political Theory of Thomas Jefferson* (Macon, Georgia: Mercer University Press, 2010), 113.

67   Thomas Jefferson, "Reply to Danbury Baptist Association," January 1, 1802, in *The Life and Selected Writings of Thomas Jefferson: Including the Autobiography, The Declaration of Independence & His Public and Private Letters*, ed. Adrienne Koch and William Peden (New York: The Modern Library, 2004), 307.

68   Alexis de Tocqueville, *Democracy in America: The Complete and Unabridged, Volumes ! and II*, trans. Henry Reeve (New York: Bantam-Dell, 2000), 355.

69   Thomas Paine, "Age of Reason," Part 2, Section 21 in *Collected Writings: Common Sense, The Crisis, and Other Pamphlets, Articles, and Letters; The Rights of Man; The Age of Reason.* Edited by Eric Foner (New York: The Library of America, 1995), 826.

70   The first quote is from Marcus Tullius Cicero, *De Re Publica (On the Republic)*, book 3 paragraph 22. Translated by Clinton W. Keyes. Loeb Classical Library (Cambridge, Massachusetts: Harvard University Press), 211; the second is from the same book, page 343; the third may be found on page 345 of the same book.

Chapter 7

71   Kelly et al., *The American Constitution*, Volume 1, 7th edition, 87–88.

72 James Madison, "Federalist No. 46," in Alexander Hamilton, James Madison, and John Jay, *The Federalist*, ed. J. R. Pole (Indianapolis, Indiana: Hacket Publishing Company, Inc., 2005), 255.

73 Gordon S. Wood, *Empire of Liberty*, 134–138, 198–198.

74 George Washington, *Washington's Farewell Address 1796*. The Avalon Project, Yale Law School. Digitized 2008: http://avalon.law.yale.edu/18th_century/washing.asp (accessed October 20, 2011).

Chapter 8

75 James Madison, "Federalist No. 14," in Alexander Hamilton, James Madison, and John Jay, *The Federalist*, ed. J. R. Pole (Indianapolis, Indiana: Hacket Publishing Company, Inc., 2005), 71.

76 Thomas Jefferson, "Kentucky Resolutions of 1798" in Thomas Jefferson and James Madison, *The Kentucky-Virginia Resolutions and Mr. Madison's Report of 1799*. Richmond, Virginia: Virginia Commission on Constitutional Government, 1960), 8.

77 John Adams, letter to John Taylor, April 15, 1814.

78 James Madison, "Federalist No. 10," in Alexander Hamilton, James Madison, and John Jay, *The Federalist*, ed. J. R. Pole (Indianapolis, Indiana: Hacket Publishing Company, Inc., 2005), 52.

79 James Madison qtd. in Kristin Waters, *Women and Men Political Theorists: Enlightened Conversations* (Hoboken, New Jersey, 2000), 175.

80 For Madison's opinions on democracy and theory of how the United States could survive as a republic, see Alan Gibson, "Inventing the Extended Republic: The Debate over the Role of Madison's Theory in the Creation of the Constitution," in *James Madison: Philosopher, Founder, Statesman*, ed. John R. Vile, William D. Pederson, and Frank J. Williams (Athens, Ohio: Ohio University Press, 2008).

81 Alexander Hamilton, "Federalist No. 21," in Alexander Hamilton, James Madison, and John Jay, *The Federalist*, ed. J. R. Pole (Indianapolis, Indiana: Hacket Publishing Company, Inc., 2005), 112.

82 James Madison, speech before the 1829 Virginia Ratifying Convention qtd. in Marvin Meyers, ed. *The Mind of the Founder: Sources of*

the Political Thought of James Madison, The American Heritage Series (New York: The Bobbs-Merril Company, Inc., 1973), 512.

83 James Madison, letter to Edmund Pendleton, January 21, 1792 in *The Papers of James Madison,* Volume 14: 6 April 1791–16 March 1793. Edited by Robert A. Rutland, Thomas A. Mason, Robert J. Brugger, Jeanne K. Sisson, and Fredrika J. Teute (Charlottesville, Virginia: University of Virginia Press, 1983), 195.

Chapter 9

84 Thomas Jefferson to Wilson C. Nicholas, September 7, 1803, *The Life and Selected Writings of Thomas Jefferson: Including the Autobiography, The Declaration of Independence & His Public and Private Letters,* ed. Adrienne Koch and William Peden (New York: The Modern Library, 2004), 525.

85 Thomas Paine, *Common Sense and Other Writings,* ed. Gordon Wood (New York: The Modern Library, 2003), 48.

86 Kelly et al., *The American Constitution,* 76.

87 James Madison, "Federalist No. 62," in Alexander Hamilton, James Madison, and John Jay, *The Federalist,* ed. J. R. Pole (Indianapolis, Indiana: Hacket Publishing Company, Inc., 2005), 335.

88 There were three constitutions for the Soviet Union, one from 1924, one from 1936, and one from 1977, all of which purported to protect rights. These constitutions may be viewed at the following links:

http://faculty.unlv.edu/pwerth/Const-USSR-1924(abridge).pdf (1924)

http://www.departments.bucknell.edu/russian/const/1936toc.html (1936)

http://www.departments.bucknell.edu/russian/const/1977toc.html (1977)

89 James Madison qtd. in Thomas F. Gordon *War on the Bank of the United States* (North Stratford, New Hampshire: Ayer Publishing, 1966), 106.

90 Thomas Jefferson, *Jefferson's Opinion on the Constitutionality of a Na-*

tional Bank: 1791. The Avalon Project. Digitized 2008, http://avalon. law.yale.edu/18th_century/bank-tj.asp (accessed October 20, 2011).

91 James Madison, Speech before Congress on the Bank Bill, February 2, 1791,*The Papers of James Madison,* Volume 13. Edited by Charles F. Hobson, Robert Rutland, William M.E. Rachal, and Jeanne K. Sisson (Charlottesville, Virginia: University of Virginia Press, 1981), 377.

92 Joseph Story qtd. in United States Supreme Court, Lawyers Co-operative Publishing Company, *United States Supreme Court Reports* (Ann Arbor, Michigan: Lawyers Co-operative Pub. Co., 1911, the University of Michigan 2006), 584.

93 Alexander Hamilton, "Federalist No. 22," in Alexander Hamilton, James Madison, and John Jay, *The Federalist,* ed. J. R. Pole (Indianapolis, Indiana: Hacket Publishing Company, Inc., 2005),115.

94 James Madison, letter to James Robertson, April 20, 1831, qtd. in Arthur E. Palumbo, *The Authentic Constitution: An Originalist View of America's Legacy* (New York: Algora Publishing), 34.

95 Thomas Jefferson to William Johnson, June 12, 1823 in *The Jeffersonian Cyclopedia: A Comprehensive Collection of the Views of Thomas Jefferson Classified and Arranged in Alphabetical Order under Nine Thousand Titles Relating to Government, Politics, Law, Education, Political Economy, Finance, Science, Art, Literature, Religious Freedom, Morals, etc.* Edited by John P. Foley (Cambridge, Massachusetts: Harvard University Press and Funk & Wagnalls Company, 1900, digitized 2008), 844.

Chapter 10

96 Thomas Jefferson, "First Annual Message—December 8, 1801," in *The Life and Selected Writings of Thomas Jefferson: Including the Autobiography, The Declaration of Independence & His Public and Private Letters,* ed. Adrienne Koch and William Peden (New York: The Modern Library, 2004), 305.

97 For an excellent brief overview of natural rights, including the right to own property, see Richard Tuck, *Natural Rights Theories: Their Origin and Development* (Cambridge University Press, 1981).

98 James Madison, *The Writings of James Madison: 1790–1802, Volume 6 of The Writings of James Madison: Comprising His Public Papers and*

His Private Correspondence, Including Numerous Letters and Documents New for the First Time Printed. Edited by Gaillard Hunt (New York: G.P. Putnam's Sons, 1906), 102.

99 The full opinion of the *Kelo v. City of New London* may be found at http://www.law.cornell.edu/supct/pdf/04-108P.ZO (accessed October 24, 2011).

100 James Madison, *Letters and Other Writings of James Madison: 1829–1836* (Charlottesville, Virginia, 1884, digitized 2010), 479.

101 The opinion of *Bennis v. Michigan* may be viewed at http://www.law. cornell.edu/supct/html/94-8729.ZO.html.

102 Full opinion of *Penn Central Transportation Co. v. New York City* may be found at http://www.law.cornell.edu/supct/html/historics/USSC_ CR_0438_0104_ZS.html.

103 An excellent discussion of how government destroys currency through inflation may be found in Murray Rothbard, *What Has Government Done to Our Money?* (Auburn, Alabama: Ludwig von Mises Institute, 2008.) It can be viewed for free at http://mises.org/books/whathasgov-ernmentdone.pdf.

104 John Emerich Edward Dalberg, 1st Baron Acton (1834–1902), British historian. Letter, April 3, 1887, to Bishop Mandell Creighton. *The Life and Letters of Mandell Creighton*, vol. 1, ch. 13, ed. Louise Creighton (1904).

105 Al Goodman, "Thousands protest economic crisis, high unemployment in Spain," May 18, 2011, in CNN. http://www.cnn.com/2011 /WORLD/europe/05/18/spain.protests/index.html (accessed October 24, 2011); Ina Dimireva, "Spain: Economy Overview," November 5, 2008 in *EUBusiness.* http://www.eubusiness.com/europe/spain (accessed October 24, 2011); "Spain: Overview," in *New York Times*, updated October 20, 2011. http://topics.nytimes.com/top/news/in-ternational/countriesandterritories/spain/index.html (accessed October 24, 2011).

106 Thomas Jefferson, letter to Joseph Milligan, April 6, 1816 in *The Life and Selected Writings of Thomas Jefferson: Including the Autobiography, The Declaration of Independence & His Public and Private Letters*, ed. Adrienne Koch and William Peden (New York: The Modern Library, 2004), 606.

107 James Madison qtd. in Ralph Ketcham, *James Madison: A Biography* (Charlottesville, Virginia: University of Virginia Press, 1971), 330.

108 John Adams, *The works of John Adams, second president of the United States: with a life of the author, notes and illustrations*, vol. 6. Edited by Charles Francis Adams (Berkeley, California: University of California Press, 1850, digitized 2009), 9.

Chapter 11

109 Thomas Jefferson, "Notes on the State of Virginia," in *The Life and Selected Writings of Thomas Jefferson: Including the Autobiography, The Declaration of Independence & His Public and Private Letters*, ed. Adrienne Koch and William Peden (New York: The Modern Library, 2004), 221–222.

110 John Adams, *The works of John Adams, second President of the United States,* Volume 6. Edited by Charles Francis Adams (Berkeley, California: University of California Press, 1850, digitized 2009), 463; James Madison, "Federalist No. 51," in Alexander Hamilton, James Madison, and John Jay, *The Federalist*, ed. J. R. Pole (Indianapolis, Indiana: Hacket Publishing Company, Inc., 2005), 281–282.

111 Stuart Leibiger, *Founding Friendship: George Washington, James Madison, and the Creation of the American Republic* (Charlottesville, Virginia: University Press of Virginia, 1999), 77; Max Farrand, *The Framing of the Constitution of the United States,*116, 119, 183–184.

112 James Madison, "Federalist No. 51," 281.

113 Timothy Gardner, "US states sue EPA to stop greenhouse gas rules," March 19, 2010 in Reuters. http://www.reuters.com/article/2010/03/19/states-climate-idUSN1916237120100319 (accessed October 24, 2011). At least 15 states have started suing the EPA over regulations; Brandon Loomis, "Utah sues feds over wildlands policy," May 14, 2011 in *Salt Lake Tribune*. http://www.sltrib.com/sltrib /politics/51720408-90/utah-lands-wild-officials.html.csp (accessed October 24, 2011) A list of the states suing the federal government over ObamaCare may be found at Brandon Stewart, "List of 27 States Suing Over Obamacare," January 17, 2011 from the Heritage Foundation. http://blog.heritage.org/2011/01/17/list-of-states-suing-over-obamacare/ (accessed October 24, 2011); the Arizona law SB 1070 is the most

notable example of states enforcing laws against illegal immigration, Randal C. Archibold, "Arizona Enacts Stringent Law on Immigration," April 23, 2010 in *New York Times*. http://www.nytimes.com/2010/04/24/us/politics/24immig.html (accessed October 24, 2011).

Chapter 12

114 Thomas Jefferson, letter to David Humphreys, March 18, 1789. *The Jeffersonian Cyclopedia: A Comprehensive Collection of the Views of Thomas Jefferson Classified and Arranged in Alphabetical Order under Nine Thousand Titles Relating to Government, Politics, Law, Education, Political Economy, Finance, Science, Art, Literature, Religious Freedom, Morals, etc.* Edited by John P. Foley (Cambridge, Massachusetts: Harvard University Press and Funk & Wagnalls Company, 1900, digitized 2008), 206.

115 Farrand, *The Framing of the United States Constitution*, 73.

116 Ibid., 111–112.

117 The Confederation Congress's response to the Constitution was somewhat ambiguous. However, states went ahead and began planning ratification conventions before Congress made an official statement on the new document. Pauline Maier, *Ratification: The People Debate the Constitution* (New York: Simon and Schuster, 2011), 61–64.

118 Philadelphia Convention qtd. in Kelly et al., *The American Constitution* Volume 1, 7th edition, 89.

119 Farrand, *The Framing of the Constitution of the United States*, 71.

120 Farrand, *The Framing of the Constitution of the United* States, 81–83; Roger Sherman qtd. in Lewis Henry Boutell, *The Life of Roger Sherman* (Chicago: McClurg & Co., 1896), 304.

121 Farrand, *The Framing of the Constitution of the United States*, 91–112.

122 Article I, Section 8, of the Constitution allows Congress "To exercise exclusive Legislation in all Cases whatsoever, over such District (not exceeding ten Miles square) as may, by Cession of particular States, and the Acceptance of Congress, become the Seat of Government of the United States, and to exercise like Authority over all Places purchased by the Consent of the Legislature of the State in which the

Same shall be, for the Erection of Forts, Magazines, Arsenals, dock-Yards, and other needful Buildings"; setting the framework for what would become Washington, D.C. Its actual location on the Potomac River was the result of a bargain stuck between James Madison and Alexander Hamilton at Thomas Jefferson's house, whereby Madison and Jefferson would allow Hamilton's fiscal plan to pass if Hamilton could guarantee that the national capital would be in the South, an agreement which was followed. For more on this agreement see Joseph J. Ellis, *Founding Brothers: The Revolutionary Generation*, Chapter Two, "The Dinner," 48–80 (New York: Vintage Books, 2000.)

123 Obviously the Confederate States of America was the greatest expression of secession practiced in American history, but the concept of a northern non-slave nation was also pushed by the abolitionist William Lloyd Garrison when he proclaimed "No Union With Slaveholders" in his *Liberator* newspaper; an electronic version of the May 31, 1844, article may be viewed at http://www.theliberatorfiles.com/no-union-with-slaveholders/. A New England nation was also contemplated by some Federalists during the War of 1812 when they gathered in Hartford, Connecticut for the infamous Hartford Convention; Wood, *Empire of Liberty*, 692–696.

124 Between 1820–1850, the states went through a frenzy of drafting new constitutions, most of which provided for more popular elections of officials and for popular elections to decide the apportionment of electoral college votes. Kelly et al., *The American Constitution*. Volume 1, 7th edition, 217–221.

125 United States Constitution, Article I, Section 8, Clause 8, the Copyright Clause.

126 George Mason qtd. in George Bancroft, *History of the United States of America, from the Discovery of the Continent to 1789*. Volume 6 (Ann Arbor, Michigan: D. Appleton and Company, 1884, digitized 2006), 256.

Chapter 13

127 James Madison qtd. in Kevin R. Gutzman, "James Madison and 'The Principles of '98'" in *Journal of the Early Republic* 15, no. 4 (Winter, 1995), 587–588.

128 James Madison, "Federalist No. 46," in Alexander Hamilton, James Madison, and John Jay, *The Federalist*, ed. J. R. Pole (Indianapolis, Indiana: Hacket Publishing Company, Inc., 2005), 255.

129 James Madison, "Federalist No. 14," in Alexander Hamilton, James Madison, and John Jay, *The Federalist*, ed. J. R. Pole (Indianapolis, Indiana: Hacket Publishing Company, Inc., 2005), 71.

130 Roger Sherman qtd. in James Madison, *The Debates in the Several State conventions on the Adoption of the Federal Constitution*. Edited by Jonathan Elliot (Berkeley, California: University of California Press and J.B. Lippincott & Co., 1836, digitized 2009), 166.

131 Education Department Budget History Table. http://www2.ed.gov/about/overview/budget/history/edhistory.pdf (accessed October 25, 2011).

132 *The Wall Street Journal*, Thursday, October 20, 2011.

133 The Cato Institute research may be viewed at http://www.downsizing-government.org/education (accessed October 25, 2011).

134 Associated Press, "Colleges spend billions on remedial classes to prep freshmen," in *USA Today*, September 19, 2008. http://www.usatoday.com/news/education/2008-09-15-Colleges-remedialclasses_N.htm (accessed October 25, 2011).

135 Most recent dropout rate is from 2009; it may be viewed at the National Center for Education Statistics and may be viewed at http://nces.ed.gov/fastfacts/display.asp?id=16 (accessed October 25, 2011); John Selegean, "Overstayers: 5th Year Seniors and 3rd Year Transfers," DUE/Assessment & Research Studies, June 2, 2009. http://www.assessment.uci.edu/reports/documents/Overstayers_Final_Report.pdf (accessed October 25, 2011).

136 10 Facts About K–12 Education Funding—U.S. Department of Education, http://www2.ed.gov/about/overview/fed/10facts/index.html (accessed October 25, 2011).

137 PTA website is www.pta.org/ (accessed October 25, 2011).

138 James Madison, "Federalist No. 46," 258.

Chapter 14

139 John Jay, letter to R. Lushington, March 15, 1786. In William Jay, *The Life of John Jay with Selections from His Correspondence* (New York: J. & J. Harper, 1833), 181–182.

140 Bruce Levine, *Half Slave and Half Free: The Roots of the Civil War* (New York: Hill & Wang, 2005), 1–16.

141 Isaacson, *Benjamin Franklin*, 456–457.

142 United States Department of Agriculture, Atlas of American Agriculture, V, Sec. A, Cotton, Table IV, 18.

143 For the stark differences in development between the North and South from the Founding to the break of the Civil War and slavery's role in it, see Bruce Levine, *Half Slave and Half Free: The Roots of the Civil War* (New York: Hill & Wang, 2005.)

144 Isaacson, *Benjamin Franklin*, 464.

145 Bruce Levine, *Half Slave, Half Free*, 136.

146 John Jay Chapman, *William Lloyd Garrison,* 1913, 9.

147 Middlekauff, *The Glorious Cause*, 572.

148 Oliver Ellsworth qtd. in Paul Leicester Ford ed. *Essays on the Constitution of the United States: published during its discussion by the people, 1787–1788* (Historical Printing Club, 1892), 164.

149 James Wilson qtd. in John P. Kaminski, *A Necessary Evil?: Slavery and the Debate over the Constitution* (Lanham, Maryland: Rowman & Littlefield, 1995), 116.

150 Benjamin Franklin qtd. in Hugh Thomas, *The Slave Trade: The Story of the Atlantic Slave Trade, 1440–1870* (New York: Simon and Schuster, 1997), 481.

151 The Slaughterhouse Cases were the first cases to interpret the Fourteenth Amendment. The opinion consolidated three separate cases, and said that the new amendment could not restrict the police powers of the states, and that the Privileges and Immunities Clause of the Fourteenth Amendment only applied to federal citizenship and not state citizenship. Therefore, the Amendment only protected rights

guaranteed by the national government, giving the states leeway to ignore racial injustices as well as other police powers. The opinion of the Slaughterhouse Cases may be viewed at http://www.law.cornell. edu/supct/html/historics/USSC_CR_0083_0036_ZO.html (accessed October 25, 2011).

Chapter 15

152 Thomas Jefferson, *The life and letters of Thomas Jefferson: being his autobiography and select correspondence, from original manuscripts.* Edited by Henry Augustine Washington (New York: Edwards, Pratt & Foster, 1858, digitized 2007), 58–59.

153 A copy of the Articles of Confederation may be found at http://www.usconstitution.net/articles.html (accessed October 25, 2011).

154 Isaacson, *Benjamin Franklin*, 447.

155 Farrand, *The Framing of the Constitution of the United States*, 110–112.

156 Ibid., 91.

157 Farrand, *The Framing of the Constitution of the United States*, 183–184.

158 Benjamin Franklin qtd. in James Madison, *Noted of debates in the Federal Convention of 1787* (London: W.W. Norton & Company, 1987), 251.

159 James Madison, "Federalist No. 53," in Alexander Hamilton, James Madison, and John Jay, *The Federalist*, ed. J. R. Pole (Indianapolis, Indiana: Hacket Publishing Company, Inc., 2005), 291.

Chapter 16

160 Alexander Hamilton, "Federalist No. 67," in Alexander Hamilton, James Madison, and John Jay, *The Federalist*, ed. J. R. Pole (Indianapolis, Indiana: Hacket Publishing Company, Inc., 2005), 359.

161 Alexander Hamilton, "Federalist No. 70," in Alexander Hamilton, James Madison, and John Jay, *The Federalist*, ed. J. R. Pole (Indianapolis, Indiana: Hacket Publishing Company, Inc., 2005), 374.

162 Benjamin Franklin qtd. in James Madison, *The Constitutional Conven-*

tion: A Narrative History From the Notes of James Madison. Edited by Edward John Larson, Michael Paul Winship, and Michael Winship (New York: Random House Inc., 2005.)

163 George Mason qtd. in *Volume 3 of Documentary History of the Constitution of the United States of America, 1786–1870: Derived from Records, Manuscripts, and Rolls Deposited in the Bureau of Rolls and Library of the Department of State* (Washington, D.C.: Department of State, 1900), 59; Mason favoring the executive council may be found in Farrand, *The Framing of the Constitution of the United States*, 171–172.

164 Farrand, *The Framing of the Constitution of the United States*, 115.

165 Alexander Hamilton, "Federalist No. 72," in Alexander Hamilton, James Madison, and John Jay, *The Federalist*, ed. J. R. Pole (Indianapolis, Indiana: Hacket Publishing Company, Inc., 2005), 388.

166 Farrand, *The Framing of the Constitution of the United States*, 115.

167 For specific protection of slavery, see Constitution of the Confederate States of America, Article 1, Section 9. For term of the Confederate President, see Constitution of the Confederate States of America, Article 2, Section 1.

168 For an excellent overview of Lincoln's relationship with his cabinet and political maneuvers during his presidency, see Doris Kearns Goodwin, *Team of Rivals: The Political Genius of Abraham Lincoln*, (New York: Simon and Schuster Paperbacks, 2005). It is particularly notable that Lincoln was expected by some to follow a recent tradition and be a one-term president. Since Andrew Jackson, who was president from 1829–1837, no president had served two terms. Lincoln's own secretary of the treasury Salmon Chase attempted to set himself up as Lincoln's replacement for the Republican nomination in 1864; Chase was, of course, unsuccessful. Similarly, Lincoln had to face former Union General George McClellan—whom Lincoln had fired—in the general election. Many assumed Lincoln would lose, but because of a series of Union victories, Lincoln was vindicated and won a second-term overwhelmingly.

169 Farrand, *The Framing of the Constitution of the United States*, 164–165.

170 The Twenty-Second Amendment was ratified in 1951, and it is notable that it occurred under a Democratic president, Harry Truman, and a Democratic-controlled Congress, as a reaction to the Democratic President Franklin Roosevelt's four terms. This shows that the amendment

was not some partisan reaction by party. A two-term tradition was supported by the Founders, and Jefferson himself said, "If some termination to the services of the chief Magistrate be not fixed by the Constitution, or supplied by practice, his office, nominally four years, will in fact become for life." Thomas Jefferson letter to Vermont Legislature, December 1807, *The Jeffersonian Cyclopedia: A Comprehensive Collection of the Views of Thomas Jefferson Classified and Arranged in Alphabetical Order under Nine Thousand Titles Relating to Government, Politics, Law, Education, Political Economy, Finance, Science, Art, Literature, Religious Freedom, Morals, etc.* Edited by John P. Foley (Cambridge, Massachusetts: Harvard University Press and Funk & Wagnalls Company, 1900, digitized 2008), 867.

171 Joseph J. Ellis, *His Excellency*, 193. John Adams in particular pushed for the president to have a title such as "His Elective Majesty" or "His Mightiness." Critics of Adams responded by saying the Vice President should be called "His Rotundity."

172 A chart of federal government spending as a percentage of gross domestic product from fiscal year 1920 to fiscal year 2010 may be found at http://www.usgovernmentspending.com/spending_chart_1920_2010USp_12s1li011mcn_F0f (accessed November 7, 2011).

173 Breakdowns and estimates of the number of people employed by the executive branch may be found at http://www.whitehouse.gov/our-government/executive-branch (accessed November 7, 2011).

174 A pdf of the text of the Budget and Accounting Act of 1921 may be accessed at http://world.moleg.go.kr/download.do?file_id=3914 (accessed November 7, 2011).

175 While executive privilege goes back to George Washington, who invoked executive privilege when refusing to give the House of Representatives documents concerning the negotiation of the controversial Jay Treaty, it is not in the Constitution and was only held up as a legitimate power in the 1974 case *United States v. Nixon*, which was over the Watergate scandal and whether President Nixon could be subpoenaed to hand over the infamous "Watergate tapes." While the Court held executive privilege as a legitimate function of the executive branch, they set certain boundaries for how it could be enacted, boundaries that it could be argued have been trampled upon in recent years. For a

brief history of executive privilege see Michael C. Dorf, "A Brief History of Executive Privilege, from George Washington through Dick Cheney," in Findlaw, February 6, 2002. http://writ.news.findlaw.com/dorf/20020206.html (accessed November 7, 2011).

176 Supreme Court opinion of this case may be found at http://www.law.cornell.edu/supct/html/historics/USSC_CR_0299_0304_ZS.html (accessed November 7, 2011).

Chapter 17

177 Alexander Hamilton, "Federalist No. 81," in Alexander Hamilton, James Madison, and John Jay, *The Federalist*, ed. J. R. Pole (Indianapolis, Indiana: Hacket Publishing Company, Inc., 2005), 429.

178 Alexander Hamilton, "Federalist No. 78," in Alexander Hamilton, James Madison, and John Jay, *The Federalist*, ed. J. R. Pole (Indianapolis, Indiana: Hacket Publishing Company, Inc., 2005), 412.

179 *Plessy v. Ferguson* is a case decided in 1896 in regards to Homer Plessy, who was one-eighth black and seven-eighths white—which under Louisiana law designated him as black—and refused to leave the white car when asked to sit in the "colored" car. He was then arrested and jailed. The Supreme Court handed down a 7 to 1 decision—with only Justice John Marshall Harlan dissenting—which said that Plessy should have moved out from the white car to the other car, and that Louisiana's law designating separate spaces for different races was legal as long as the facilities were of equal quality. For more on *Plessy v. Ferguson*, see Charles A. Lofgren, *The Plessy Case: A Legal-Historical Interpretation* (New York: Oxford University Press, 1987.)

180 Franklin Roosevelt, letter to Samuel B. Hill, July 6, 1935, qtd. in Jeff Shesol, "Supreme Power: Franklin Roosevelt Vs. the Supreme Court." (London: W.W. Norton & Company, Inc., 2011), 166.

181 Paul Gewritz and Chad Golder, "So Who Are the Activists?" in *New York Times*, July 6, 2005. http://www.nytimes.com/2005/07/06/opinion/06gewirtz.html (accessed October 17, 2011).

182 Stephen Breyer qtd. in Robert A. Levy, "Judicial Appointments: What's on Tap from Obama or McCain?" October 2, 2008. Levy is chairman of the libertarian Cato Institute; the article is from the Cato Institute:

http://www.cato.org/pub_display.php?pub_id=9687 (accessed October 17, 2011).

183 Paul Gewritz, "Supreme Court Press," in *New York Times*, July 2, 2010. http://www.nytimes.com/2010/07/06/opinion/06gewirtz.html (accessed October 17, 2011).

184 Thomas Jefferson, letter to Spencer Roane, September 6, 1819. *The Jeffersonian Cyclopedia: A Comprehensive Collection of the Views of Thomas Jefferson Classified and Arranged in Alphabetical Order under Nine Thousand Titles Relating to Government, Politics, Law, Education, Political Economy, Finance, Science, Art, Literature, Religious Freedom, Morals, etc.* Edited by John P. Foley (Cambridge, Massachusetts: Harvard University Press and Funk & Wagnalls Company, 1900, digitized 2008), 190.

185 James Madison, speech to the House of Representatives, June 8, 1789, in Jack N. Rakove, *Declaring Rights: A Brief History with Documents* (New York: Palgrave Macmillan, 1998), 179.

186 James Madison qtd. in John J. Patrick and Gerald P. Long, *Constitutional Debates on Freedom of Religion: A Documentary History* (New York: Greenwood Publishing Group, 1999), 61.

Chapter 18

187 Alexander Hamilton qtd. in Ron Chernow, *Alexander Hamilton* (New York: The Penguin Press, 2004), 60.

188 James Madison, *Writings*, edited by Jack N. Rakove (New York: Literary Classics of the United States, Inc., 1999), 441.

189 Alexander Hamilton, "Federalist No. 84," in Alexander Hamilton, James Madison, and John Jay, *The Federalist*, ed. J. R. Pole (Indianapolis, Indiana: Hacket Publishing Company, Inc., 2005), 455.

190 Middlekauff, *The Glorious Cause*, 682–683; Kelly et al, *The American Constitution*, Volume 1, 7th edition, 110.

191 Kelly et al., *The American Constitution*, Volume 1, 7th edition, 76.

192 Thomas Jefferson, letter to James Madison, December 20, 1787, *The Life and Selected Writings of Thomas Jefferson: Including the Autobiography, The Declaration of Independence & His Public and Private Letters,*

ed. Adrienne Koch and William Peden (New York: The Modern Library, 2004), 405; Richard Henry Lee qtd. in Pauline Maier, *Ratification*, 66; Patrick Henry qtd. in David Wootton ed., introduction to *The Essential Federalist and Anti-Federalist Papers* (Indianapolis, Indiana: Hackett Publishing, 2003), xxxi.

193 Ralph Ketcham, *James Madison: A Biography*, 280. James Madison actually had to run against his old friend James Monroe in this election. He had originally been considered for a Senate seat but was blocked by Patrick Henry in the Anti-Federalist-controlled Assembly.

194 James Madison qtd. in Ralph Ketcham, *James Madison: A Biography*, 290.

195 James Madison qtd. in Scott J. Hammond, Kevin R. Hardwick, and Howard Leslie Lubert, *Classics of American Political and Constitutional Thought*, 528.

196 The two cases that struck down gun control laws are *District of Columbia v. Heller* and *McDonald v. City of Chicago*. The Heller opinion may be viewed at http://www.law.cornell.edu/supct/html/07-290.ZS.html (accessed October 26, 2011), and the McDonald opinion may be viewed at http://www.supremecourt.gov/opinions/09pdf/08–1521.pdf (accessed October 26, 2011).

197 The opinion of *Griswold v. Connecticut* may be viewed at http://www.law.cornell.edu/supct/html/historics/USSC_CR_0381_0479_ZO.html (accessed October 26, 2011).

198 Alexander Hamilton, "Federalist No. 1," in Alexander Hamilton, James Madison, and John Jay, *The Federalist*, ed. J. R. Pole (Indianapolis, Indiana: Hacket Publishing Company, Inc., 2005), 3.

199 Aristotle in *Politics*, translated by Benjamin Jowett, Forgotten Books Edition, 126.

200 Gordon Wood, *Empire of Liberty: A History of the Early Republic, 1789–1815*. Oxford History of the United States (Oxford: Oxford University Press, 2009), 68–70.

201 Terry Frieden, "FBI recovers original copy of Bill of Rights." March 19, 2003. http://www.cnn.com/2003/LAW/03/19/bill.of.rights/ (accessed October 26, 2011).

202 Order and dates of constitutional amendments. http://caselaw.

lp.findlaw.com/data/constitution/amendments.html (accessed October 26, 2011).

203 Gordon Wood, *Empire of Liberty: A History of the Early Republic, 1789–1815.* Oxford History of the United States (Oxford: Oxford University Press, 2009), 69. The Supreme Court case *Coleman v. Miller* allowed for any proposed amendment that did not have a set deadline to be ratified at any time. For the full story of the Twenty-Seventh Amendment, see John W. Dean, *Telling the Tale of the Twenty-Seventh Amendment: A Sleeping Amendment Concerning Congressional Compensation Is Later Revived.* September 27, 2002. http://writ.news.findlaw.com/dean/20020927.html (accessed October 14, 2011). The other proposed amendment was the Congressional Apportionment Amendment.

Chapter 19

204 Harry Truman qtd. in Matthew Spalding, *We Still Hold These Truths: Rediscovering Our Principles, Reclaiming Our Future.* The Heritage Foundation (Wilmington, Delaware: Intercollegiate Studies Institute, 2009), 5.

205 Thomas Mucha, "US debt: What would George Washington do?" May 5, 2011. http://www.globalpost.com/dispatches/globalpost-blogs/macro/us-debt-what-would-george-washington-do (accessed November 7, 2011); Daniel Indiviglio, "The U.S. Debt Ceiling: A Historical Look," in *The Atlantic*, April 29, 2011. http://www.the-atlantic.com/business/archive/2011/04/the-us-debt-ceiling-a-historical-look/238061/ (accessed November 7, 2011).

206 Wood, *Empire of Liberty*, 92–103.

207 William E. Leuchtenburg, "New Faces of 1946," in *Smithsonian* magazine, November 2006. http://www.smithsonianmag.com/history-archaeology/newfaces.html?c=y&page=5 (accessed November 8, 2011).

208 For an overview of the postwar period, see Stephen A. Marglin and Juliet B. Schor, ed. *The Golden Age of Capitalism: Reinterpreting the Postwar Experience* (Oxford: Oxford University Press. 1992.)

209 Historical measures of the misery index can be traced back to 1948 and may be viewed at http://inflationdata.com/articles/misery-index/

(accessed November 7, 2011); historical inflation rates back to 1979 may be viewed at http://inflationdata.com/inflation/inflation_rate/historicalinflation.aspx (accessed November 7, 2011).

210 Bruce Bartlett, "Warriors Against Inflation: Volcker *and* Reagan got the job done." In *National Review Online*, June 14, 2004. http://old.nationalreview.com/nrof_bartlett/bartlett200406140846.asp (accessed October 14, 2011); "1984 Presidential General Election Results," *U.S. Election Atlas*. http://uselectionatlas.org/RESULTS/national.php?year=1984 (accessed October 14, 2011). The only state Reagan did not win was his opponent Walter Mondale's home state of Minnesota.

211 These four principles compose the foundation of what has come to be called "Reaganomics." A full discussion of Reaganomics may be found in a book copublished with the Cato Institute: William A. Niskanen, *Reaganomics: An Insider's Account of the Policies and the People* (Oxford: Oxford University Press, 1988.) A shorter overview of Reaganomics by Niskanen may be found at the website *The Concise Encyclopedia of Economics* and the article "Reaganomics," which may be viewed at http://www.econlib.org/library/Enc1/Reaganomics.html (accessed November 7, 2011). Niskanen was a member of Reagan's Council of Economic Advisors from 1981–1985, and was both a supporter and internal critic of the economic program, as well as involved in many of its major policies.

212 G.C. Mays, "The Relationship Between Corporate Profits and U.S. GDP Growth Appears to Have Ended," July 31, 2011. http://seekingalpha.com/article/283425-the-relationship-between-corporate-profits-and-u-s-gdp-growth-appears-to-have-ended (accessed November 8, 2011). This article takes corporate profits as a whole as a percentage of GDP, but when the profits are divided by 500, the average is about 0.5 percent.

213 George Washington, *Volume 1 of The Writings of George Washington: Being His Correspondence, Addresses, Messages, and Other Papers, Official and Private, Selected and Published from the Original Manuscripts; with a Life of the Author, Notes, and Illustrations*. Edited by Jared Sparks (Charlottesville, Virginia: The University of Virginia Press, 1837, digitized 2010), 426.

214 Abraham Lincoln. *Great Speeches*, ed. John Grafton (New York: Dover Publications, Inc., 1991), 50–51.

215 Gregory Korte, "Proposals for balanced-budget amendment vary," in *USA Today,* October 31, 2011. http://www.usatoday.com/news /washington/story/2011-10-31/balanced-budget-amendment-pro-posals/51021020/1 (accessed November 7, 2011). There are currently eighteen proposed balanced budget amendments pending in Congress.

216 An visual of the U.S. debt and amount owed by each individual citizen may be found at http://www.usdebtclock.org/ (accessed November 7, 2011).

Chapter 20

217 Ronald Reagan qtd. in Peggy Noonan, *What I Saw at the Revolution: A Political Life in the Reagan Era* (Random House Digital, Inc., 2003), 335.

218 John Winthrop qtd. in Joseph A. Conforti, *Imagining New England: Explorations of Regional Identity from the Pilgrims to the Mid-Twentieth Century* (Chapel Hill, North Carolina: University of North Carolina Press Books, 2001), 28.

Appendix

219 Thomas Paine, *Common Sense and Other Writings,* ed. Gordon Wood (New York: The Modern Library, 2003), 48.

220 Alexander Hamilton, "Federalist No. 31," in Alexander Hamilton, James Madison, and John Jay, *The Federalist,* ed. J. R. Pole (Indianapolis, Indiana: Hacket Publishing Company, Inc., 2005), 164.

221 William Paterson qtd. in William Mack and William Benjamin Hale, *Corpus juris: being a complete and systematic statement of the whole body of the law as embodied in and developed by all reported decisions,* vol. 12 (Cambridge, Massachusetts: Harvard University Press and the American Law Book Co., 1917, digitized 2007), 676.

222 Thomas Jefferson qtd. in Scott A. Nelson, *The Discourses of Algernon Sidney* (Madison, New Jersey: Farleigh Dickinson University Press, 1993), 146.

223 Thomas Jefferson, letter to Henry Dearborn, March 1821. *The Jeffersonian Cyclopedia: A Comprehensive Collection of the Views of Thomas*

Jefferson Classified and Arranged in Alphabetical Order under Nine Thousand Titles Relating to Government, Politics, Law, Education, Political Economy, Finance, Science, Art, Literature, Religious Freedom, Morals, etc. Edited by John P. Foley (Cambridge, Massachusetts: Harvard University Press and Funk & Wagnalls Company, 1900, digitized 2008), 678.

224 Montesquieu qtd. in Geoff Mulgan, *Good and Bad Power: The Ideals and Betrayals of Government* (New York: Allen Lane, 2006), 200.

225 Dwight Eisenhower, *The Inaugural Addresses of the American Presidents: From Washington to Kennedy.* Edited by Davis Newton Lott (Chicago: Holt, Rinehart, and Winston, 1961), 261.

226 Ronald Reagan, *Ronald Reagan: The Great Communicator.* Edited by Frederick J. Ryan (New York: HarperCollins Publishers, 2001), 78.

227 John Adams, letter to Abigail Adams, July 17, 1775. *The Letters of John and Abigail Adams.* Edited by Frank Shuffelton (London: Penguin, 1876), 50.

228 James Madison, *Selected Writings of James Madison.* Edited by Ralph Ketcham (Indianapolis, Indiana: Hackett Publishing, 2006), 213.

229 Alexander Hamilton, "Federalist No. 8," in Alexander Hamilton, James Madison, and John Jay, *The Federalist*, ed. J. R. Pole (Indianapolis, Indiana: Hacket Publishing Company, Inc., 2005), 37.

230 Benjamin Franklin qtd. in Andrew P. Napolitano, *Constitutional Chaos: What Happens When Government Breaks Its Own Laws* (Nashville, Tennessee: Thomas Nelson, Inc., 2006), 126.

231 James Madison "Federalist No. 47," in Alexander Hamilton, James Madison, and John Jay, *The Federalist*, ed. J. R. Pole (Indianapolis, Indiana: Hacket Publishing Company, Inc., 2005), 261.

232 James Madison "Federalist No. 10," in Alexander Hamilton, James Madison, and John Jay, *The Federalist*, ed. J. R. Pole (Indianapolis, Indiana: Hacket Publishing Company, Inc., 2005), 49.

233 John Adams, letter to William Cushing, June 9, 1776, *Papers of John Adams: Volume 4-February–August 1776.* Edited by Robert J. Taylor, Gregg L.Lint, and Celeste Walker (Cambridge, Massachusetts: Harvard University Press, 1979), 245

234 Thomas Paine, "The American Crisis Number 4," in *Collected Writings: Common Sense, The Crisis, and Other Pamphlets, Articles, and Letters; The Rights of Man; The Age of Reason*. Edited by Eric Foner (New York: The Library of America, 1995), 150.

235 John Adams qtd. in Sydney E. Ahlstrom and David D. Hall, *A Religious History of the American People* (New Haven, Connecticut: Yale University Press, 2004), 262.

236 Samuel Adams qtd. in Paul Della Valle, *Massachusetts Troublemakers: Rebels, Reformers, and Radicals from the Bay State* (Guilford, Connecticut: Globe Pequot, 2009), 38.

237 Thomas Jefferson, letter to Henry Lee, May 8, 1825 in *The Life and Selected Writings of Thomas Jefferson: Including the Autobiography, The Declaration of Independence & His Public and Private Letters*, ed. Adrienne Koch and William Peden (New York: The Modern Library, 2004), 656.

238 George Mason, letter to George Mason, Jr., June 1, 1787. *The Papers of George Mason, 1725–1792, Volume III 1787–1792*. Edited by Robert A. Rutland (Chapel Hill, North Carolina: University of North Carolina Press, 1970), 892–893.

239 George Mason qtd. in George Bancroft, *History of the United States of America, from the discovery of the continent to 1789*. Volume 6 (Ann Arbor, Michigan: D. Appleton and company, 1884, digitized 2006), 256.

240 James Madison, "Federalist No. 51," 281.

241 Alexander Hamilton, "Federalist No. 1," in Alexander Hamilton, James Madison, and John Jay, *The Federalist*, ed. J. R. Pole (Indianapolis, Indiana: Hacket Publishing Company, Inc., 2005), 1.

242 James Madison, "Federalist No. 46," in Alexander Hamilton, James Madison, and John Jay, *The Federalist*, ed. J. R. Pole (Indianapolis, Indiana: Hacket Publishing Company, Inc., 2005), 255.

243 Thomas Jefferson, First Inaugural Address, *The Jeffersonian Cyclopedia: A Comprehensive Collection of the Views of Thomas Jefferson Classified and Arranged in Alphabetical Order under Nine Thousand Titles Relating to Government, Politics, Law, Education, Political Economy, Finance, Science, Art, Literature, Religious Freedom, Morals, etc.* Edited by John P.

Foley (Cambridge, Massachusetts: Harvard University Press and Funk & Wagnalls Company, 1900, digitized 2008), 798.

244 John Adams, letter to John Taylor, April 15, 1814.

245 George Washington qtd. in Susan Dunn, *Something That Will Surprise the World: The Essential Writings of the Founding Fathers* (New York: Basic Books, 2006), 51.

246 James Madison, *The Writings of James Madison: 1790–1802, Volume 6 of The Writings of James Madison: Comprising His Public Papers and His Private Correspondence, Including Numerous Letters and Documents New for the First Time Printed.* Edited by Gaillard Hunt (New York: G.P. Putnam's Sons, 1906), 102.

247 James Madison, "Federalist No. 62," in Alexander Hamilton, James Madison, and John Jay, *The Federalist*, ed. J. R. Pole (Indianapolis, Indiana: Hacket Publishing Company, Inc., 2005), 333.

248 Ibid., 335.

249 Alexander Hamilton, "Federalist No. 6," in Alexander Hamilton, James Madison, and John Jay, *The Federalist*, ed. J. R. Pole (Indianapolis, Indiana: Hacket Publishing Company, Inc., 2005), 24.

250 James Madison, letter to Edmund Pendleton, January 21, 1792, in *The Papers of James Madison,* Volume 14: 6 April 1791–16 March 1793. Edited by Robert A. Rutland, Thomas A. Mason, Robert J. Brugger, Jeanne K. Sisson, and Fredrika J. Teute (Charlottesville, Virginia: University of Virginia Press, 1983), 195.

251 James Madison, "Federalist No. 53," in Alexander Hamilton, James Madison, and John Jay, *The Federalist*, ed. J. R. Pole (Indianapolis, Indiana: Hacket Publishing Company, Inc., 2005), 291.

252 James Madison, "Federalist No. 10," 51.

253 Benjamin Franklin qtd. in Martin H. Manser, *The Facts on File Dictionary of Proverbs*, edited by Rosalind Fergusson and David Pickering, edition 2 (New York: Infobase Publishing, 2007), 206.

254 Thomas Paine, "Common Sense," *Foundations of Freedom: Common Sense, the Declaration of Independence, the Articles of Confederation, the Federalist Papers, the U.S. Constitution* (Radford, Virginia: Wilder Publications, 2008), 19.

255 James Madison, speech before the 1829 Virginia Ratifying Convention qtd. in Marvin Meyers, ed. *The Mind of the Founder: Sources of the Political Thought of James Madison*, The American Heritage Series (New York: The Bobbs-Merril Company, Inc., 1973), 512.

256 George Washington qtd. in Warren L. McFerran, *The Principles of Constitutional Government: Political Sovereignty* (Gretna, Louisiana: Pelican Publishing, 2009), 12.

257 Thomas Jefferson, letter to David Humphreys, March 18, 1789. *The Jeffersonian Cyclopedia: A Comprehensive Collection of the Views of Thomas Jefferson Classified and Arranged in Alphabetical Order under Nine Thousand Titles Relating to Government, Politics, Law, Education, Political Economy, Finance, Science, Art, Literature, Religious Freedom, Morals, etc.* Edited by John P. Foley (Cambridge, Massachusetts: Harvard University Press and Funk & Wagnalls Company, 1900, digitized 2008), 206.

258 John Adams qtd. in Clinton Rossiter, ed., *1787: The Grand Convention* (New York: Macmillan, 1966), 11.

259 George Washington qtd. in Orville James Victor, *The History, Civil, Political, and Military, of the Southern Rebellion: From Its Incipient Stages to Its Close. Comprehending, Also, All Important Syaye Papers, Ordinances of Secession, Proclamations, Proceedings of Congress, Official Reports of Commanders, Etc, Etc.* Volume 1 (Ann Arbor, Michigan: University of Michigan Press and J.D. Torrey, 1861, digitized 2008), 7.

260 Thomas Paine qtd. in Matthew Spalding, *We Still Hold These Truths: Rediscovering Our Principles, Reclaiming Our Future.* The Heritage Foundation (Wilmington, Delaware: Intercollegiate Studies Institute, 2009), 89.

261 Thomas Jefferson to Wilson C. Nicholas, September 7, 1803, *The Life and Selected Writings of Thomas Jefferson: Including the Autobiography, The Declaration of Independence & His Public and Private Letters*, ed. Adrienne Koch and William Peden (New York: The Modern Library, 2004), 525.

262 James Madison, "Federalist No. 45," in Alexander Hamilton, James Madison, and John Jay, *The Federalist*, ed. J. R. Pole (Indianapolis, Indiana: Hacket Publishing Company, Inc., 2005), 253.

263 James Madison, letter to James Robertson, April 20, 1831 qtd. in Ar-

thur E. Palumbo, *The Authentic Constitution: An Originalist View of America's Legacy* (New York: Algora Publishing), 34.

264 Thomas Jefferson, "Kentucky Resolutions of 1798" in Thomas Jefferson and James Madison, *The Kentucky-Virginia Resolutions and Mr. Madison's Report of 1799* (Richmond, Virginia: Virginia Commission on Constitutional Government, 1960), 8.

265 James Madison, "Federalist No. 14," in Alexander Hamilton, James Madison, and John Jay, *The Federalist*, ed. J. R. Pole (Indianapolis, Indiana: Hacket Publishing Company, Inc., 2005), 71.

266 Thomas Jefferson, *Jefferson's Opinion on the Constitutionality of a National Bank: 1791.* The Avalon Project. Digitized 2008, http://avalon.law.yale.edu/18th_century/bank-tj.asp (accessed October 20, 2011).

267 Roger Sherman qtd. in James Madison, *The Debates in the Several State Conventions on the Adoption of the Federal Constitution.* Edited by Jonathan Elliot (Berkeley, California: University of California Press and J.B. Lippincott & Co., 1836, digitized 2009), 166.

268 Joseph Story qtd, in United States Supreme Court, Lawyers Co-operative Publishing Company, *United States Supreme Court Reports* (Ann Arbor, Michigan: Lawyers Co-operative Pub. Co., 1911, the University of Michigan 2006), 584.

269 James Madison, "Federalist No. 46," in Alexander Hamilton, James Madison, and John Jay, *The Federalist*, ed. J. R. Pole (Indianapolis, Indiana: Hacket Publishing Company, Inc., 2005), 255.

270 Thomas Jefferson, letter to Spencer Roane, September 6, 1819. *The Jeffersonian Cyclopedia: A Comprehensive Collection of the Views of Thomas Jefferson Classified and Arranged in Alphabetical Order under Nine Thousand Titles Relating to Government, Politics, Law, Education, Political Economy, Finance, Science, Art, Literature, Religious Freedom, Morals, etc.* Edited by John P. Foley (Cambridge, Massachusetts: Harvard University Press and Funk & Wagnalls Company, 1900, digitized 2008), 190.

271 James Madison, "Federalist No. 48," in Alexander Hamilton, James Madison, and John Jay, *The Federalist*, ed. J. R. Pole (Indianapolis, Indiana: Hacket Publishing Company, Inc., 2005), 268–269

272 James Madison, "Federalist No. 51," 282.

273 Thomas Jefferson, *The life and letters of Thomas Jefferson: being his autobiography and select correspondence from original manuscripts*. Edited by Henry Augustine Washington (New York: Edwards, Pratt & Foster, 1858, digitized 2007), 58–59.

274 James Madison, "Federalist No. 48," 272.

275 George Washington qtd. in Matthew Spalding and Patrick J. Garrity, *A Sacred Union of Citizens: George Washington's Farewell Address and the American Character* (Lanham, Maryland: Rowman & Littlefield), 76.

276 Thomas Jefferson, "Notes on the State of Virginia," in *The Life and Selected Writings of Thomas Jefferson: Including the Autobiography, The Declaration of Independence & His Public and Private Letters*, ed. Adrienne Koch and William Peden (New York: The Modern Library, 2004), 221–222.

277 Roger Sherman, letter to John Adams, July 20, 1789. *The works of John Adams, second president of the United States: with a life of the author, notes and illustrations*, vol. 2. Edited by Charles Francis Adams (Berkeley, California: University of California Press, 1850, digitized 2009), 441–442.

278 James Madison, "Federalist No. 51," 281.

279 Gouverneur Morris qtd. in David Womersley, *Liberty and American experience in the eighteenth century* (Indianapolis, Indiana: Liberty Fund, 2006), 246.

280 Thomas Jefferson, "Kentucky Resolutions of 1798" in Thomas Jefferson and James Madison, *The Kentucky-Virginia Resolutions and Mr. Madison's Report of 1799* (Richmond, Virginia: Virginia Commission on Constitutional Government, 1960), 8.

281 James Madison, "Federalist No. 46," 258.

282 Benjamin Franklin qtd. in James Madison, *The Constitutional Convention: A Narrative History from the Notes of James Madison*. Edited by Edward John Larson, Michael Paul Winship, and Michael Winship (New York: Random House Inc., 2005.)

283 Thomas Paine, *Common Sense and Other Writings*, ed. Gordon Wood. (New York: The Modern Library, 2003), 10.

284 Alexander Hamilton, "Federalist No. 21," in Alexander Hamilton, James Madison, and John Jay, *The Federalist*, ed. J. R. Pole (Indianapolis, Indiana: Hacket Publishing Company, Inc., 2005), 112.

285 James Madison, "Federalist No. 44," in Alexander Hamilton, James Madison, and John Jay, *The Federalist*, ed. J. R. Pole (Indianapolis, Indiana: Hacket Publishing Company, Inc., 2005), 247.

286 John Adams qtd. in David Womersley, *Liberty and American experience in the eighteenth century* (Indianapolis, Indiana: Liberty Fund, 2006), 247.

287 Thomas Jefferson, letter to James Madison, December 20, 1787, qtd. in Richard E. Labunski, *James Madison and the Struggle for the Bill of Rights* (New York: Oxford University Press, 2006), 104.

288 James Madison, speech to the Virginia Constitutional Convention, 1829, qtd. in Scott J. Hammond, Kevin R. Hardwick, and Howard Leslie Lubert, *Classics of American Political and Constitutional Thought: Origins through the Civil War* (Indianapolis, Indiana: Hackett Publishing, Inc., 2007), 757.

289 James Madison, *Writings*, edited by Jack N. Rakove (New York: Literary Classics of the United States, Inc., 1999), 441.

290 James Madison qtd. in Scott J. Hammond, Kevin R. Hardwick, and Howard Leslie Lubert, *Classics of American Political and Constitutional Thought*, 528

291 Alexander Hamilton, "Federalist No. 1," in Alexander Hamilton, James Madison, and John Jay, *The Federalist*, ed. J. R. Pole (Indianapolis, Indiana: Hacket Publishing Company, Inc., 2005), 3.

292 Alexander Hamilton, "Federalist No. 84," in Alexander Hamilton, James Madison, and John Jay, *The Federalist*, ed. J. R. Pole (Indianapolis, Indiana: Hacket Publishing Company, Inc., 2005), 455.

293 James Madison qtd. in Jennifer Nedelsky, *Private Property and the Limits of American Constitutionalism: The Madisonian Framework and Its Legacy* (Chicago, University of Chicago Press, 1994), 19.

294 James Madison qtd. in Ralph Ketcham, *James Madison: A Biography* (Charlottesville, Virginia: University of Virginia Press, 1971), 330.

295 Thomas Jefferson qtd in Luigi Marco Bassani, *Liberty, State, & Union:*

The Political Theory of Thomas Jefferson (Macon, Georgia: Mercer University Press, 2010), 113.

296 Thomas Jefferson, "Summary View of the Rights of British America," in *The Life and Selected Writings of Thomas Jefferson: Including the Autobiography, The Declaration of Independence & His Public and Private Letters*, ed. Adrienne Koch and William Peden (New York: The Modern Library, 2004), 289.

297 Alexander Hamilton qtd. in Ron Chernow, *Alexander Hamilton* (New York: The Penguin Press, 2004), 60.

298 John Adams qtd. in Bruce A. Findlay, *Your Rugged Constitution* (Stanford: Stanford University Press, 1969), 216.

299 Thomas Jefferson, "Notes on the State of Virginia," in *The Life and Selected Writings of Thomas Jefferson: Including the Autobiography, The Declaration of Independence & His Public and Private Letters*, ed. Adrienne Koch and William Peden (New York: The Modern Library, 2004), 258.

300 George W. Bush qtd. in Peter H. Irons, *God on Trial: Dispatches from America's Religious Battlefields* (New York: The Penguin Press, 2007), 242.

301 James Madison qtd. in Kristin Waters, *Women and Men Political Theorists: Enlightened Conversations* (Hoboken, New Jersey, 2000), 175.

302 John Jay, letter to R. Lushington, March 15, 1786. In William Jay, *the Life of John Jay with Selections from His Correspondence* (New York: J. & J. Harper, 1833), 181–182.

303 Thomas Jefferson qtd. in Peter A. Dorsey, *Common Bondage: Slavery as Metaphor in Revolutionary America* (Knoxville, Tennessee: University of Tennessee Press, 2009), 145.

304 George Washington qtd. in Peter Henriques, *Realistic Visionary: A Portrait of George Washington* (Charlottesville, Virginia: University of Virginia Press, 2008), 158.

305 Gouverneur Morris qtd. in John P. Kaminski, *A Necessary Evil?: Slavery and the Debate over the Constitution* (Lanham, Maryland, 1995), 56.

306 Oliver Ellsworth qtd. in Paul Leicester Ford ed. *Essays on the Constitu-*

tion of the United States: published during its discussion by the people, 1787–1788 (Historical Printing Club, 1892), 164.

307 Roger Sherman qtd. in William O. Blake, *The history of slavery and the slave trade, ancient and modern: The forms of slavery that prevailed in ancient nations, particularly in Greece and Rome. The African slave trade and the political history of slavery in the United States. Compiled from authentic materials* (J. and H. Miller, 1857), 397.

308 George Mason qtd. in Michael W. Cluskey, *The political text-book, or encyclopedia: Containing everything necessary for the reference of the politicians and statesmen of the United States* (C. Wendell, 1857), 509.

309 James Wilson qtd. in John P. Kaminski, *A Necessary Evil?: Slavery and the Debate over the Constitution* (Lanham, Maryland: Rowman & Littlefield, 1995), 116.

310 John Adams qtd. in Thomas G. West, *Vindicating the Founders: Race, Sex, Class, and Justice in the Origins of America* (Lanham, Maryland: Rowman & Littlefield, 2000), 5.

311 Benjamin Franklin qtd. in Hugh Thomas, *The Slave Trade: The Story of the Atlantic Slave Trade, 1440–1870* (New York: Simon and Schuster, 1997), 481.

312 Thomas Jefferson, "Jefferson's Draft with Revisions," in Joseph J. Ellis ed. *What Did the Declaration Declare?* (New York: Bedford/St. Martin's, 1999), 10.

313 Frederick Douglass qtd. in Peter Lawler and Robert Martin Schaefer, *American Political Rhetoric: Essential Speeches and Writings on Founding Principles and Contemporary Controversies* (Lanham, Maryland: Rowman & Littlefield, 2010), 212.

314 Elbridge Gerry qtd. in James Madison, *The Debates in the Federal Convention of 1787: Which Framed the Constitution of the United States of America*. Edited in Gaillard Hunt and James Brown Scott (Clark, New Jersey: The Lawbook Exchange, Ltd.), 391.

315 Benjamin Franklin qtd. in James Madison, *Notes of Debates in the Federal Convention of 1787* (London: W.W. Norton & Company, 1987), 251.

316 Thomas Jefferson, *The Jeffersonian Cyclopedia: A Comprehensive Collection of the Views of Thomas Jefferson Classified and Arranged in Alphabetical Order under Nine Thousand Titles Relating to Government, Politics,*

Law, Education, Political Economy, Finance, Science, Art, Literature, Religious Freedom, Morals, etc. Edited by John P. Foley (Cambridge, Massachusetts: Harvard University Press and Funk & Wagnalls Company, 1900, digitized 2008), 852.

317 Thomas Jefferson, *The Jeffersonian Cyclopedia: A Comprehensive Collection of the Views of Thomas Jefferson Classified and Arranged in Alphabetical Order under Nine Thousand Titles Relating to Government, Politics, Law, Education, Political Economy, Finance, Science, Art, Literature, Religious Freedom, Morals, etc.* Edited by John P. Foley (Cambridge, Massachusetts: Harvard University Press and Funk & Wagnalls Company, 1900, digitized 2008), 854.

318 Alexander Hamilton, "Federalist No. 21," in Alexander Hamilton, James Madison, and John Jay, *The Federalist*, ed. J. R. Pole (Indianapolis, Indiana: Hacket Publishing Company, Inc., 2005), 113.

319 James Madison qtd. in F. Forrester Church, *So Help Me God: The Founding Fathers and the First Great Battle over Church and State* (Boston, Massachusetts: Houghton Mifflin Harcourt, 2007), 355.

320 Thomas Jefferson, *The Jeffersonian Cyclopedia: A Comprehensive Collection of the Views of Thomas Jefferson Classified and Arranged in Alphabetical Order under Nine Thousand Titles Relating to Government, Politics, Law, Education, Political Economy, Finance, Science, Art, Literature, Religious Freedom, Morals, etc.* Edited by John P. Foley (Cambridge, Massachusetts: Harvard University Press and Funk & Wagnalls Company, 1900, digitized 2008), 855.

321 Thomas Jefferson to William Johnson, June 12, 1823, in *The Jeffersonian Cyclopedia: A Comprehensive Collection of the Views of Thomas Jefferson Classified and Arranged in Alphabetical Order under Nine Thousand Titles Relating to Government, Politics, Law, Education, Political Economy, Finance, Science, Art, Literature, Religious Freedom, Morals, etc.* Edited by John P. Foley (Cambridge, Massachusetts: Harvard University Press and Funk & Wagnalls Company, 1900, digitized 2008), 844.

322 Thomas Jefferson, letter to Spencer Roane, September 6, 1819. *The Jeffersonian Cyclopedia: A Comprehensive Collection of the Views of Thomas Jefferson Classified and Arranged in Alphabetical Order under Nine Thousand Titles Relating to Government, Politics, Law, Education, Political Economy, Finance, Science, Art, Literature, Religious Freedom,*

Morals, etc. Edited by John P. Foley (Cambridge, Massachusetts: Harvard University Press and Funk & Wagnalls Company, 1900, digitized 2008), 190.

323 James Madison qtd. in Thomas F. Gordon, *War on the Bank of the United States* (North Stratford, New Hampshire: Ayer Publishing, 1966), 106.

324 James Wilson, *The Works of the Honourable James Wilson, L.L.D., Late One of the Associate Justices of the Supreme Court of the United States, and Professor of Law in the College of Philadelphia.* Edited by Bird Wilson (Ann Arbor, Michigan: Lorenzo Press and University of Michigan Press, 1804, digitized 2007), 14.

325 Alexander Hamilton, "Federalist No. 81," in Alexander Hamilton, James Madison, and John Jay, *The Federalist*, ed. J. R. Pole (Indianapolis, Indiana: Hacket Publishing Company, Inc., 2005), 429.

326 James Madison, speech to the House of Representatives, June 8, 1789, in Jack N. Rakove, *Declaring Rights: A Brief History with Documents* (New York: Palgrave Macmillan, 1998), 179.

327 John Adams qtd. in Scott J. Hammond, Kevin R. Hardwick, and Howard Leslie Lubert, *Classics of American Political and Constitutional Thought,* (Indianapolis, Indiana: Hackett Publishing, 2007), 294.

328 Alexander Hamilton, "Federalist No. 78," in Alexander Hamilton, James Madison, and John Jay, *The Federalist*, ed. J. R. Pole (Indianapolis, Indiana: Hacket Publishing Company, Inc., 2005), 412.

329 Joseph Story, *Commentaries on the Constitution of the United States: With a preliminary review of the Constitutional History of the Colonies and States, Before the Adoption of the Constitution.* Volume 3 (New York: Hilliard, Gray, and Company, 1833), 476.

330 Ronald Reagan in Jim Hayes, *The Original Reagan Conservative: Ronald Reagan's Conservative Ideas in His Own Words* (Jim Hayes Publishing, 2008), 72.

331 Alexander Hamilton, "Federalist No. 8," in Alexander Hamilton, James Madison, and John Jay, *The Federalist*, ed. J. R. Pole (Indianapolis, Indiana: Hackett Publishing Company, Inc., 2005), 38.

332 Benjamin Franklin, letter to Dr. Priestley, June 7, 1782, in Benjamin Franklin, William Temple Franklin, and William Duane, *Memoirs of*

Benjamin Franklin. Volume 1 (New York: M'Carty & Davis, 1834, digitized 2007), 432.

333 Alexander Hamilton, "Federalist No. 34," in Alexander Hamilton, James Madison, and John Jay, *The Federalist*, ed. J. R. Pole (Indianapolis, Indiana: Hackett Publishing Company, Inc., 2005), 178.

334 James Madison, "Federalist No. 41," 220.

335 Alexander Hamilton qtd. in Morton J. Frisch and Richard G. Stevens, *American Political Thought: The Philosophic Dimensions of American Statesmanship* (Piscataway, New Jersey: Transaction Press, 2011), 97.

336 George Washington, "Washington's Farewell Address 1796." The Avalon Project, Yale Law School. http://avalon.law.yale.edu/18th_century/washing.asp (accessed November 12, 2011).

337 Alexis de Tocqueville, *Democracy in America*, 355.

338 Thomas Paine, "Age of Reason," Part 2, Section 21, in *Collected Writings: Common Sense, The Crisis, and Other Pamphlets, Articles, and Letters; The Rights of Man; The Age of Reason*. Edited by Eric Foner (New York: The Library of America, 1995), 826.

339 John Witherspoon qtd. in L. Gordon Tait, *The Piety of John Witherspoon: Pew, Pulpit, and the Public Forum* (Louisville, Kentucky: Westminster John Knox Press, 2001), 158.

340 Thomas Jefferson, "Reply to Danbury Baptist Association," January 1, 1802, in *The Life and Selected Writings of Thomas Jefferson: Including the Autobiography, The Declaration of Independence & His Public and Private Letters*, ed. Adrienne Koch and William Peden (New York: The Modern Library, 2004), 307.

341 John Adams qtd. in Robert A. Gross, "Reading for an Extensive Republic," in *The History of the Book in America: An Extensive Republic: Print, Culture, and Society in the New Nation, 1790–1840*. Volume 2 of *History of the Book in America*. Edited by Robert A. Gross and Mary Kelley (Charlotte, North Carolina, University of North Carolina Press, 2010), 516.

342 Benjamin Franklin qtd. in Stacy Schiff, *A Great Improvisation: Franklin, France, and the Birth of America* (New York: Henry, Holt, and Company, 2006), 350.

343 George Washington, letter to Steptoe Washington, December 5, 1790, *The Writings of George Washington*, Volume II, 1785–1790. Edited by Worthington Chauncey Ford (New York: G.P. Putnam's Sons, 1891), 509.

344 John Adams, *The Political Works of John Adams*. Edited by George Wescott Carey. Volume 6 of Conservative Leadership Series (Washington, D.C.: Regnery Gateway, 2000), 285.

345 Thomas Jefferson, "First Annual Message—December 8, 1801," in *The Life and Selected Writings of Thomas Jefferson: Including the Autobiography, The Declaration of Independence & His Public and Private Letters*, ed. Adrienne Koch and William Peden (New York: The Modern Library, 2004), 305.

346 Thomas Jefferson, letter to Joseph Milligan, April 6, 1816, in *The Life and Selected Writings of Thomas Jefferson: Including the Autobiography, The Declaration of Independence & His Public and Private Letters*, ed. Adrienne Koch and William Peden (New York: The Modern Library, 2004), 606.

347 James Madison, *Selected Writings of James Madison*, 60.

348 Benjamin Franklin, *Memoirs of Benjamin Franklin*, Volume 1, 38.

349 Ibid., Volume 4, 157.

350 Ibid., Volume 2, 430.

351 James Madison, *Letters and Other Writings of James Madison: 1829–1836* (Charlottesville, Virginia, 1884, digitized 2010), 479.

352 James Madison qtd. in Bernard H. Siegan, *Property Rights: From Magna Carta to the Fourteenth Amendment* (Piscataway, New Jersey: Transaction Press, 2001), 81.

353 John Adams, *The Works of John Adams*, Volume 1, 113.

354 Calvin Coolidge qtd. in William J. Bennet and John T. E. Cribb, *The American Patriot's Almanac* (Nashville, Tennessee: Thomas Nelson, Inc., 2008), 147.

355 Woodrow Wilson, *Woodrow Wilson: The Essential Political Writings*. Edited by Ronald J. Pestritto (Lanham, Maryland: Lexington Books, 2005), 121.

356 Franklin Roosevelt qtd. in Roger LeRoy, Frank B. Cross, and Gaylord A. Jentz, *Essentials of the Legal Environment* (Florence, Kentucky: Cengage Learning, 2010), 90.

357 Lyndon B. Johnson qtd. in J. Scott Harr and Karen M. Hess, *Constitutional Law and the Criminal Justice System* (Florence, Kentucky: Cengage Learning, 2007), 368.

358 Felix Frankfurter qtd. in Burt Solomon, *FDR v. the Constitution: The Court-Packing Fight and the Triumph of Democracy* (New York: Bloomsbury Publishing, 2009), 213.

359 Stephen Breyer qtd. in Christopher S. Kelley, *Executing the Constitution: Putting the President Back into the Constitution* (Albany, New York: State University of New York Press), 180.

360 Thurgood Marshall qtd. in Bernard K. Duffy and Richard W. Leeman, *American Voices: An Encyclopedia of Contemporary Orators* (Cheektowaga, New York: Greenwood Group, 2005), 304.

361 Francis Biddle qtd. in William H. Rehnquist, *All Laws but One: Civil Liberties in Wartime* (New York: Random House, Inc., 2000.)

362 Harry Truman qtd. in Matthew Spalding, *We Still Hold These Truths*, 5.

363 Antonin Scalia qtd. in James Joyner, "Scalia Slams Judicial Activism," March 15, 2005. http://www.outsidethebeltway.com/scalia_slams_judicial_activism/ (accessed November 12, 2011).

364 Joseph Biden qtd. in "Chief Justice at the Bedside: John Roberts and the End of Life," *The New Atlantis-Journal of Technology & Society*. http://www.thenewatlantis.com/publications/chief-justice-at-the-bedside (accessed November 12, 2011).

365 Calvin Coolidge, *Foundations of the Republic*. Essay Index Reprint Series (North Stratford, New Hampshire: Ayer Publishing, 1926), 84.

366 Gerald R. Ford qtd. in Eric J. Mitnick, *Rights, Groups, and Self-invention: Group-Differentiated Rights in Liberal Theory* (London: Ashgate Publishing, Ltd., 2006), 51.

367 Dwight D. Eisenhower qtd. in John Cook, Leslie Ann Gibson, *The Book of Positive Quotations* (Binghamton, New York: Fairview Press, 2007), 507.

368 Milton Friedman with William Richard Allen, *Bright Promises, Dismal Performance: An Economist's Protest* (San Diego, California: Harcourt Brace Jovanovich, 1983), 197.

369 Alexander Hamilton, *The works of Alexander Hamilton: Containing his correspondence, and his political and official writings, exclusive of the Federalist, civil and military.* Volume 6. Edited by John Church Hamilton (Oxford: Oxford University Press, 1851, digitized 2006), 163.

370 George Washington, *The writings of George Washington: Being his correspondence, addresses, messages, and other papers, official and private.* Volume 9.Edited by Jared Sparks (Berkeley, California: University of California, 1835, digitized 2009), 167.

371 Alexander Hamilton, "Federalist No. 11," in Alexander Hamilton, James Madison, and John Jay, *The Federalist*, ed. J. R. Pole (Indianapolis, Indiana: Hackett Publishing Company, Inc., 2005), 57.

372 John Boehner qtd. in John R. Parkinson, "Emotional Boehner Promises New Way Forward for GOP," in *ABC News*, November 3, 2010. http://abcnews.go.com/Politics/john-boehner-emotional-house-republican-leader-promises-gop/story?id=12040640 (accessed November 12, 2011).

Index

A

Adams, John, xiii, 3, 7, 26, 30, 36,
37, 42, 43, 44, 45, 47, 54, 66,
85, 86, 87, 120, 180, 181, 183,
185, 190, 192, 193, 197, 199,
200, 201, 205, 209, 211, 212,
214, 217, 218, 225, 232, 233,
235, 237, 238, 239, 240, 242,
243, 244

Anti-Federalist Papers, 27, 50, 74

B

balanced, 11, 14, 18, 65, 69, 86,
87, 88, 102, 108, 135, 167, 173,
174, 175, 188, 230

Biden, Joe, 203, 245

Bill of Rights, viii, 14, 18, 27, 29,
39, 41, 54, 55, 70, 101, 103,
132, 143, 149, 151, 152, 153,
154, 155, 156, 158, 159, 161,
228, 238

Boehner, John, 204, 246

Breyer, Stephen, 146, 202, 226,
245

Bush, George W., 192, 239

C

checks, 11, 17, 41, 43, 49, 50, 54,
56, 57, 66, 69, 70, 86, 87, 88,
91, 92, 93, 101, 102, 104, 115,
127, 128, 131, 135, 153, 159

checks and balances, 17, 41, 43,
49, 50, 57, 70, 86, 92, 93, 101,
115, 135, 153, 159

Congress, vii, xiv, 3, 22, 24, 31, 34,
35, 36, 37, 38, 39, 41, 43, 49,
55, 57, 61, 62, 63, 69, 70, 76,
82, 87, 91, 92, 97, 98, 99, 102,
106, 119, 120, 121, 123, 124,
125, 126, 128, 134, 135, 136,
138, 139, 140, 146, 147, 151,
153, 155, 158, 159, 161, 167,
175, 184, 186, 188, 193, 194,
215, 219, 224, 231, 235

Constitution, vii, xi, xiv, 4, 10, 12,
13, 14, 15, 16, 18, 23, 24, 26,
27, 29, 32, 33, 35, 38, 39, 40,
41, 45, 46, 48, 49, 50, 54, 55,
57, 60, 62, 63, 64, 66, 67, 69,
70, 71, 72, 73, 74, 75, 77, 78,
85, 86, 87, 88, 89, 90, 92, 98,
101, 102, 103, 106, 107, 108,

H

Hamilton, Alexander, 21, 25, 26, 30, 32, 38, 39, 41, 42, 46, 61, 68, 77, 98, 100, 101, 130, 133, 142, 151, 152, 159, 166, 179, 180, 183, 184, 190, 191, 192, 195, 196, 197, 198, 204, 207, 210, 213, 214, 215, 216, 218, 219, 220, 223, 224, 226, 227, 228, 231, 232, 233, 234, 235, 236, 237, 238, 239, 241, 242, 245, 246

J

Jay, John, 26, 39, 116, 120, 192, 207, 213, 214, 215, 216, 218, 220, 221, 222, 223, 224, 225, 226, 227, 228, 231, 232, 233, 234, 235, 236, 237, 238, 239, 241, 242, 246

Jefferson, Thomas, xii, 18, 25, 26, 30, 35, 36, 37, 38, 40, 43, 46, 53, 54, 56, 57, 66, 72, 75, 77, 79, 85, 86, 97, 116, 120, 123, 134, 148, 153, 156, 180, 182, 183, 185, 186, 187, 188, 189, 190, 191, 192, 194, 195, 196, 199, 200, 207, 209, 211, 212, 213, 214, 215, 216, 217, 218, 219, 223, 224, 225, 227, 231, 233, 235, 236, 237, 238, 239, 240, 241, 243, 244

Johnson, Lyndon, 202, 216, 241, 244

judiciary, 56, 89, 91, 92, 98, 100, 123, 124, 128, 142, 145, 147, 148, 149, 160, 181, 196

M

Madison, James, v, xi, xii, 16, 17, 18, 24, 26, 27, 30, 32, 33, 38, 39, 40, 43, 44, 46, 50, 56, 61, 65, 66, 67, 68, 69, 70, 73, 74, 76, 77, 81, 82, 85, 86, 87, 90, 92, 98, 99, 100, 101, 106, 107, 108, 109, 115, 120, 126, 129, 131, 133, 149, 151, 152, 153, 154, 156, 157, 161, 180, 181, 182, 183, 184, 185, 186, 187, 188, 189, 190, 191, 192, 195, 196, 198, 200, 201, 205, 207, 210, 213, 214, 215, 216, 217, 218, 219, 220, 221, 223, 224, 226, 227, 228, 231, 232, 233, 234, 235, 236, 237, 238, 239, 240, 241, 242, 244, 246

Marshall, Thurgood, 202, 226, 245

Mason, George, 10, 18, 26, 38, 46, 54, 104, 132, 182, 193, 206, 214, 220, 223, 224, 233, 234, 239

Montesquieu, xiii, 47, 54, 87, 180, 212, 232

Morris, Gouverneur, 30, 39, 40, 41, 46, 128, 189, 193, 210, 237, 239

P

Paine, Thomas, 9, 16, 22, 25, 47, 57, 59, 72, 179, 181, 184, 185, 189, 199, 206, 207, 213, 215, 231, 232, 234, 235, 237, 243

Paterson, William, 12, 179, 207, 231

president, 21, 63, 104, 109, 118, 130, 134, 137, 139, 167, 180, 192, 201, 202, 203, 218, 224, 225, 245

About the Author

JAMES D. BEST is the author of *The Digital Organization*, *Tempest at Dawn*, *The Shopkeeper*, *Leadville*, *Murder at Thumb Butte*, and *The Shut Mouth Society*. James has also written two regular magazine columns and numerous journal articles. He was CIO for AlliedSignal and was COO of Grand Circle Travel, the Scottsdale Center for Business Technology, and Vista Software. Best lives in Paradise Valley, Arizona, with his wife, Diane, and maintains a summer home in Omaha, Nebraska.

Made in the USA
Middletown, DE
17 May 2020